OLD ENGLISH LITERATURE IN CONTEXT

OLD ENGLISH LITERATURE
IN CONTEXT

TEN ESSAYS

Edited by John D. Niles

D. S. BREWER · ROWMAN & LITTLEFIELD

© Contributors 1980

Published by D. S. Brewer, 240 Hills Road, Cambridge
an imprint of Boydell & Brewer Ltd,
PO Box 9, Woodbridge, Suffolk IP12 3DF
and by Rowman and Littlefield
81, Adams Drive, Totowa, New Jersey, N.J. 07512, USA

First published 1980

British Library Cataloguing in Publication Data

Old English literature in context.
1. Anglo-Saxon literature – History and criticism
 I. Niles, John D
 829   PR173   79-41515

ISBN (UK) 0 85991 061 X
(US) 0 8476 6770 7

The illustrations from Corpus Christi College, Cambridge
MS. 41 on pp. 16–18 are reproduced by kind permission
of the Master and Fellows of Corpus Christi College.

Erratum: the caption to the jacket illustrations should read:
Back: BL MS Cotton Tiberius B. v, f6ᵛ: mowing hay.

Phototypeset in Great Britain by
Rowland Phototypesetting Ltd, Bury St Edmunds, Suffolk
and printed by St Edmundsbury Press, Bury St Edmunds, Suffolk

Contents

Introduction

INTO what context should a given work of Old English literature be placed if it is to be understood well?

In its own way, each of the essays in this volume takes its departure from this question. Taken together, the ten responses should provide an efficient rebuttal to anyone who would claim that the question of contextuality in Old English literature has a simple answer. In the Anglo-Saxon period as in any other, we can speak not of any one context for a particular literary work, but only of a variety of interlocking contexts. The present book can do no more than articulate a few features of the vast cultural matrix that underlies the earliest English literature.

In the Old English period, texts do not often explain themselves. Sometimes debate must center on distressingly basic questions: Is the speaker of a given poem a man or a woman? Alive or dead? Is there one speaker, or are we to posit two or three? Is the text a lyric poem, or could it be something quite different—a wen charm, for instance, or a sort of medieval crossword puzzle? Is the text a purely personal expression of joy or grief, or does it draw on well-established literary conventions that now are lost to sight? The answers to these and a multitude of other questions are seldom self-evident, and an attempt to interpret a text solely on the basis of 'what it means to me' is likely to strike most scholars as narcissistic. Any text is part of a cultural continuum. Whether composed for public performance or private instruction, an archaic poem is likely to have had some social function, and if so this function may provide a key to its meaning. In addition, the Old English cultural continuum extends back into the past in at least two great dimensions encompassing the Latin traditions of the learned and the more obscure Germanic traditions of the race. Underlying both is a more shadowy inheritance which may date back to common Indo-European times. The more one understands of the complex range of early English culture, the more accurately one can hope to interpret a given text by placing it in its contemporary social setting as well as in relation to its intellectual sources in the past. Without such an attempt at historical reconstruction, the critic's methods and conclusions are likely to be colored by tacit assumptions based on present-day realities—or worse, on the authoritative judgments of a prior generation of scholars whose vision was equally culture-bound.

The study of Old English literature, in other words, is a field for the scholar who looks upon language and literature as parts of a cultural whole. Complicating the task of such a scholar is the fact that the cultural system in which he is interested ceased to exist (or took on radically different forms) many centuries ago. To reconstruct the Old English cultural matrix is a job for the humanist of many talents. Among these is the talent of reconstructing much from little: a twisted brooch, a few indentations in the sand, some curt annals or charters, and an occasional brilliant poem whose text was saved almost at random from the much larger corpus of which it must have been a part.

Criticism of the earliest English literature has often been devoted to a few of these poetic texts to the exclusion of a large body of documents thought to be of only passing interest. We would do well to remember that heroic poems such as *Beowulf* and *The Battle of Maldon*, however great their appeal, represent a small minority of Old English poetic texts that have come down to us, most of which are of a devotional nature. Poetry, in turn, represents a small minority of the totality of Old English literature, most of which consists of devotional or utilitarian texts in prose. English literature itself represents only a part of the total body of literature to have survived from the Anglo-Saxon period, most of which was written in Latin. The reason for these proportions is not hard to find. For most of the period, the technology of writing was in the hands of a class of persons who—nominally, at least—had renounced secular concerns to devote themselves to the service of God. It is to the hands and minds of these persons that Fred C. Robinson directs his attention in the essay that introduces this volume. By reference particularly to the scribal colophon, or brief notice or prayer by which a scribe takes leave from the labors of writing, Robinson shows that a useful or even indispensable guide to the meaning of a medieval text can be provided by its setting within the manuscript in which it appears.

Scribes trained in Latin letters did not invent Old English literature, of course. Antedating our earliest recorded texts is a native Germanic poetic tradition that did not happen to be written down because it traveled from mouth to mouth. In the next essay, Jeff Opland discusses the revolution in sensibility that occurred when the introduction of Latin letters to England permitted the development of a kind of literature unknown before: literature of the eye, not of the ear.

As all Old English recorded literature postdates the coming of Christian missionaries from Rome and Iona, there scarcely exists a text that does not in some way reflect Christian attitudes or Latin learning. The next three essays share a common concern with the Christian and Latin tradition in Anglo-Saxon literature. My own essay on *Æcerbot* attempts to clarify the character and setting of one of the most intriguing of early magical texts. Thomas D. Hill turns his attention to the Old English poetic paraphrase of the story of Exodus. By focussing his analysis on the single image of the *virga* ('rod') of Moses, Hill not only solves a local crux in the poem; he discovers a key that unlocks the meaning of a set of disputed passages. James W. Earl sets himself in emphatic opposition to those who would read the saint's life *Andreas* as an expression of early Germanic storytelling tradition. Instead, he offers a systematic reading of the poem in terms of a cluster of related *figurae* having to do with the themes of baptism and conversion.

No other Old English poem has attracted so much attention as *Beowulf*, and none has been such a shape-changer in the hands of the critics. The remaining essays in this book suggest five different reading contexts for this unique surviving example of early Germanic epic poetry. The different approaches could be characterized as Germanic (Andersson), structuralist (Damon), oral-formulaic (Foley), and mythic (Lord and Nagler). One approach that is not taken is the exegetical or typological approach that Earl illustrates so well in his study of *Andreas*. This omission is by chance rather than choice, and yet the shape of the present volume accords with an apparent swing of the pendulum in *Beowulf* criticism away from elaborately symbolic views of the poem toward a view of it as a Christian product or offshoot of a deep-rooted native verse-making tradition. While none of the five authors seeks to discount Latin or Christian influence on the poem, none takes this as a point of departure. Instead, the authors look for clues to the poem's design in Germanic antiquity, in 'primary' or oral-traditional epic poetry, and—venturing on ground less easily charted—in the storytelling traditions of the Indo-European past. Whatever their differences, the five authors agree in seeing the poet as standing rather late, not at the beginning, of a long tradition of human storytelling. Nagler pursues the question of contextuality toward its limits as he claims that the ultimate context for understanding *Beowulf* is nothing more or less than the human psyche.

Such, in brief, are the main concerns of the essays included in this volume. The book has no pretensions of standing alone as a companion to Old English literature. Its intention is to illustrate how certain modes of inquiry—textual, philological, social, folkloristic, exegetical, structural, comparative, oral-formulaic, mythic, and so on—can be drawn on to develop a reading context for certain key literary texts that have come down to us from the early Middle Ages. If space permitted, other equally valid essays might be included by historians, archaeologists, theologians, and other persons with an interest in rediscovering the meaning of Old English literature in its native cultural setting. As it is, the responses to the question of contextuality range from the most narrow, as in Fred Robinson's essay on manuscript transmission, to the most eclectic, as in Michael Nagler's mythological and psychological reading of *Beowulf*. The Germanic and the Latin/Christian traditions in Old English literature receive equal attention, in a cooperative effort which is hoped to reflect progress in a field that has suffered too long from antagonisms drawn along the lines of a false 'pagan vs. Christian' dichotomy. A concern with theory surfaces throughout the book, explicitly in the essays by Damon and Foley and implicitly elsewhere, but this concern tends to be practical rather than abstract as the authors direct their attention to how narrative theory can help identify the special characteristics of particular texts. It is hoped that taken together, the ten essays will witness to the liveliness that characterizes current work in the field of Old English.

The editor would like to express his gratitude to his nine co-contributors for their cheerful willingness to take part in this cooperative venture, and to D. S. Brewer for offering the book his encouragement. Special thanks are due Ms. Anita Hernández and the other student members of the Berkeley Old English Colloquium—in particular Laurel Brinton, Sarah Higley, and Peter Ting—for their heroic efforts in helping to organize a conference in May, 1978, at which seven of these essays were presented in preliminary form. Thanks are also due my research assistant Barbara Grossman, whose editorial skills and patience deserve equal praise, and my colleague Alain Renoir, for acts of kindness too numerous to mention.

Old English Literature in Its Most Immediate Context

FRED C. ROBINSON

CRITICS concerned to understand an Old English literary text usually begin by trying to ascertain some facts about its context—the genre of which it is a specimen, the approximate date of its composition, its sources, the cultural milieu in which the author wrote, and, where possible, the identity of the author. Even critics whose interests are restricted to the aesthetic appreciation of Old English poetry can usually be relied on to give some attention to data of this kind, for such information can be helpful in establishing the main course of a poem's thought and in determining the most relevant meanings of individual words within the text. But there is another aspect of a literary work's context which often can be of equal or even greater help in understanding it and which both critics and scholars frequently neglect to investigate. That is, the poem's context within the manuscript in which it is preserved—its most immediate context.

My thesis is that when we read an Old English literary text we should take care to find out what precedes it in its manuscript state and what follows it. We should know whether it is an independent text or part of another, larger text. We should have some sense of the poem's *mise en page* and some conception of the manuscript as a whole. For medieval books often constituted composite artifacts in which each component text depended on its environment for part of its meaning. If a text is detached from its codicological environment (as texts normally are in our modern editions), we risk losing that part of its meaning. In the observations that follow I shall try to illustrate my thesis by examining an Old English poem first in the isolated state in which we encounter it in the standard edition (where it has been imperfectly understood by modern readers) and then by examining the same poem in its manuscript context and seeing what help this gives us in interpreting the poem. Following this detailed study of a single text within its manuscript environment, I shall deal more briefly with further examples of the importance of reading texts in their 'most immediate context' and shall suggest some broader implications of this approach.

The poem to be considered first is 'The Metrical Epilogue to Manuscript 41, Corpus Christi College, Cambridge.' This unprepossessing title was assigned to the poem by E. V. K. Dobbie in volume VI of *The Anglo-Saxon Poetic Records*.[1] Dobbie's is the most recent and standard edition of the poem; his text is as follows:

THE METRICAL EPILOGUE TO MS. 41,
CORPUS CHRISTI COLLEGE, CAMBRIDGE

Bidde ic eac   æghwylcne mann,
brego, rices weard,   þe þas boc ræde
and þa bredu befo,   fira aldor,
þæt gefyrðrige þone writre   wynsum cræfte
þe ðas boc awrat   bam handum twam,
þæt he mote manega gyt   mundum synum
geendigan,   his aldre to willan,
and him þæs geunne   se ðe ah ealles geweald,
rodera waldend,   þæt he on riht mote
oð his daga ende   drihten herigan. Amen. Geweorþe þæt.

The ensuing translation is a literal rendering of Dobbie's text except that I have incorporated two departures from his edition in lines 2 and 4:[2]

I also beseech each man—ruler of the realm, lord of men—who might read this book and hold the volume[3] that he support with kindly power the scribe who wrote this book with his two hands so that he might complete yet many [more copies] with his hands according to his lord's desire; and may He Who reigns over all, the Lord of the Heavens, grant him that so that he might rightly praise the Lord until the end of his days. Amen. So be it.

Even a slight performance like this one requires editorial guidance and some scholarly commentary if it is to be understood, but *The Anglo-Saxon Poetic Records*, like previous editions,[4] provide little of either. Dobbie's textual notes say only that the initial capital letter was left out by the scribe. The editor's spare commentary adds that three lines in the poem are metrically irregular and that a previous editor misread one word in line 8 when he transcribed the text. Interesting data, perhaps, but a slim basis on which to build an interpretation.

If we want to recover the context in which this poem was written, we would do well to begin with an examination of its apparent genre—i.e., the scribal colophon. That colophons were ubiquitous can be verified by a glance at the collection of *Colophons de manuscrits occidentaux des origines au xvie siècle* now in preparation by the Benedictines of Le Bouveret in Switzerland.[5] The four volumes which have appeared thus far contain nearly fifteen thousand colophons, and some thirty thousand are promised in the complete series. Many of these are very simple, consisting of little more than the name of the scribe, a brief prayer or anathema, or a grateful declaration that the copyist's task is finished. Other colophons are more elaborate and artful. A ninth-century scribe named Heriveus ends his manuscript with a 28-line acrostic poem of considerable originality.[6] Colophon poems of comparable length and complexity, including some with acrostic signatures, are published under the title 'Versus libris adiecti' in the *Monumenta Germaniae historica*.[7] Some colophons, like the Old English poem 'Thureth,' give recognition to the man who ordered the book made, while others, like that of the glossator Aldred, purport to identify the scribe and the binder of the manuscript and give other details about the book's production.[8] Frequently colophons beg for the reader's prayers in behalf of the scribe or author of the book. Yet others comment on the contents of the work just copied or bewail the labor and discomfort entailed in the copying of the book. While the quality of verse colophons is uneven, there is a sufficiently large number of subtle and thoughtful specimens to warrant our taking a poem like the 'Metrical Epilogue' seriously, granting the possibility that it could be the product of careful reflection and not merely the doggerel of a trifling scribe.

That colophons are not merely spontaneous exclamations at the end of a job of copying is shown by their frequently formulaic quality. Many are mere repetitions of the same tags that had been appearing in manuscripts for centuries. Others are creative adaptations of old formulas and motifs by individual scribes for individual poetic purposes. Such jingles as 'Qui scripsit scribat, semper cum domino vivat' ('May he who wrote write; may he always live with the Lord') appear with little variation in manuscripts from many times and lands, as do less reverent tags such as 'Explicit hoc totum; pro Christo da mihi potum' ('This whole thing is finished; for Christ's sake give me a drink') or 'Detur pro penna scriptori pulcra puella' ('May a beautiful girl be given to the scribe for his pen').[9] But occasionally such time-worn fillers are worked into verse statements of a more personal sort. The pretty simile

Sicut nautes desiderat portum videre
Ita scriptor desiderat librum complere[10]

13

(As the seafarer longs to see the port
So the scribe longs to finish the book)

is to be found in various forms in manuscripts datable as early as the
seventh century. But a ninth-century scribe in Fleury alters the simile to
suit his own concerns (*Colophons*, no. 12, 892):

Sicut desiderat navigator ad ripam venire
Sic desiderat scriptor Maganarius ad regnum dei venire . . .

(As the sailor longs to come to the shore
So does Maganarius the scribe long to come to the kingdom of God . . .)

while another ninth-century scribe (from Ivrea) makes the simile the
starting point for a 26-line poem which he writes in gold at the end of his
manuscript (*Colophons*, no. 315). Engelbodus, a tenth-century scribe
writing in Ghent, makes a 4-line poem out of the simile (*Colophons*, no.
3795), and an eleventh-century scribe in Monte Cassino includes it among
a series of commonplaces out of which he makes his scribal poem
(*Colophons*, no. 8370). The simile is also adopted by Alcuin in one of his
poems (Wattenbach, p. 280): here we see the formulas of the colophon
writers emerging in serious Anglo-Latin poetry.

Consideration of the colophon tradition out of which the Old English
'Metrical Epilogue' seems to have come not only is useful in clarifying the
poem's general strategies in combining old formulas with new intentions
(as we shall see later), but it can even contribute toward the solution of
individual textual cruces. Line 5, for example, has been the subject of
scholarly dispute. Jacob Schipper was convinced that 'ðas boc awrat bam
handum twam' meant that the scribe was ambidextrous, and on this
assumption he rested his theory that the two distinct scribal hands in the
foregoing text (which paleographers have subsequently explained as
contrasting earlier and later scripts by two different copyists)[11] were in fact
the work of a single scribe who sometimes wrote with his left hand and
sometimes with his right.[12] But attention to the way in which other
colophons refer to the craft of writing suggests that this theory is misguided. Scribes often referred to themselves as writing *per manus* or
propriis manibus ('with their hands' or 'with their own hands'),[13] and the
Anglo-Saxon who copied the Old English version of Bede's *De temporibus anni* in MS. Cotton Tiberius B.v (fol. 28ᵛ) writes pathetically at the
end of his labors, 'God helpe minum handum' ('God help my hands'), not
'God helpe minre handa' ('God help my hand').[14] This feeling that both
hands are involved in the act of writing is probably related to the scribes'
oft repeated complaint in their colophons that when one writes the whole
body toils:

Scribere qui nescit, nullum putat esse laborem:
Tres digiti scribunt, totum corpusque laborat.[15]

(He who does not know how to write thinks it is no labor; three fingers write, and the whole body labors.)

Comments in the colophons like 'propriis manibus totum scripsit' ('he wrote it all with his own hands'), 'scripsit suis manibus istum' ('he wrote this with his own hands'), 'ut pene calamum in manibus tenere poteram' ('that I was hardly able to hold the pen in my hands'), and 'duabus manibus et decem cum digitis scripsi' ('I wrote with two hands and ten fingers')[16] leave little doubt that the Old English poet's 'bam handum twam' is merely a scribal formula and has nothing to do with ambidexterity.

While other images and allusions in the 'Metrical Epilogue' also become clearer in the light of the colophon tradition,[17] the real problems of interpretation posed by this poem as it appears in Dobbie's edition arise not so much from inattention to its generic precursors as from inattention to the codicological context in which it is preserved. A case in point is the opening verse, where the poem begins with 'Bidde ic eac'—'I *also* beseech.' 'Also' in addition to what? The notes in our standard edition (and in previous editions) make no allusion to this curiosity, although it is surely an unusual way to begin a poem. Of course the title Dobbie has assigned to the poem implies that something has gone before, but neither his textual nor his explanatory notes tell the reader what text or what words precede the poem in the manuscript.

A search through the introductory material in Dobbie's volume does reveal the helpful datum that our poem comes 'at the end of the Anglo-Saxon text of Bede's *Ecclesiastical History*' (p. cxvii), but even this information is less exact than it might have been, since the surviving manuscripts of Bede's *History* do not all end in the same way.[18] Also, Dobbie gives us no indication of what relation, if any, the verses in the manuscript bear to the foregoing text of Bede. Is the poem visually integrated with the main text of the manuscript, or does it stand separate? Is it an independent text, or are there verbal or other links between the *History* and the poem? For answers to these questions we must return to the manuscript in which the verses are preserved and study them in their original context.

What we find when we turn to the manuscript is that the poem is one in a series of three petitions with which this copy of Bede's *History* ends. The three petitions immediately follow Bede's list of his previous writings, the list with which he concludes the *History* proper in virtually all manuscripts. The list closes with the words 'be gesettnessum 7 be gemetum spræccynna ðam þæt halige gewrit se canan awriten' ('concern-

15

Corpus Christi College, Cambridge MS. 41, page 482

þæt he mote maneȝa ȝyt mundū
rynum ȝeendiȝan hir aldre copi
lan ⁊ him þær ȝeunne rede aheal
ler ȝeþeald þo deþa þaldens þæt
he onriht mote oð hir daȝa ende
ophihȝen hepiȝan · AMEN
ȝe p e o n þ e þ æt is

MENDI ȝehiþað nu hu ... ophten þæs spurende on þaſ ʒɪɚ ɚ ɚ... ⁊ hu he
prezede þ ær sæp cþam hinȝum eastron þreþon þ þæsse mannes sunu ȝesealo ɚ à honñ Sens
hælend nened þa hi þa ȝeȝaðopuoe þreþon þabi steopas ⁊ þa ealdopinen þæs þolces inanum
cafepcune ⁊ se biscepp þæs nenes scís as haðioon hi spiþe micele þeahcunȝe in þe upine hæbeñ
þ hi hine yoloon mio inpicæ bespican to þam þ hie hine ucpealoon þacpeoon Sæne þamen
tala nelle þe on þisne simbel ooȝ þileſ pensy simicel unȝeþre si on þissuſ solce mio þiþe hæleno
þæſ in bethania lanoe onsimonys h use þæſ unȝuman þa ȝe eooe him an pisco ɚos hir þæſ
de elescet on hanoa þær þæſ oeon þrþope ... simin ȝe sull þa ȝæt heo hir oȝenþaſ
hælenes heaþoo be ȝitenoum þa þæs ȝe sa ... þon hiſ ȝin ȝeþan þapun oon hi spiþe
unpæte ⁊ hi cpeoon hpæt iſ þeos saptopienes þ ðiſ þtð ɚós hpæt heo hiſ mihte on micel
penið becýpan ⁊ þon þeansmouum mannum ȝe ... oꞃe lan þapicte hiþa ȝe þancaſ ⁊
cýþþa to þim hpæte iſ eop un eaoe æt þissum piſſe ... heo þæſ ȝoo þonð þiicenoe
onne simble ȝe habbað þeanȝan mio eop æt ȝe ... ne habbað me Simble þær
heo oioe minum lichoman to spinsinesse ⁊ heo ... neoe þ he scealoe beon anþyp
ȝenne aleȝeo Sod iſ þ eop seccȝ þæn hiſ ȝoo spell ... bio inne þeo ȝeono calle
mioo an ȝeapo bio hi þie ȝemino hþæt heo oioe ... onne ȝemino þa eooe an oꞃ xii
ȝeon ȝenum þæs nana þuſ iupaſ scapuoð iooe to ... þapa sacenoa ealoon mannum
⁊ he cpæo to him hpæte pille ȝeme sillan ȝi ic hine ... ȝe þte þ he laȝe upne ophten
hi þa calle anmooduce him to ȝenel oneþæoon þe þe ... ȝe sillað · ꞃꞃꞃ sullinȝa on silſþe
⁊ hu þanen þasahte heþa ȝebmplican ... ooð ȝe sillan þa seþcheno ær
... ȝepeonoum · Sæ mio hiſ ſpell ȝeonȝum on ȝan þa ... ſpþecan to hiſ ȝeonȝum · ⁊ heſpa
cpæo · Soð ic eop sec ȝe oæt an iſ mio eop þeme hiꞃ ð ȝe seal ... ne þaþ ðe ȝe hiþ oon hiſ ȝeonȝe
pan þapunoon hie spioe ... þæ ſooꞃ ꞃæle cpæo ſuꞃ ... þꞃ ... þom ic hnȝ ꞇa an ſpa
þoðe him hæleno · ⁊ he cpæo ſeþe me mio hiſ hanoum ... þuneð ſpa hir be him apꞃiꞇ iſ on þiſ
ſum oiſce Sæne belæþeð þon sonannes sunu ȝeð þala þam men þo mannes ȝe sealo ne hæð
ſel þe him þaþe þ hena næþe oa ſiþeð ⁊ ſpanoðe him se iuoa ſeðe hine ȝesealo ne hæþe ⁊
he cpæo ſæcȝſt · hu laþ eoþ þ ic þæt ſi þa cpæð him hæleno to þu þæt cpæoe · he þa hæleno ⁊ þan
æꞇeꞃ ȝeþeonoum an ꞃenȝ h laþe ⁊ þane ȝebleoſaoe ꞃeo þiþæc ⁊ ſealoe hiſ ȝinȝꞃum ⁊ cpæð · æꞇ ȝe calle

ing the figures and modes of speech in which the Canon, the Holy Writ, [is] written'). Thereupon ensue the three petitions:

ANd ic bidde ðe nu goda hælend þæt þu me milde forgeafe swetlice drincan þa word ðines wisdomes þæt þu eac swylce forgyfe þæt ic æt nyhstan to ðe þam wylle ealles wisdomes becuman mote symle ætywan beforan þinre ansyne

EAC þonne ic eaðmodlice bidde þæt on eallum ðam þe ðis ylce stær to becume ures cynnes to rædenne oððe to gehyrenne þæt hi for minum untrumnessum modes 7 lichaman gelomlice 7 geornlice þingian mid ðære upplican arfæstnesse godes ælmihtiges 7 on gehwylcum heora mægðe þas mede heora edleanes me agyfan þæt ic be þe syndrigum mægðum oð þam hyhrum stowum, ða þe ic gemyndelice 7 þam bigengum þancwyrðlice gelyfde Geornlice ic tilode to awritenne þæt ic mid eallum þingum þone westm arfæstre þingunge gemete

BIDDe ic eac æghwylcne mann brego rices weard þe þas boc ræde 7 þa bredu befo fira aldor þæt gefyrðrige þone writre wynsum cræfte þe ðas boc awrat bam handum twam þæt he mote manega gyt mundum synum geendigan his aldre to willan 7 him þæs geunne se ðe ah ealles geweald rodera waldend þæt he on riht mote oð his daga ende drihten herigan.   AMEN

ge   weorþe   þæt

Translated literally, the petitions would read as follows:

And now I beseech Thee, Good Savior, that Thou [Who] hast graciously permitted me to drink sweetly the words of Thy wisdom, that Thou also permit that I be allowed to come at last to Thee, the fountain of all wisdom, [and] to be present eternally before Thy face;

I also humbly beseech that among all those to whom this same history of our nation might come—either for reading or for hearing—that they will frequently and zealously intercede with the celestial mercy of God Almighty for my defects both of mind and of body, and that in each province of theirs they will grant me this meed of recompense: that I, who strove zealously to record whatever I found memorable or pleasing to the inhabitants concerning their various provinces [or] more important places, might obtain the fruits of their pious intercession in all things;

I also beseech each man—ruler of the realm, lord of men—who might read this book and hold the volume that he support with kindly power the scribe who wrote this book with his two hands so that he might complete yet many [more copies] with his hands according to his lord's desire; and may He Who reigns over all, the Lord of the Heavens, grant him that so that he might rightly praise the Lord until the end of his days. Amen. So be it.

If we notice how closely related these three petitions are, it will seem curious indeed that the third of the three should have been detached from its place in the sequence and printed separately by editors under the title 'Metrical Epilogue to Manuscript 41.' Each petition begins with the same subject and verb: *ic bidde.* The same connective, *eac,* is used to link the third petition to the second and the second to the first, as well as for internal linkage in the first. The introductory *and* of the first petition links the entire sequence of requests to the foregoing context. The petitions themselves form a connected series of appeals for access to God—through direct admission to the Presence, through intercessory prayers of readers, and through devotion to God expressed through pious labor. The three prayers are, in fact, even more closely linked than that: they are all parts of a single, loosely constructed sentence: 'And now I beseech . . . ; I also beseech . . . ; I also beseech . . . .' The concluding 'Amen, geweorþe þæt,' which Dobbie (like the other editors) prints as an awkward, extra-metrical appendage to his 'Metrical Epilogue,' in fact refers to all three of the foregoing prayers and should not be associated with the poem alone.

The verbal and syntactic linkages between the closing sections of the manuscript are reinforced strongly by the visual presentation of the text. If we examine the reduced facsimiles in the three plates accompanying this essay, we will note that the scribe wrote the three petitions in the same stately script he used for the text of the *History* itself, thus suggesting a continuum from the *History* through the last of the petitions. (The monumental script he uses may be compared with the more normal-sized scripts of the texts which have been added by a later scribe in the margins and the originally unused space which followed the three petitions and 'geweorþe þæt.') The scribe left large spaces for illuminated capital letters to introduce each of the three petitions, just as he did to set off sections and subdivisions of the *History* preceding. As the facsimiles show, the illuminator never completed his task, however, and so each of the three petitions begins with a blank space (which in my transcription I have filled in with the intended letter). The triad of appeals ends with the generously spaced concluding formula 'Geweorþe þæt,' and below this is 'a fine figure of Christ crucified,'[19] now overwritten by the Old English homiletic text which a later scribe copied into the blank spaces preserved by the original scribes to enhance the stately effect of their pages. In the closing petition, moreover, the scribe of the poem has written every other line in red ink ornamented with gold rather than in the usual brown ink. It is clear from the presentation of the three petitions in the manuscript that something rather grand was intended, a ceremonial coda to Bede's great work. And the Old English poem is an integral part of that coda, not an independent bit of scribal verse.

The verbal and visual integration of the triad of petitions with each other and with the foregoing text—a triad which appears in this precise form in no other surviving manuscript of Bede's *History*—suggests the question, What is the source of this three-part prayer? To what extent is this material Bede's, and to what extent is it someone else's elaboration? The first of the three is indubitably Bede's, of course. It appears at this point in virtually every non-fragmentary copy of the *History*, both Latin and Old English. The second petition, though just as certainly by Bede, is quite another matter. In one whole family of manuscripts (what Plummer calls the 'M-type manuscript'), it appears not at the end of the *History* but as part of the Preface to Book I, and this is the position it occupies in the standard modern editions of the Latin version. In the 'C-type' manuscripts, however, this prayer is located at the end of the entire work, where we see it in the manuscript we are considering here.[20] The Old English poem, which makes up the third of the prayers in our manuscript, appears to have been added by a later versifier who thought it would make a fitting conclusion to the preceding prayers and to the work as a whole.

Having restored the poem to its manuscript context, we can now begin to read it and to deal with the problems it has posed for previous editors and scholars. The adverb *eac* at the beginning of the Old English poem (the third word in the first line) is no longer puzzling: it merely continues the sequence of *eac* connectives in the preceding two sections of the prayer. More important, we are now able to identify the speaker of the poem. Heretofore scholars have uniformly identified the speaker as the scribe who wrote the manuscript. Dobbie (p. cxvii) states that the poem is spoken by 'one of the scribes . . . beseeching the help and encouragement of his noble readers.' Thomas Miller in his edition of Bede's *History* says, 'At the end . . . the scribe addresses the reader in six [!] verses.'[21] C. L. Wrenn, who appears to have misunderstood the poem's contents in several respects, says, 'At the end of a version of the Alfredian Bede in MS. Corpus Christi College, Cambridge, 41, . . . a scribe has added what is apparently his own metrical prayer inviting his aristocratic readers to pray for the book's copyist.'[22] But a reading of the poem in its manuscript context makes clear that it is not the scribe who speaks in these verses. It is the Venerable Bede.

Once we recognize that the sequence of *ic bidde*'s occurs in a single sentence rhetorically connected to Bede's autobiographical conclusion to the *History* (that is, his brief account of his life, followed by the list of his works and his two prayers), we realize that the same voice must be speaking throughout the entire three-part 'coda' culminating in the poem. There has never been any doubt that the first two sections of the coda are spoken by Bede; how then can the first person pronoun of the last of the three sections be read as referring to anyone else? The poet who first attached these verses to the conclusion of the *History* clearly intended us to take the third section as Bede's words as well, the verses thus forming an author's *envoi* rather than a scribe's colophon. To be sure, the author of these verses may very well have been a scribe (though not very likely the scribe of this particular manuscript),[23] and he or she[24] used the conventions of scribal colophons in much of the phrasing in the poem. But the dramatic voice speaking in the poem is that of Bede, not of the versifying scribe responsible for the poem. Its genre is that of the Cynewulfian signatures rather than that of the colophons.[25]

Another fundamental question which could not be dealt with until the poem was restored to its context can also be raised now: to whom are these ten verses addressed? The first petition of the three is addressed to the Savior, the second to anyone who ever reads the *History* or even hears it read ('to rædenne oððe to gehyrenne'). The third limits its appeal to those who actually have the book in their possession and can read it ('þe þas boc ræde ond þa bredu befo'), and it requests not intercessory prayers but rather material support for the scribe ('gefyrðrige þone writre wynsum[um] cræfte'). Only someone of power can supply such support to scribes, and the poet's epithets *bregorices weard* and *fira aldor* make clear that he is indeed addressing a man of power—a king.

At this point we need to reflect once again on where the poem stands within the context of Bede's *History* as a whole. The immediately preceding petition, as we have already noticed, occurs in many manuscripts of the Latin *History* not here at the end of the work but in a prefatory letter which Bede placed at the very beginning of the *History*. This letter is addressed, of course, to King Ceolwulf. Bede says in this letter that he is sending his *History* to the King so that Ceolwulf can read it himself ('þe sylfum to rædenne' in the Old English version) and then have it copied and more widely published among his subjects.[26] The Old English poem which now stands after the second petition is, then, simply a restatement at the end of the *History* of the appeal which Bede had originally placed at the beginning of his book in his Preface to Ceolwulf. But by the eleventh century, when many scholars think this poem was written,[27] King Ceolwulf was long past promoting scribal work. Therefore the poet appropriately generalizes the appeal to include 'each king, (each) ruler of men.'

What are we to make of a poet—whether a scribe or another—who usurps the voice of Bede to restate in a completely new form and modified terms Bede's original appeal for promulgation of his book? To the scholarly modern reader, with his anxieties over accurate authorial attribution, the whole procedure could seem a little fraudulent. But this, of course, is a modern attitude. The luxuriant pseudepigraphy of pious intent circulating in the medieval world implies a less anxious attitude toward a writer's appropriation of an authoritative voice to enunciate Godly verities, while the Anglo-Saxon poets' fondness for assuming dramatic voices to speak their verses (as in *Widsith, The Dream of the Rood, The Wife's Lament, Wulf and Eadwacer,* and *The Wanderer,* among others) shows that they were alert to the artistic possibilities of this device. Colophon writers shared in this relaxed attitude, as is shown by the closing inscription in the Book of Durrow claiming that that codex was produced by St. Columba himself in only twelve days. Indeed, the poet who wrote the 'Metrical Epilogue' was doing so within a well-documented tradition of colophons and envois placed at the end of Bede manuscripts, some of which purport to be addressed to the reader by Bede himself. Two poetic colophons dealing with Bede are quoted by Colgrave and Mynors in their edition of the *History* (p. lxxiv). But probably the most famous of the colophons purporting to be spoken by Bede is that written in alternate black and red letters (like the 'Metrical Epilogue') at the end of the Leningrad Bede:

> Explic*it* D*omi*no ivvante
> Lib*er* qvintvs Historiae
> Ecclesiasticae Gentis
> Anglorvm
> Beda famvlvs Chr*isti* indignvs.[28]

(Here with the aid of God ends the fifth book of the *Ecclesiastical History of the English People*—Bede, unworthy servant of Christ.)

Paul Meyvaert has demonstrated persuasively that this is not a genuine autograph of the Venerable Bede but is rather the effort of a later scribe to convince medieval readers of the manuscript that the concluding line consists of Bede's own words written in his own hand[29]—a deception similar to that intended by the author of the 'Metrical Epilogue' in the Cambridge manuscript. But in the case of the Leningrad colophon the later scribe's artifice was so successful that he has fooled even some modern scholars.[30] Several other Bede manuscripts also contain colophons which claim descent directly 'de manu Bedae' but which modern paleographers have shown to be ungenuine.[31] Such pious appropriations of the authority of the Church Father give to these manuscripts what Meyvaert has called ' "a relic" value in connection with Bede.'[32] Not all such colophons are dismissed by modern specialists as forgeries; one which appears at the end of some manuscripts of Bede's redaction of Paulinus' *Vita Felicis* is thought by modern scholars to go back to a genuine colophon by Bede, even though it is now preserved only in late manuscripts.[33]

'Ðvs Beda ðe broema boecere cuęð' ('Thus said the renowned scholar Bede'), writes the Lindisfarne Gospels glossator in the margin of folio 255ʳ, and he may be quoting a line from a lost Old English poem on Bede.[34] The authority of the Northumbrian Father was immense, and more than a few Anglo-Saxons could not resist invoking its power in support of a text, a gloss, or a manuscript. But the tradition of Bedan (and pseudo-Bedan) *colophons*, as we have just seen, was especially strong, and in completing our assessment of what the poet of the 'Metrical Epilogue' was trying to suggest when he grafted his verses so skillfully onto the pre-existing words of Bede's own colophon,[35] we must reflect for a moment on the significance which scribal activity held for Anglo-Saxons and, more specifically, for Bede himself.

As we have seen, the 'Metrical Epilogue' is an appeal for royal support of the publication of Bede's *History*, an appeal made now in behalf of the vernacular version, just as Bede himself had appealed in his *Prefatio* for promulgation of the Latin *Historia*. But the poem further states that if the scribe is granted an opportunity to make copies of the book he will thereby praise the Lord ('drihten herigan'). This statement invokes the often enunciated medieval view of the nobility of scribal work, which, even more than other monastic activities, is an effective means of honoring God. *Laborare est orare*, but, as Alcuin makes clear, some types of work are a higher form of devotion than others:

> Est opus egregium sacros iam scribere libros,
> Nec mercede sua scriptor et ipse caret.
> Fodere quam vites melius est scribere libros,
> Ille suo ventri serviet, iste animae.[36]

> (To copy sacred books is a noble work,
> Nor does the scribe himself fail to receive his reward.
> It is better to copy books than to cultivate the vine,
> The one serves his belly, the other his soul.)

Cassiodorus, in the first sentence of his chapter on scribes, had already stated that of all forms of physical toil performed by monks scribal work is the most preferable, and his reason was that scribes were so effective in disseminating the precepts of God.[37] They preach with their hands, release tongues with their fingers and so, 'O spectaculum bene considerantibus gloriosum!' ('Oh sight glorious to those considering it well!'), it is through the scribe's fingers that the power of the Trinity is given expression.[38]

This conception of the scribe as a medium through which the Godhead speaks is a potent metaphor which had appeal among early Anglo-Saxon writers. The phrase 'dictante Deo' ('with God dictating') occurs more than once in Alcuin's poems,[39] and the scribe depicted in Æthelwulf's ninth-century treatise *De abbatibus* was able to perform his incomparable feats of calligraphy and ornamentation because 'digitos sanctus iam spiritus auctor rexit' ('the Creator, the Holy Spirit, was ruling his fingers').[40] God Himself set the example for scribes, says Cassiodorus, when He used His omnipotent finger to write the Law,[41] an observation repeated later by Rabanus Maurus.[42] And among the Church Fathers who devoutly followed the Lord's example in this respect stands the Venerable Bede, who, in the Preface to his commentary on Luke, describes himself as both author and scribe: 'Ipse mihi dictator simul notarius et librarius' ('Myself at the same time author, stenographer, and scribe').[43] In the person of Bede the roles of author and of scribe converge, just as the genres of authorial envoi and scribal colophon seem to converge in the 'Metrical Epilogue.' And this is the source of the poem's charm and spiritual force. When the poet has Bede speak in behalf of the scribe, he is using the voice of an author who has himself served as scribe on occasion and who understands that both authors and scribes are nothing more (or less) than intermediaries through whom God speaks. This virtual equivalence of scribal and authorial roles seems to be suggested by the poet's use of the ambiguous verb *awrat* ('composed' or 'copied') to describe the scribe's work of copying, for a form of this same verb is used in the preceding petition (*awritenne*) in reference to Bede's composition of the *Historia ecclesiastica*, and in the section of Bede's history just before the three petitions begin, *awrat* is used repeatedly in Bede's list of his literary works ('ic awrat . . . ic awrat . . . ic awrat . . . ic geornlice awrat . . .'). The last word before the petitions begin, moreover, is *awriten*, only this time in reference to Holy Writ. This repetitive and polysemic use of the verb seems to emphasize that Holy Writ, the writings of Bede, and the humble scribe's work with 'his two hands' are all expressions of God's intentions, a fact which exalts the scribe's work and lends a spiritual dimension to the support which the poem asks powerful worldly men to give to that work. It also gives special meaning to the poet's adoption of the voice of the erstwhile scribe Bede when he makes his appeal for that support.

As was stated at the outset of this essay, my intention is not solely to clarify the meaning of the 'Metrical Epilogue' but rather to suggest the importance of considering manuscript context when reading any Old English text. In the interest of this more general concern, my remaining pages will be devoted to a summary account of a group of other texts which might gain clarity when studied in the light of their codicological environments. One such text is the poem called *Maxims II* by Dobbie in his edition[44] and *The Cotton Gnomes* by previous editors. *Maxims II* is a versified list of sententious sayings strung together, it would appear, more or less *ad libitum*. A mere listing of items has seemed to some modern tastes an unworthy structure for a poem, however,[45] and so scholars have tried now and again to discern organic unity in the list, positing thematic, associational, imagistic, or other structures, or else dividing the poem into subsections or 'movements' that are unified by style or content.[46] Since there is more diversity than congruence in the structures posited, one wonders whether we are not approaching the problem in the wrong way when we limit our attention to the *Maxims* in isolation rather than consider them in their manuscript context. For in the manuscript *Maxims II* is the second in a series of three texts, each of which has the structure of a list. British Library MS. Cotton Tiberius B.i, fols. 112^r–64^r, contains the verse calendar *Menologium*, *Maxims II*, and *The Anglo-Saxon Chronicle* in that order. All three texts are written in the same scribal hand, and 'the evidence of the capitalization in the manuscript,' says Dobbie (p. lx), 'makes it probable that the scribe, at least, regarded the *Menologium* and *Maxims II* as preliminary matter to the Chronicle.' Having made this observation, Dobbie then proceeds nonetheless to discuss the two texts separately from the *Chronicle* and from each other, remarking, 'The *Menologium*, to be sure, has some connection with the subject matter of the Chronicle, being itself an account of the seasons and festal days of the Christian year; but *Maxims II*, like *Maxims I* in the Exeter Book, has no relationship in subject matter to either the *Menologium* or the Chronicle' (pp. lx–lxi).

The diversity of the subject matter of these texts cannot be denied,[47] and yet they do have in common a catenulate structure: that is, they are all essentially lists. And at this point it is of interest to examine the manuscript environment of other texts similar to, or identical with, those in Cotton Tiberius B.i. *Maxims I* is the poem most like *Maxims II*, of course, and when we turn to the Exeter Book we find that there it is grouped with *Widsith* and *The Fortunes of Men*—two list-poems *par excellence*. The poem in the Old English corpus most like *Menologium* in structure is probably *The Seasons for Fasting*. This text survives in MS. Cotton Otho B.x, which also contains a West-Saxon genealogy, *The Anglo-Saxon Chronicle*, a list of popes and other churchmen, Anglo-Saxon laws, a burghal hidage, and a group of herb recipes—again, essentially a collection of lists. When we examine other manuscripts of

The Anglo-Saxon Chronicle, we find that they too usually combine the annals with texts which are catenulate in structure. *The Parker Chronicle* (MS. Corpus Christi College, Cambridge, 173) appears along with a genealogical list and a list of laws. The manuscript now preserved as Cotton Tiberius A.vi and A.iii also combines the *Chronicle* with a genealogy of the West-Saxon kings. Cotton Caligula A.xv has the annals combined with a paschal table and other miscellaneous lists. While it must be conceded that there is an element of subjectivity in judging whether a text's structure is basically that of a list—as the *Chronicle*'s entries become increasingly substantial, for example, it begins to look less like a list—there does seem to be a strong tendency to anthologize lists, and this suggests in turn that the Anglo-Saxons acknowledged and accepted the list as a structural principle.

It is hardly surprising that they did, for the list is a very popular form in the Middle Ages in general and in Anglo-Saxon England in particular. Isidore's *Etymologies* are but the most famous of many influential list-works in medieval Europe, and the Anglo-Saxons' numerous glossaries, regnal lists, episcopal lists, martyrologies, lapidaries, law codes, genealogies, herbaria, leechdoms, and other lists attest to the popularity of the form in England. And since the list-form suggested by the Latin encyclopedia tradition conforms so well with the additive style of poetry inherited from the Germanic oral tradition, it is hardly surprising that listing should have been the structural principle of so many Old English poems (such as *The Fates of the Apostles*, *The Gifts of Men*, *The Fortunes of Men*, *Precepts*, *The Rune Poem*, and *Widsith*).[48]

To say that *Maxims II* (along with *Menologium* and the *Chronicle*) is, after all, a list and that lists were a popular medieval form may seem a rather uninteresting way to 'solve' the problem of the poem's structure. But if we go on to study the three texts together, as they are presented by the scribe in the manuscript, we may find evidence of other, more interesting structural features which were not apparent so long as scholars limited their analyses to *Maxims II* in isolation. The beginning and end of each of the three works bear close attention. *Menologium* begins with Christ the King and, coming full circle through the calendar year, closes with Him. *Maxims II* then begins with the powers of the king and of Christ ('Cyning sceal rice healdan . . . þrymmas syndan Cristes myccle' ['The king shall have dominion[49] . . . great are the powers of Christ']) and, after moving through the seasons of the year and the various characteristics of men and matter, ends with Christ the Lord. The *Chronicle* then begins by naming Christ ('Ær Cristes geflæscnesse' ['Before Christ's incarnation']) and, if it ran its course to its predestined end, would presumably end with Christ in Judgment, the event that marks the end of human time. The conclusion of *Menologium* and the beginning of

Maxims II are also linked by a curious verbal echo: *healdan sceal . . . geond Brytenricu . . . kyninges* at the end of *Menologium* is immediately followed by *Cyning sceal rice healdan* at the beginning of *Maxims II*. This repetition could be the result of a compiler's adapting the phrasing of his texts to forge a verbal link between them.

Besides these rather mechanical connections the three texts seem to be thematically united by a shared concern with time. The account of the seasons and the 'fruits of the year' in *Maxims II*, lines 5–9, evokes both the calendar theme of *Menologium* and the annalistic development of the *Chronicle*. Also, all three texts reveal a similar perspective on historical time, each calling attention to the relation between antiquity and the (Anglo-Saxon) present. *Maxims II* mentions near its beginning the Roman ruins 'which are on this earth' ('enta geweorc þa þe on þysse eorðan syndon') and thus binds the Anglo-Saxon moving 'hider under hrofas' ('hither under [our] roofs' [line 64]) with architectural relics of the ancient world. In *Menologium* references to Christ and His early saints are repeatedly interspersed with phrases directing attention to present times 'in Brytene her' ('here in England'),[50] and the relation between the two worlds is made concrete and historical by the figure of St. Augustine of Canterbury, who 'on Brytene her' proclaimed the teachings of the Roman church (lines 95–106). The *Chronicle* begins with Christ and Julius Caesar and then spells out year by year the historical links between that world and the Anglo-Saxon present. Bollard and others have discerned yet other unifying themes,[51] and some or all of these may also be present in the texts, although thematic similarities by their nature are less demonstrable than the verbal links mentioned above and the catenulate structure shared by the three texts. These more overt signs of relationship would seem to argue by themselves the value of reading the texts in association, as they are presented in the manuscript, rather than as isolated texts.

This is not to say, of course, that every juxtaposition of texts in every manuscript is deliberate and meaningful. Some manuscripts are grab-bags, with texts on various subjects from various periods collected and copied into a single manuscript for no discernible reason. Sometimes a scribe will copy a text into a pre-existent manuscript by another scribe simply because there is unused space available there. The facsimiles of Corpus Christi College, Cambridge, MS. 41 included in this article provide an excellent example: the Latin and vernacular texts penned into the margins of Bede's *History* have no relation whatever with the manuscript's original text. Recent discussions of the 'booklet theory' of manuscript compilation suggest yet another reason for caution in drawing inferences from the juxtaposition of texts in a codex.[52]

But often there clearly is an organizational principle behind the arrangement of texts in an Old English codex, and we may even suspect that compilers sometimes adapted one text to another when they were adjacent. The degree of interdependence of texts within a manuscript can vary widely. A poem like the 'Metrical Epilogue' cannot really be understood as long as it is read in isolation. In other cases, such as the juxtaposition of *Maxims II*, *Menologium*, and the *Chronicle* in Cotton Tiberius B.i, a consideration of the codicological aspects of the texts might suggest new and more fruitful questions to ask about works which have proven unresponsive to critical analysis when they are studied in isolation. In yet other cases a return to manuscript contexts might suggest new ways to examine old questions about authorship and textual integrity, such as the unity of *Christ* or the relation of *Guthlac A* to *Guthlac B* or of *Genesis A* to *Genesis B*. In all cases, however, interpreters of Old English literature would be prudent when they consider the various contexts of a poem not to neglect its position and appearance within the manuscript in which it is preserved, for its most immediate context can sometimes be its most important context.

Yale University

From Horseback to Monastic Cell: The Impact on English Literature of the Introduction of Writing

JEFF OPLAND

IN the course of the seventh and eighth centuries, the pagan Anglo-Saxons in England were converted to Christianity by Celtic and Roman missionaries.[1] Although the Anglo-Saxons had in the runic alphabet a system of writing, its use was never widespread and was restricted to inscriptions; the use of writing to record literature was introduced to the early English by the Christian missionaries. We are accustomed to think of the introduction of printing as the event of greatest significance in the history of English literature. Certainly Caxton and his successors initiated profound social and educational changes; but in the history of English literature, the introduction of writing has had even more profound an effect than the introduction of printing. Printing merely facilitates the dissemination of literary works, whereas writing initiates a change in attitude among audience and artists alike that is revolutionary. Written literature introduced the Anglo-Saxons to a new kind of artist, a different relation between artist and artifact, an altered function of the artifact in society. Consider two Anglo-Saxon poets, one a king's thane riding a horse, the other a monk labouring at night in his cell.[2]

On the morning following Beowulf the Geat's triumphant victory over the monster Grendel, the Danish retainers ride out to the monster's lake dwelling to survey the signs of Grendel's defeat. Old and young retainers ride joyfully back from the lake on their horses, and well they might rejoice, for Beowulf has finally rid the Danish court of the unwanted attentions of the gluttonous Grendel, who for the past twelve years has delighted in drinking the blood of drowsy Danes, up to thirty at one sitting. As the retainers ride along, they discuss Beowulf's deed; many of them remark that there is no finer warrior alive, no one more worthy to be

king, though of course in so doing they are not casting aspersions on their
own king Hrothgar. At times, on the level sandy plains, they raced their
horses; at other times a thane of the king, a man well versed in oral
tradition, found new words properly linked. He began to shuffle with
words, skilfully to stir up again Beowulf's exploit, and to create quickly an
apt account. He mentioned all the heroic deeds of Sigemund and referred
to the unhappy reign of king Heremod:

> Þanon eft gewiton ealdgesiðas,
> swylce geong manig of gomenwaþe
> fram mere modge mearum ridan,
> beornas on blancum. Ðær wæs Beowulfes
> mærðo mæned; monig oft gecwæð
> þætte suð ne norð be sæm tweonum
> ofer eormengrund oþer nænig
> under swegles begong selra nære
> rondhæbbendra, rices wyrðra.
> Ne hie huru winedrihten wiht ne logon,
> glædne Hroðgar, ac þæt wæs god cyning.
> Hwilum heaþorofe hleapan leton,
> on geflit faran fealwe mearas
> ðær him foldwegas fægere þuhton,
> cystum cuðe. Hwilum cyninges þegn,
> guma gilphlæden, gidda gemyndig,
> se ðe ealfela ealdgesegena
> worn gemunde, word oþer fand
> soðe gebunden; secg eft ongan
> sið Beowulfes snyttrum styrian
> ond on sped wrecan spel gerade,
> wordum wrixlan. Welhwylc gecwæð
> þæt he fram Sigemundes secgan hyrde
> ellendædum, uncuþes fela,
> Wælsinges gewin, wide siðas . . .
> Se wæs wreccena wide mærost
> ofer werþeode, wigendra hleo,
> ellendædum (he þæs ær onðah),
> siððan Heremodes hild sweðrode,
> eafoð ond ellen. He mid Eotenum wearð
> on feonda geweald forð forlacen,
> snude forsended . . . (853–77, 898–904a).[3]

(The aged retainers turned back again, and also many a gallant
youth returned from that gay hunting, riding back from the mere on

their glossy steeds. Beowulf's glory was proclaimed; many a man declared that nowhere in the wide world, north or south, from sea to sea, was there another shield-bearer nobler than he beneath the broad sweep of the brilliant sky, nor any more worthy of kingship. Yet indeed they did not find any fault in their kindly lord, the gracious Hrothgar, for he was a good king.

Sometimes these famous fighters would set their tawny steeds to gallop in rivalry, wherever the paths seemed fair and were known to be good. Sometimes one of the king's thanes, a man with a rich store of high-sounding words and a memory filled with lays, one who remembered a whole host of tales from olden times, would devise some new poem linked in true metre. Or again, this man would set out to relate Beowulf's exploit according to his art, reciting the well-wrought tale to good effect, and varying his words.

He spoke too of all he had heard tell about Sigemund and his valiant deeds, and much that was not known, about the warfare of the son of Wæls, his wide journeyings. . . . Of all exiles, Sigemund, shield of fighting men, was most renowned among many nations for his valiant deeds, for by these he had prospered—after the prowess, the strength and the valour of Heremod dwindled away.

Heremod was lured into the power of his foes among the Jutes, and speedily sent to his death. . . .)[4]

This passage is a notorious crux, the occasion of much scholarly debate particularly as to the character of the thane's performance.[5] I believe that we have here a description of a Danish thane giving vent to his emotion in the production of a spontaneous poem. The emotion is occasioned by the particular social circumstance in which the thane finds himself. The stimulus for the performance has been established for us quite carefully. The party of Danes has travelled to the lake and viewed the grisly scene. On their return the retainers discuss Beowulf's glory, and they assert that there is no better warrior alive anywhere on earth, no one more worthy of being a king. It is within this specific social context that the thane, drawing on his knowledge of ancient stories, performs. I believe that the thane on this occasion produces one poem, not a cycle of poems, and that the poem is not a narrative at all. He utters a eulogy in praise of Beowulf.[6] He skilfully rehearses Beowulf's conquest of the monster; he refers to every famous deed of Sigemund that he has heard of; and he reviews the career of Heremod. The thane's poem derives directly from the discussion of Beowulf's glorious prowess and his fitness to be king: Beowulf's exploit is mentioned, his prowess is placed alongside that of Sigemund, another monster-killer, and his potential as a king evokes the admonitory example of Heremod, a promising young king who ultimately oppressed his own people. Sigemund and Heremod serve as poetic metaphors of Beowulf: his prowess is as great as Sigemund's, but he should beware of inviting a fate similar to Heremod's. In both cases the real referent is Beowulf: the Danish thane produces a spontaneous eulogy in praise of the young hero whose recent exploit has liberated the Danish court, and in so doing provides us with an example of what I take to be a typical Anglo-Saxon oral performance by a poet who does not employ the medium of writing, the kind of poet who operated among the Anglo-Saxons before the arrival of the Christian missionaries.[7]

Cynewulf will serve as an exemplar of the kind of English poet who emerged as a result of the Conversion, the Anglo-Saxon literate poet. Cynewulf is one of the very few Anglo-Saxon poets known to us by name, and we know that only because he ingeniously devised a means of signing the four poems of his that are now extant.[8] Runes had syllabic as well as phonemic values, and Cynewulf managed to work into his poems passages that contained the runes whose phonemic values spelt out his name and whose syllabic values allowed them to be read logically in context, thereby earning undying glory if not as a great poet certainly as the father of all English crossword puzzlers. His motive in contriving this singular feat is apparent: he wants his readers to know his name so that those who enjoy poetry might solicit the help of the Lord or of the apostles on his behalf:

> Nu ic þonne bidde beorn se ðe lufige
> þysses giddes begang þæt he geomrum me
> þone halgan heap helpe bidde,
> friðes ond fultomes. . . .
> Her mæg findan foreþances gleaw,
> se ðe hine lysteð leoðgiddunga,
> hwa þas fitte fegde. ᚠ þær on ende standeþ . . . (88–91a, 96–98).[9]

(Now then I ask the man who may love the study of this song, that he will pray to the hallowed band for help, peace, and aid for me in my sadness. . . . Here can the man shrewd in perception, who delights in songs, discover who wrought this measure. *Wealth* (F) comes at the end. . . .)[10]

Cynewulf's four signed poems are narratives treating the invention of the true cross by St. Helena, the fates of the apostles, the sufferings of St. Juliana, and the Ascension. By his own admission, Cynewulf's poems are the product of his night-time labours. Alone in his cell, weaving his compositions through his skill with words, pondering and carefully searching his mind, Cynewulf cuts a figure significantly different from that of the Danish thane galloping back from Grendel's mere:

> Þus ic frod ond fus þurh þæt fæcne hus
> wordcræftum wæf ond wundrum læs,
> þragum þreodude ond geþanc reodode
> nihtes nearwe. Nysse ic gearwe
> be ðære rode riht ær me rumran geþeaht
> þurh ða mæran miht on modes þeaht
> wisdom onwreah. Ic wæs weorcum fah,
> synnum asæled, sorgum gewæled,
> bitrum gebunden, bisgum beþrungen,
> ær me lare onlag þurh leohtne had
> gamelum to geoce, gife unscynde
> mægencyning amæt ond on gemynd begeat,
> torht ontynde, tidum gerymde,
> bancofan onband, breostlocan onwand,
> leoðucræft onleac. Þæs ic lustum breac,
> willum in worlde. Ic þæs wuldres treowes
> oft, nales æne, hæfde ingemynd
> ær ic þæt wundor onwrigen hæfde
> ymb þone beorhtan beam, swa ic on bocum fand,
> wyrda gangum, on gewritum cyðan
> be ðam sigebeacne . . . (1236–56a).[11]

(Thus, I, aged and about to depart hence because of this frail body, have woven the art of words and have wondrously gathered my matter, have pondered at times and sifted my thought in the anguish of the night. I knew not clearly the truth about the cross till wisdom by its glorious strength revealed to the thought of my mind a larger view. I was stained by deeds, bound by sins, pained by sorrows, bitterly bound, beset by troubles, before the mighty King, to comfort me in my old age, taught me in glorious manner, bestowed fair grace, and poured it into my mind, revealed it in its beauty, enlarged it once and again, unbound my body, opened my heart, unlocked the art of song which I have used gladly, with joy, in the world. Not once but often, before I had revealed the marvel concerning the radiant tree, I pondered on the tree of glory, as I found it in the course of events, set forth in books and writings concerning that sign of victory. . . .)

A consideration of the distinctive characteristics of the productions of these two poets elucidates some of the changes wrought on the Anglo-

Saxon oral poetic tradition by the introduction of writing. I do not intend to suggest that the poet on horseback was superseded by the monk in his cell as soon as Augustine or Aidan commenced their English missions. Although of course the oral poet ultimately comes to be supplanted almost entirely by the writer of poetry, the process of change is gradual; I suspect that oral poets of one kind or another remained numerically superior to literate poets throughout the Anglo-Saxon period at least. However, in the course of English literature, the arrival of poets like Cynewulf constitutes an innovation, a radical departure from English tradition. It is the purpose of this paper to explore the magnitude of that innovation using for convenience the king's thane and Cynewulf as representative examples of poets who produced their work orally and those literate poets who committed their work to writing.

First, can we effectively compare the creative products of the Danish thane and of Cynewulf? After all, we have four of Cynewulf's poems, but we do not have the thane's poem, we have only the *Beowulf* poet's account of his performance. Folklorists teach us that in some respects our approach to oral performances should differ from our approach to written texts. As Bruce Jackson eloquently put it in commenting on the analogous difference between illiterate folksong and the musically literate art song,

> Art song requires that we perceive the nature of the art involved; folk song requires not only perception of the art but also the generating or supporting musical, social, and historical contexts. Folk song is not simply textual, but *con*textual: it does not exist—save for historians and scholars—on pages in books, or even on shiny black discs. It exists in a specific place at a specific time, it is sung by specific people for whom it has specific meanings and functions.[12]

Elsewhere, approaching the same distinction from a different direction, Jackson characterises the differing responses of the literary critic and of the folklorist to the material they study:

> Although the literary critic may focus on the act of creation, he is far more interested in the fact of it—the thing created, the object as forever fixed, the artist's final issue. Most critics consider focus on the creative act ancillary to their main task—analyzing the product— and the reason for that is the product is the only thing that makes the process meaningful in the first place, and it is only the product they can ever possess entirely. The various drafts and their meanings, the psychic states of the artist along the way are never fully open to the critic. Only the finished work is available, and the finished work

justifies the attention paid. But for the folklorist, the creative act is
part of the product; each redaction of the text, each re-creation of the
event is to some extent controlled or influenced by the situation.
And the situation—involving all participants, their physical and
psychological relationships to one another and to the material—can
be very complex indeed.[13]

It is these complex relationships that inhere in the oral performance and
distinguish it from a written production that I wish to explore.

For a start, we could consider some of the physical contexts of the two
kinds of verbal productions. In order to appreciate Cynewulf's art, an
Anglo-Saxon would have had to possess a manuscript of Cynewulf's
poetry; today, scholars all over the world can pick up an edition of that
poetry and read it in the privacy of their studies or torment their students
with it. In order to appreciate the thane's art, not only would you have had
to be present in Denmark on the morning after Beowulf's defeat of
Grendel, but you would also have had to be a member of the party that rode
to the lake. The oral performer is present before his audience: they see
him and hear him perform; the thane is kinetically involved in the production of his poem: he cannot be separated from the performance.
Cynewulf on the other hand generates a poem that takes on a life apart
from him: the literate poet can be separated from his artifact. The thane's
audience is physically and temporally limited: only those present before
him as he performs can appreciate his poem. Cynewulf's audience is not
limited in time or space, not even limited to his own lifespan: *verba
volant, scripta manent*. The thane's performance is unique, a response to a
particular set of circumstances, an integral part of the experience of riding
back from a Danish lake on a particular morning. Cynewulf's products are
universal, accessible—in theory at least—to everyone who can read or
listen to a poem being read to him anywhere and at any time.

We can pursue the physical differences between oral performance and
written composition by considering the audience's response to the productions. Cynewulf wrote his poetry for readers: the only way his runic
signatures can be interpreted is by seeing the runes in the manuscript and
solving the anagram. If an Anglo-Saxon monk were to read the poems to a
literate or to an illiterate audience, he would have difficulty in conveying
the significance of the runic passages, for he would be constrained by the
metre to give the runes their syllabic value. It *is* possible, of course, that
the poetry could have been appreciated by listeners cued to the presence of
the runes by a sympathetic lector, but for our purposes we can take it that
the poems are designed to be read rather than heard. The medium of
communication is writing, symbols of the spoken word: the appeal is
visual. The appeal of the thane's poem on the other hand is primarily

aural—the audience hears the sound of his words direct, without recourse to the written word as intermediary—but the appeal is also visual, since the audience witnesses him performing his poem. Part of the total experience of the thane's poem for the audience might also have come through the sense of smell: the sweaty horses, perhaps, or the sandy plains. In the same way, part of our appreciation of a high mass would come from the smell of incense, a sensual experience that one would not recapture subsequently by reading the words in the missal. The oral performance as compared to the written text, like the live musical performance as compared to a recording, appeals simultaneously to more of our senses.

Let us pursue for a moment the smell of the incense. Our total appreciation of the mass derives in part too from witnessing the drama of the ritual, the traditional gestures of the celebrant, the ornate robes: a complex of elements contributes to our impression. With Cynewulf's poetry, it is the words alone that we concentrate our attention on, the text. But the words that the thane uttered would be only one aspect of his performance. He might have hunched his shoulders as he spoke of the misshapen monster Grendel, mimed the violent movements as he alluded to the wrestling match, complemented the words of his poem with any number of gestures, facial expressions or vocal inflexions that would have been part of his performance, that would have helped to convey his meaning. The text is only one aspect of the oral performance. This is why different stage directors may produce differing effects with the same play, or why different actors may read the same lines to differing effect: the text is only one aspect of the theatrical experience. We react today to the text of Cynewulf's poems; the thane's companions reacted to the context, not to the words alone but to the whole performance.

Indeed, the thane's audience provides the context. Their conversation about Beowulf's prowess occasioned the poem. They are part of the performance, and the text of the performance might well reflect this fact. The thane, for example, would not need to set the scene for his companions or to create the atmosphere, since they had all experienced exactly what he had, the joy of liberation that Beowulf's victory brought, the admiration of his heroic achievement. All of them had seen Beowulf and Grendel: the thane would not need to describe either protagonist in great detail, but could simply light on salient features. The text of a traditional oral performance tends to be elliptical, suggestive, because the performer and his audience usually share common experiences and values. The performer can see his audience before him, usually he knows them, and usually they are members of the same group; certainly our performer is one of King Hrothgar's thanes, and his companions are all retainers of Hrothgar. He can rely on a common social background and on the suggestive qualities of certain words: the very name of Grendel alone, for example, might be enough to conjure up in the minds of his audience all the feelings of horror he would wish to suggest to them. The literate poet on the other hand cannot see his audience and may never see them: he must visualise his readers. Cynewulf explicitly states that he has deployed his runic signature so that his readers might know the name of someone formerly unknown to them; the Danes need not ask the name of the performer, for they can see him in the act of performance. As Walter J. Ong put it in a recent article, the writer's audience is always a fiction.[14] He must expand his text for that audience in an effort to create the desired effects. A collection of the late A. C. Jordan's written versions of traditional Xhosa folktales well illustrates this point.[15] In his introduction to the volume, Harold Scheub discusses the problem confronting Jordan of capturing on paper for readers the aural or visual aspects of the traditional oral performances:

> Jordan did not attempt to do this, because he knew it was impossible. Instead, he fleshed out the scenario with words. He used techniques of the short story to bring life to the skeletal outlines, and he thereby moved away from the original [folktale] performances into the hybrid art form that exists on the pages of this book (p. 13).

This point should be apparent to anyone who has ever read a scholarly edition of an oral performance: intended originally for its usual audience, the text of the performance requires heavy annotation in order to be made universally intelligible. The thane could depend upon the experience he shared with his audience, the suggestive qualities of words common to his social group; Cynewulf, whose subjects are removed in time and whose audience is not before him, must in effect incorporate the footnotes into his text.

Performer and audience are united in a social relationship that does not exist between writer and reader, even though the reader and writer might be members of the same social group. The thane's poem is an emanation of a particular set of circumstances and is directed towards a known audience. It refers to a recent event that has affected both the thane and his companions. He responds to this situation poetically, producing a poem that is relevant, that is socially integrated: it is about a common experience of concern to both performer and audience. As he utters his poem, his companions have the opportunity to influence it, to participate in the performance perhaps by shouting encouragement, laughing in appreciation, or begging for more. The thane's performance is a social act. Cynewulf's compositions, on the other hand, are asocial. Alone in his cell, he cannot be influenced by his audience in the act of creation, only by his assessment of how his audience will react. His poetry is not socially integrated: it does not derive from an experience he shares with his readers, it refers to Biblical or historical characters remote in time from both him and his readers. The thane's poem is public: he is a member of the public and his poetry is an expression of the ethos of his society. The literate poet's products tend to be private, they become introspective and meditative, they become personal. John Pepper Clark has traced an analogous process in Nigerian literature:

> In this process Nigerian poetry has moved from the pages of daily newspapers, from the soapbox and platform of popular political meetings, held in cinema halls and the open market-place, to the private study of the individual and the exclusive confines of senior common-rooms. . . . Recluse or aristocrat, the poet no longer was of the people. Withdrawn into himself, his problems had become his own, his language one constantly geared to express issues personal to his own sensibility. The day of short circuit for both poet and public had set in.[16]

The thane's poem is as unique as the set of circumstances that inspired it. It is ephemeral: it is dead as soon as it is uttered. In order to appreciate it, you have to be one of the thane's riding companions, and you have to respond immediately to the performance, for when it is over all you will have left will be your recollection of it. The act of composition or creation coincides with the act of performance, and this in turn must coincide with the act of appreciation on the part of the audience. There is no gap in time between spontaneous artistic creation and critical response. A member of the audience may enhance his appreciation by discussing the performance subsequently with another member of the audience, but they will both be forced to base their discussion on their own imperfect recollections of the event. The thane might have spent some time before his performance marshalling his thoughts, but he could not have had more time to do this than had elapsed since he awoke that morning to the news of Beowulf's triumph. If, as I believe, his performance was a response to the conversation on horseback, he had very little time indeed to prepare his poem. All his creative faculties are brought to bear on the performance, for that is when he finally shapes his product. He might well draw on a poetic talent exercised by similar performances in the past; he probably exploits his knowledge of Germanic legend to produce his eulogy of Beowulf swiftly in acceptable Anglo-Saxon form. In the case of Cynewulf's poetry, on the other hand, there is a gap in time between the act of creation and the critical response of the reader, a gap in time now extending to some eleven centuries. His readers can and could mull over the text, return to favourite passages, grow in their understanding and appreciation through constant rereading. They may stimulate their own appreciation by reading commentaries on the text. Every act of critical response returns to the fixed text, stable and permanent: the text is established and has a primacy. Just as Cynewulf's creative action is asocial, so too is the act of critical response: the reader may read the text in the privacy of his study, an activity that involves him in personal interaction with no one. The thane's performance constitutes a social situation: for the oral performance there must be a performer and at least one listener. Unlike the thane, Cynewulf in the act of composition has time to deliberate, to improve. His objective is to produce a work that will be as stable as a work of sculpture or a painting. Since it will exist permanently, he works at it, refining it until it is as good as his talent permits: his medium affords him the opportunity to do this. In his own words, Cynewulf was tormented at times in carefully searching his thoughts (*þragum þreodude ond geþanc reodode*).

The function of the literary work in society differs too. Cynewulf probably wants to inform or educate his readers, inspire them to devotion, solicit their prayers on his behalf. The ambit of his poetry is Christian, participating in a Latin tradition that has transmitted to him discussions of the significance of the cross amongst other matters. The thane's motives are more obscure: perhaps he has a didactic motive, like Cynewulf, perhaps he simply wants to express his emotion. In any event, the ambit of his performance is Germanic, participating in an oral tradition that has transmitted to him the stories of Sigemund the Volsung and the Danish Heremod. It seems unlikely that he bursts into poetry merely in order to entertain his companions. There is one curious aspect of his performance: it seems clearly designed to praise Beowulf and to issue him a word of warning about the dictatorial tendencies of certain kings, yet Beowulf himself is not present at the performance. This suggests the possibility—and it is no more than that—that the thane's poetry might have had a ritual function, as eulogy has amongst the Zulus and Xhosas in contemporary South Africa.[17] Perhaps the eulogy served to strengthen Beowulf, whether or not he was present to hear it.

The matter of the thane's poem is Germanic. Before the Conversion traditional Anglo-Saxon poets by and large could draw only on their own native traditions; after their conversion they still had this source of material available to them, but they were also introduced to the world of Latin literature and thereby they joined a wider literary community. As members of this community they were subject to the influence of works not Anglo-Saxon or Germanic in origin, and of forms other than their traditional native forms. Cynewulf's runic signature, unlike the Danish thane's eulogy, is designed to appeal primarily to the eye. So too are the runic riddles, which, like the signature, require the reader to say the names of the runes as well as to rearrange the order of the letters the runes represent to produce the solution. Anglo-Saxons educated in Latin sometimes forego their native tradition and compose Latin poetry, some of it acrostic and as such visual in impact: the disciples or pupils of St. Boniface, for example, were fond of sending their Latin compositions to Aldhelm or to each other for comment and criticism. Some Old English poems adopt Latin rhyme; the passage in Cynewulf's *Elene* containing the description of his nocturnal poetic labours is one such. Some poems have one verse in English, one in Latin. There is a remarkable amount of experimentation with poetic forms in Anglo-Saxon England.[18] The conversion to Christianity initiates the development of offshoots of the vernacular tradition of poetry. It introduces the Anglo-Saxon to a new literary culture, to new cultural influences: in Latin the Christian Anglo-Saxon can read epics or philosophical poems, and he now has the means to imitate them. Perhaps the long narrative poem, often considered the most typical form in the corpus of Anglo-Saxon poetry that survives, is the product of this new cultural impetus. Perhaps Cynewulf's four signed poems and *Beowulf* itself are the results of the interaction of the native tradition of eulogistic poetry within which the thane's poem operates and Latin narratives like the *Aeneid*. And having tossed my hat into the ring with that supposition, I put aside Cynewulf and Hrothgar's thane to turn finally and briefly to consider Cædmon and the epic poem *Beowulf*. Is *Beowulf* an example of a traditional form current among the pre-Christian Anglo-Saxons, or does its composition need the use of writing and the model of the Latin epic to inspire it? First, let us consider Cædmon, the first English poet known to us by name and the author of the earliest English poem we possess.

Bede tells us that Cædmon was an aged illiterate shepherd in the Northumbrian monastery of Whitby.[19] He was the first Englishman to compose poems in English on Christian themes, and by his example he inspired others to follow suit. He hit on this novel idea under the inspiration of a divine vision that came to him one night. He had left a beer-drinking party at which his associates were amusing themselves by singing in turn to the harp, and had gone out to tend the cattle, whose care had been entrusted to him for the night. In the byre he fell asleep and dreamt that he was confronted by a visitor who ordered him to sing about the Creation; Cædmon dutifully complied. We know nothing about the performances earlier that evening at the party, except that they were designed to entertain and were produced to the accompaniment of a harp. Cædmon's nine-line hymn, which he produces in response to his dream, is never accompanied by a harp and hardly seems to be designed to amuse. It is in fact a eulogy: it is not so much an account of the Creation as it is a poem in praise of God the Creator. Bede explicitly says so: *statim ipse coepit cantare in laudem Dei Conditoris uersus* ('at once he began to sing verses in praise of God the Creator'). It may well be that in Cædmon we have the first Anglo-Saxon to extend the native tradition of eulogistic poetry in praise of lords to poetry in praise of the Lord.[20] Certainly he impresses the abbess the next morning when he rehearses his experience to her. She devises a test for him. The scholars at Whitby read him a passage from the Bible and ask him to convert it to metrical form. He passes the test with flying colours, and enters the monastery, where he has the scriptures read to him. He then produces poems on Genesis, Exodus, the incarnation, passion, resurrection, and ascension of Jesus, the descent of the Holy Spirit, and the work of the apostles, amongst other subjects. Now it should be noted that Cædmon produces narrative poems in English on Biblical themes because he is asked to do so by his colleagues. He gains the ability to do so through his remarkable dream, but his first response to that dream was to produce a eulogy; all his subsequent poems are command performances solicited by literate Christians rather than by heavenly apparitions. A native tradition of eulogistic poetry could have provided the matrix for Cædmon's Biblical narrative poems. Narrative is embryonically present in eulogy; all that is required for the development of an explicitly narrative tradition out of a eulogistic tradition is an impetus. Perhaps the Whitby monks, informed by their knowledge of Latin narrative poems, supplied that impetus to the native Anglo-Saxon tradition.

One implication of this hypothesis is that the epic is not native to Anglo-Saxon or even to Germanic society. What of *Beowulf*, the earliest Germanic epic we have? It deals basically with Beowulf's three great fights against monsters, the first of whom is Grendel. There is also much additional material about Beowulf's early career, and about contemporary historical events, which has puzzled critics: is history the focus of interest and the monster fights a set of diversions, are the monster fights at the centre and is the rest extraneous, or is the whole unified? What is the nature of the source material? One folktale about Beowulf's three fights; two folktales; more? The fact that we will never know the answer to these questions, of course, does little to stem the rising tide of scholarly speculation;[21] so let me add a little speculation of my own. Africa can be a fruitful source of inspiration when thinking of medieval literature, and from central Africa comes a provocative circumstance. In 1956 Daniel Biebuyck encountered Shé-kárịsị Rureke, a Nyanga bard who knew the stories about the hero Mwindo.[22] Like a monk from Whitby confronting Cædmon, Biebuyck asked Rureke to dictate for him a complete version of the exploits of Mwindo: 'Rureke sat down with us for twelve days, singing, narrating, dancing, miming, until the present text was completely written down (p. vi).' Now this command performance was unique: Biebuyck writes that 'The interesting point is that the narrator would never recite the entire story in immediate sequence, but would intermittently perform various select passages of it. Mr Rureke, whose epic is presented here, repeatedly asserted that never before had he performed the whole story within a continuous span of days (p. 14).' This comment demonstrates one of the consequences of the meeting between an oral tradition and writing: the issue may well be a longer and fuller text, a version that could never have any oral existence among the people. *Beowulf* might well be such a product.

Cædmon's narrative poetry and *Beowulf* itself are products of the meeting between traditional Anglo-Saxon society and the literacy introduced by the Christian missionaries. They stand squarely at the crossroads, participating in both the Christian and the native Anglo-Saxon traditions. As such they are works, like the poems of Cynewulf, significantly different in many respects from traditional oral performances such as might have been produced by a thane on horseback. We may stand closer today to the literate Christian tradition that collides with the oral traditions of seventh and eighth century England, and we may be uncertain now as to the exact character of those ancient oral traditions, but we should not entirely overlook the oral context from which the hybrid products now extant in Anglo-Saxon manuscripts derive. In any event, for the very existence of those manuscripts we are indebted ultimately to the Christian missionaries who introduced writing to Anglo-Saxon England. In so doing they initiated a revolution in taste and attitude unrivalled in the long history of English literature.

Institute of Social and Economic Research
Rhodes University, Grahamstown, South Africa

The Æcerbot *Ritual in Context*

JOHN D. NILES

MANKIND lives on the fruits of the field. But by what right, what arrogance, does he claim power over the productivity of the earth? God fashioned Adam of the same earth which men till. Mankind and the earth are brothers: 'Dust art thou, and to dust shalt thou return.' Whence comes the dominion that mankind claims over nature, the dominion by which he says 'Grow,' and the crops grow?

In an age when the fruits of the field overflow from the supermarket shelves, such a question rarely is asked. We worship a new god, technology, and to question technology is to risk being accused of the most dangerous apostasy. In the Middle Ages matters were different. Fields did not always respond to the touch of the plow, and the brows of men were crowned with sweat at the same time as their tables remained bare. In Anglo-Saxon England, social life essentially meant village life, and village life meant life directly dependent on the vicissitudes of the agricultural cycle. Surrounding each village were open fields where wheat, barley, and other essential grains were cultivated. If these crops grew well in a given year, the village flourished. If they failed, the consequences were soon visible in the form of dearth and possible starvation. Life in such circumstances was more precarious than we like to remember, as we can see from the repeated references to famine and dearth in the annals of *The Anglo-Saxon Chronicle*. Sometimes pestilence and famine worked hand in hand and fell on the people with a vengeance, as in the entry in chronicle 'E' for the year 1087:

A thousand and eighty-seven years after the birth of our Lord Jesus Christ . . . it became a very severe and pestilential year in this country. Such a disease came on people that very nearly every other person was in high fever—and that so severely that many people

44

died of the disease. Afterwards because of the great storms . . . there came so great a famine over all England that many hundreds of people died a miserable death because of the famine. Alas, how miserable and pitiable a time it was then. Then the wretched people lay driven very nearly to death, and afterwards there came the sharp famine and destroyed them utterly. Who cannot pity such a time? Or who is so hard-hearted that he cannot weep for such misfortune? But such things happen because of the people's sins, in that they will not love God and righteousness. [1]

The eleventh-century English text that is known as the *Æcerbot* charm— the field remedy—reads as though it may have been one response to the kind of disaster that is described by the annalist in vivid terms. *Æcerbot* attempts to pose an answer to the question of how mankind can control the productivity of the earth. This unparalleled document prescribes the exact procedures to be taken in a complex, day-long ritual designed to convert barren land to fruitful land. It shows that in Anglo-Saxon England, crop failure was a matter of concern not to agricultural engineers, with their soil samples and their systems of irrigation and crop rotation, but to priests with their chants and holy water.

Let us begin by making a few distinctions. The *Æcerbot* charm is not a pagan address to Mother Earth, 'the Goddess Earth in the capacity of Ceres,' in the words of Felix Grendon. Nor is it a pagan hymn to Father Sun, as Godfrid Storms has claimed. It is not a piece of magic to be performed by some eleventh century 'shaman or churl,' to quote Bruce Rosenberg. Nor is it an invocation of the primeval Indo-European *Ur*-deity and the mythic *hieros gamos* (sacred marriage) of mother earth and father sky, as Gert Sandman would have it. [2] The *Æcerbot* charm is not exactly a charm at all, in fact, although all editors have called it so. It is a charm and it is more; it is the text of a solemn Christian ritual. It has little in common with the pieces with which modern editors have grouped it, the household remedies of Bald's *Leechbook* or the *Lacnunga* manuscript, these simple charms and spells that are designed to counteract disease, theft, miscarriage, or a host of other private misfortunes. Unlike these remedies, which any householder could perform, the *Æcerbot* text is the script of a major communal rite. In brief space I would like to probe first the social setting and then the mythic background of this rite, taking the text for what it is, and not for what it might have been had it been composed for members of an imagined proto-Germanic horde instead of for sober Saxon farmers of the age of King Cnut.

1. At what time of year was the rite performed?
According to Storms, Rosenberg, and Sandman, the ritual was probably

enacted at a certain time of year every year, very likely as part of a set of spring fertility rituals. As a consequence, these scholars have discounted the charm's value as a way of combating witchcraft. According to Rosenberg (p. 434), 'its aspect as a counter-witching charm has been overrated, for it could only be performed at one time of year and would hardly be effective against enchantment leveled upon the ground in summer, for instance, or in autumn.' And yet the text itself specifies no date on which the rite is to be performed. On the other hand, its very first lines claim emphatically that the rite is effective against witchcraft. 'Here is the remedy by which you can improve your fields, if they will not grow properly, or if any harm has been done to them by sorcery or witchcraft (*on dry oðe on lyblace*).'' A clause specifically intended to counteract the effects of witchcraft is included later, in a prayer for favor for the owner of the land: 'May the eternal Lord grant him [the landowner] . . . that his produce may be safe against every foe, and secure against every harm from witchcraft (*lyblac*) sown throughout the land' (lines 63–66). However sadly the sect of witches may be diminished today, evidently it was still flourishing in late Saxon England, or at least non-witches thought it was. That witchcraft and black magic were real concerns to eleventh-century Englishmen is shown by numerous documents,[3] section 5 of the *Laws of Cnut*, for example:

> And we earnestly forbid every heathen practice.
> It is heathen practice if one worships idols, namely if one worships heathen gods and the sun or the moon, fire or flood, wells or stones or any kind of forest trees, or if one practices witchcraft. . . .

Or sections 48–50 of the eleventh-century *Law of the Northumbrian Priests*:

> If, then, any man is discovered who henceforth carries on any heathen practice, either by sacrifice or divination, or practices witchcraft by any means, or worship of idols, he is to pay, if he is a king's thegn, 10 half-marks, half to Christ [i.e. the Church], half to the king.
> If it is otherwise a landowner, he is to pay six half-marks, half to Christ and half to the lord of the estate.
> If it is a *færbena* [landless freeman], he is to pay 12 ores.

Given the specificity of *Æcerbot* and the lively contemporary concern with witchcraft, the text is best taken as a countercharm against black magic. In addition, it claims to be effective against 'every sort of evil' (line 65), whether this evil afflicted the land through witchcraft or through other causes.

The character of *Æcerbot* as a counter-witching charm in no way counts against the rite being performed seasonally, of course. It is *last* year's crops which have failed, and the rite is designed to prevent a recurrence of failure in the *coming* year. *Æcerbot* is a plowing rite, among other things, and we know from the references to the opening of the first furrow (lines 70, 77) that the ceremony is to be performed on an actual or symbolic 'first' day of plowing. We need only inquire which day this was. Under the two-field system of agriculture that was practised widely in early Anglo-Saxon England, the arable land was divided into two halves.[4] One half lay fallow each year, while the other half grew both summer and winter crops. Under the three-field system that later came to be the norm, one field lay fallow each year; one field grew wheat and rye, long-growing crops which required winter planting; and one field grew short-growing crops which were sown in the spring (chiefly barley and oats). In either case, plowing for wheat began not long after the fall harvest and continued through the fall, while plowing for barley and oats began sometime during the winter, whenever the weather and the demands of other labor permitted. In addition, certain parallels to *Æcerbot* in the modern English agricultural calendar suggest that one special date in midwinter was set aside as a day of consecration of the work of the fields. The day known as 'Plough Monday,' falling on the first Monday after Epiphany (January 6), was formerly the day on which farm work was resumed after the twelve days of Christmas. Up to the present day in parts of rural England, Plough Sunday and Plough Monday have been the occasion of special ceremonies reminiscent of *Æcerbot*. According to Christina Hole, the principal feature of Plough Sunday is the blessing of the plough and the farm laborers in church:

> . . . A plough is brought into the church by farmers and ploughmen who come, in the words of the service, 'to offer the work of the countryside to the service of God.' Prayers are offered for a plentiful harvest, that the people may be fed, and finally the plough is blessed, and with it the ploughmen and all who work on the farms of the parish.[5]

In former days the principal feature of Plough Monday was 'the ritual dragging about of a decorated plough . . . by bands of young men' (Hole, p. 157). Ceremonies of the kind are recorded throughout the eastern half of England from Norfolk to Northumbria and are best documented in East Anglia and Lincolnshire. In Doddington, Cambridgeshire, the Plough Monday ceremonies that were observed until the early 1900s were known as 'Plough Witching' (Porter, p. 100). The young men who dragged the plow were known variously as 'plough stots' (from an old word for 'horse' or 'young ox'), 'plough bullocks,' 'bullock lads,' 'plough boys,' 'plough jags,' and 'plow-lads'. The plow is referred to as the 'stot plough,' 'white plough,' 'fond plough,' 'fond pleeaf,' or 'fool plough'. In the nineteenth and twentieth centuries the Plough Festival has tended to include a good deal of merriment in the form of mumming plays and dancing, particularly the sword-dance, but the author of the most detailed study on the subject concludes that only the plough mass and the plough-stotting are likely to have been part of the original celebration. 'The dancing is basically insignificant and subsidiary,' writes Geoffrey Ridden (p. 364). 'The "stots" (and only the "stots") were part of the religious ceremony which was, ostensibly, the nucleus of the celebration, and to which all the other customs were merely attendant trappings' (p. 355). One persistant feature of the day has been the taking up of a collection. In pre-Reformation times the chief aim of the collection seems to have been to raise money for the Plough Lights, wax candles lit by husbandmen during the plough mass. More recently the funds have gone for drink or charity. The collectors, often masked or blackfaced or dressed as women, followed the plough boys or dancers from door to door. The function of the procession seems to have been to spread luck, specifically agricultural luck, to judge from a comment by one nineteenth century observer: 'When they are well paid they raise a huzza; where they get nothing they shout "Hunger and starvation!" '⁶

Although one cannot project modern British folk customs back over the centuries into Anglo-Saxon England, the Plough Festival ceremonies of modern England have enough in common with *Æcerbot* for us to imagine that the Anglo-Saxon text describes not a unique event but a general custom. Both the ancient and the modern ceremonies have in common (a) a church service specially dedicated to the agricultural process, (b) solemn prayers for a good harvest, (c) a blessing of special tools or substances (the plough, in the modern rite; oil, honey, yeast, milk, four sods, and assorted greenery, in the old), and (d) an offering of the farmwork to the service of God (note *Æcerbot* 46–47, 'and commend it [the land, or the agricultural labor] to Christ and Holy Mary and to the Holy Rood in praise and worship'). In addition, both ceremonies feature (e) the decoration of a symbolic plow (note *Æcerbot* 51–52, which call for incense, fennel, hallowed soap, and hallowed salt to be placed in a hole bored into the plough-beam), and both conclude with (f) the ritual dragging about of the plough. That the modern rite takes place on two days rather than one does not count against the analogy, as there is no indication in *Æcerbot* that the ceremony of the plow is to take place on the same day as the preliminary church service and prayers. If present custom is any guide, the medieval ritual may likewise have taken place over a period of two days. The fact that the author of *Æcerbot* is silent on this point may simply reflect his confidence that Anglo-Saxon farmers would have been familiar with the customary sequence of the rite.

2. *Who performed the rite?*

The text is addressed to an unidentified 'you.' 'Here is the remedy by which you can improve your fields.' Who was this 'you,' whom I shall call the celebrant of this open-air drama, and what can we tell about his social standing?

Earlier studies of *Æcerbot* have tended to work from the assumption that the celebrant is some kind of yeoman farmer. This assumption fits in well with the romantic stereotype of the stout, self-sufficient Saxon farmer, but it has little to do with the body of evidence now at hand that points to the central importance of the manor, and not the individual landowner, in the Anglo-Saxon agricultural system from an early date. Particularly in the eleventh century—the date of our text—occurred the growth of the large secular and ecclesiastical estates which made possible the rise of feudalism. Under the manorial system, agriculture was essentially a communal enterprise. In order to understand this enterprise, we must banish from our minds preconceptions which are based on familiarity with capitalist economies and with the modern English landscape. In the great open fields of medieval England, no fences or hedges walled off one man's holdings from another's. Crop failure would have cut right across the private holdings of individual farmers. As a rule, each man's holdings were in the form of narrow plow-strips scattered widely in different parts of the arable, so that no one farmer had a monopoly of the good land. The arable was plowed in common, and it was sown by common agreement. Given such scattered holdings in fields which were worked communally, there is no way that a single farmer could have demarcated his land by taking four sods from four corners of the estate, as the celebrant of *Æcerbot* is instructed to do in lines 4–5. The only person who could have thus demarcated his land was the lord of the manor himself. Such a lord, in his probable capacity as patron of the parish church, easily could have arranged for a priest to sing four masses over the sods (lines 16–17), so that the cure was conducted at a single time for all members of the community.

Concerning the more exact identity of the celebrant, there are two real choices: he was either a layman or an ecclesiastic. Either alternative is possible, but on the basis of other evidence in the text the second choice seems more likely. The celebrant is assumed to be so well acquainted with the liturgy that he will be prepared to intone not only the Paternoster, which anyone would know by heart, but also the Tersanctus from the Mass, the Benedicite from the office of morning prayer, and the Magnificat, all in good Latin (for it is an essential part of any magic that the

49

charms be uttered correctly). Few secular landlords would have been able to peform these tasks in person. Most likely we are dealing either with the head of an ecclesiastical estate or—more likely, given the unorthodox nature of the rite—with a priest in the service of a secular lord. In either case, the same charm which modern scholars have tended to treat as a heathen document seems to have been intended for the use of a churchman of some learning.

3. *Why are hardwood trees excluded from the rite?*

In lines 7–8, the celebrant is instructed to gather a sample of every sort of tree which grows on the land 'except for hardwood trees' (*butan heardan beaman*). What is the reason for this exception? Grendon (p. 220) explains that by 'hardwood trees' is meant specifically the oak and the beech. He suggests that these trees did not require sanctification because they already were held sacred. Rosenberg (p. 432) accepts this general line of interpretation and adds that the oak and the beech formerly were viewed with such veneration that they could not be broken: 'Felling an oak was tantamount to destroying its god, or the soul of the god who dwelled within its bark.' Such an approach to the problem would be convincing if our text were the work of an ancient Germanic tribesman or an unbaptized Dane, but if *Æcerbot* is to be read as an eleventh-century English document, then appeals to tree-worship seem fanciful. One of the commonest sounds during the later Old English period would have been the sound of iron axehead meeting hardwood oak or beech. If eleventh-century Englishmen secretly believed in gods within the bark, they did not scruple to dispatch these gods right and left in the interests of augmenting their acreage of arable land. I would advance a less arcane explanation.[7] Hardwood trees—probably all hardwood trees, not just the oak and the beech—were excluded from the rite because they played no part in the agricultural cycle. They were important as a source of firewood, lumber, and winter forage for swine, not as a source of food for human beings. Furthermore, in the open fields hardwood trees would have been a positive hindrance to agriculture. In any event, the deep root systems of hardwood trees are unaffected by drought, hence even if one wished to encourage their growth there would be no need to engage in the sympathetic magic of sprinkling their twigs with holy water.

4. *What is the function of burying the four crosses?*

After the sods are blessed, the celebrant is instructed to make four crosses out of *cwicbeam* (variously interpreted as the aspen or the rowan) and to have the names of the four evangelists inscribed on the four ends of each cross. He then is to bury the crosses face down (*neopeweardne*) in the pit from which the sods were cut. The sods are then replaced, to the accompaniment of elaborate prayers. Rosenberg (pp. 429–30) speculates that the purpose of this part of the rite is to encourage growth by burying the rowan, a tree sacred to Thor. He sees the four evangelists as Christian substitutes for four Germanic gods of the 'original' rite, and he interprets the act of burial as an act of sympathetic magic analogous to the ritual burials of Osiris, Adonis, and other ancient gods of death and resurrection. My own view is less Frazerian. The idea of the cross as a prophylactic device is one of the most fundamental concepts underlying Christian ritual and custom. No Christian symbol is more ancient or widespread than the cross. In the words of St. John Chrysostom, 'Everything is done by the cross. Baptism is given by the cross—we must receive the *sphragis*. The laying on of hands [in exorcism or healing] is done by the cross. Wherever we are, travelling or at home, the cross is a great good, a saving protection, an impregnable shield against the devil.'[8] In baptism, the great importance of signing with the cross can be attributed to the belief that the *sphragis* will defend the neophyte against unclean spirits and devils. Marking out a church with the sign of the cross during the ceremonies of dedication serves an analogous function. Signing with the cross becomes equivalent to an exorcism, hence the frequency with which we encounter this motif in the charms of the Anglo-Saxon corpus. At crossroads, at graveyards, and at other places where evil spirits are believed to congregate, the image of the cross traditionally is erected or displayed as a way of purifying the ground. Even in Puritan New England, houses were marked with the sign of the cross to keep out witches. The amulet is a similar defense set on the 'house' of a person's body. In *Æcerbot*—a charm specifically directed against witchcraft, as we have seen—the burial of the four crosses serves the similar function of guarding the greater 'house' of the earth against the entry of malign influences. By 'sowing' the crosses in the earth, the celebrant seeks directly to annul the influence of whatever witchcraft may be 'sown throughout the land' (line 66). In this way he purifies the soil into which the seeds of the new crops are literally to be sown during the coming weeks.

In addition, the act of fashioning and burying the crosses has another function specifically appropriate to an agricultural rite, namely to call up the idea of the cross as an emblem of fertility. The association of the cross with the Tree of Life (*lignum vitae* or *arbor vitae*) is a commonplace of medieval Christian thought. Stevens (p. 63) cites examples of this association from Bede and from the Benedictional of Æthelwold and notes that the correlation 'is found all through the Anglo-Saxon literature of the cross, and also in the sacramentaries.' In particular, the cross and the Tree of Life are linked by several related sets of quaternities.[9] According to early belief, from the foot of the Tree of Life in the earthly paradise emerged four rivers flowing toward the four cardinal points of the compass and thus marking the horizontal cross on the surface of the terrestrial world. (We may compare the passage in *Æcerbot* which concerns the four quarters of the land, as the celebrant is instructed to demarcate the area to be included under the blessing by marking it out as a giant cruciform shape.) From the cross, in like manner, Christ's glory radiated in four directions. An anonymous text formerly attributed to Alcuin describes as follows a visionary cross reminiscent of that which appears in *The Dream of the Rood*: 'Indeed as it lay, the cross stretched out toward the four quarters of the world, east and west, north and south, because even so Christ by his passion draws all people to him.'[10] Stevens (p. 9) cites a later medieval legend that a twig (or a seed, or three seeds) from the Tree of Life was the source of the wood used for the beam of the cross. Whether or not this legend was known in Anglo-Saxon England, clearly the four arms of the cross were thought to embody a spiritual power cognate with the terrestrial fructifying power of the Tree of Life and its associated rivers. By burying the four crosses in the ground, the celebrant of *Æcerbot* is planting symbolic replicas of the Tree of Life, the archetypal source of earthly fruitfulness. Simultaneously, he is invoking the powers of the four arms of the cross not as the instruments of Christ's passion, but as symbols of the cosmic extent of His reign.

5. *Why is unknown seed taken from beggars?*

After the preliminary ceremonies are concluded and before the blessing of the plough, the celebrant is instructed to take unknown seed from beggars and to return them twice as much. The logic of this trade has been interpreted in several ways. Storms (p. 185) takes a mystical view: 'The unknown seed is an offering to Mother Earth and its value is enhanced by the magical flavour of its mysteriousness.' Hill (pp. 219–21) prefers a practical explanation: once planted, the unknown seed might prove more successful than the farmer's previous seed, and so the new strain could be saved and used in subsequent years. Without excluding either of these approaches, I would advance a different explanation, namely that the celebrant is engaged in an act of magic by transference. He is making a symbolic trade of his own 'bad' seed for the 'good' seed of the almsmen. The logic of the trade is that of symbolic transference of bad luck from one party to another. Magic by transference is a commonplace of folk belief from early times and is well illustrated by other Anglo-Saxon charms, Storms 10, for example, a charm to prevent the recurrence of miscarriage. Here the woman who has not been able to give birth to a live child is instructed to take some earth from her child's grave and hide it well in a wrapping of wool. She then sells the wool to a chapman. Because the chapman has bought the wool, symbolically he has 'bought' the bad luck as well. In this charm as in *Æcerbot*, the importance of the trade lies not in what is gained but in what is given away. To some moderns, the logic of magic by transference may seem ungenerous; and yet magic in general is not noted for its generosity. The point is to effect a cure. From a purely practical point of view, of course, the celebrant's seed is 'bad' only symbolically, and so he is doing the almsmen a small favor by giving them twice as much as he receives. In this respect the celebrant is indeed a model of generosity. By his outwardly magnanimous gesture of giving seed to the poor, he qualifies himself for the Lord's favor according to the terms of the charm itself (cf. lines 40–42, 'as the prophet said, that he would have favors on earth who dealt out alms judicially').

6. *What is the function of the* Crescite *prayer?*

The key part of the spoken rite is the threefold repetition of the formula *Crescite et multiplicamini et replete terram* ('Grow and multiply and fill the earth'). This prayer is to be intoned three times at dawn, when the gathered sods, twigs, herbs, and other items are sprinkled with holy water; nine times during the afternoon, when the sods are set back in place; and three times during the plowing rite, after the first furrow has been opened and a small loaf placed within. Each time, the formula is followed by the exhortation *In nomine patris et filii et spiritus sancti sitis benedicti* ('In the name of the Father and the Son and the Holy Ghost, be ye blessed'). These words in turn are followed by the Paternoster, a prayer which appropriately includes the appeal 'Give us today our daily bread.' The whole *Crescite* prayer thus consists of three parts: (1) an exhortation to the fields to be fruitful (*Crescite*), (2) a blessing in the name of the Trinity (*sitis benedicti*), and (3) an appeal for personal well-being (the Paternoster). Prior scholarship has not tended to stress the importance of the threefold *Crescite* prayer within the rite as a whole, perhaps because what is obviously Christian in the charm has been taken for granted, and yet clearly this prayer is central to the whole procedure. Of previous commentators, only Thomas D. Hill has paid great attention to this prayer and its source, Genesis 1.28, when God blessed Adam and commanded him to 'Grow and multiply and fill the earth.' As Hill points out (p. 215), the intonation of the *Crescite* prayer in the here-and-now of Saxon England serves in effect 'to reiterate . . . the creation,' so that the barren fields may be reintegrated into the world which God made good and fruitful.

Hill's penetrating comments leave little to be said on the subject of the mythic background of *Æcerbot*. Still, in brief space I shall try to go a step beyond Hill in probing the intention behind the *Crescite* prayer. A rite could be defined as a solemn communal action performed to the accompaniment of a myth; and in *Æcerbot* as in other rites, the myth serves as ultimate authority for the communal action. The command to 'grow and multiply' in *Æcerbot* is based not only on the authority of Genesis 1.28, to be precise, but also on the authority of Genesis 8.17, when God spoke to Noah after the Flood and commanded him in the same words to 'grow and multiply and fill the earth.' From Genesis 1 to Genesis 8, from Adam to Noah, occurs a progression of events so critical to the understanding of *Æcerbot* that we would do well to review these events briefly here.[11]

There are four stages in the agricultural myth which is recounted in Genesis 1–8. (I) When God first makes man out of the dust of the field, he gives him all plants and fruits as food: 'Behold, I have given you every plant yielding seed which is upon the face of all the earth, and every tree with seed in its fruit; you shall have them for food' (Gen. 1.29). (II) When Adam and Eve fall from Paradise, God curses the earth and makes Adam a tiller of the soil: 'Cursed is the ground because of you; in toil you shall eat of it all the days of your life; thorns and thistles it shall bring forth to you, and you shall eat the plants of the field' (Gen. 3.17–18). (III) After Cain, the plowman, kills Abel, the herdsman, God renews his curse on the earth in emphatic terms: 'When you till the ground, it shall no longer yield to you its strength' (Gen. 4.12). (IV) With the coming of Noah, God lifts his curse. As it is prophesied at the time of Noah's birth, 'Out of the ground which the Lord has cursed this one shall bring us relief from our work and from the toil of our hands' (Gen. 5.29). After the waters of the Flood have subsided, God addresses Noah with the same command to be fruitful and multiply that he issued to Adam at the beginning of creation. Most important, God pledges never to curse the earth again: 'I will never again curse the ground because of man. . . . While the earth remains, seedtime and harvest, cold and heat, summer and winter, day and night, shall not cease' (Gen. 8.21). At this point the agricultural myth is complete. After the Flood has ended and Noah has begun planting his vines, God establishes for all time the sequence of seasons and the alternation of seedtime and harvest that are at the heart of the agricultural process.

To conclude that the function of the ritual is 'to reiterate the creation' is therefore true, yet a slight simplification. More precisely, the rite seeks to invoke that entire process of events by which God made man a tiller of the good earth. The deity addressed in *Æcerbot* is not only the God of Creation. He is the God of the Covenant, the Lord who spoke his eternal decree that summer should follow winter, that harvest should follow planting, that good times should follow lean times in a perpetual merciful sequence. It is for this reason that the celebrant of the rite is instructed to intone the magnificent prayer *Benedicite omnia opera Domini Domino*, with its call to all the works of the Lord—angels and man, winter and summer, nights and days, dews and frosts, mountains and hills, and all green and growing things—to praise the Lord and magnify him forever.[12]

It is probably for like reason that late fifteenth-century inventories of expenses on Plough-days for the town of Kingston-upon-Hull, Yorkshire, list expenditures for the performance of a Play of Noah and for 'a rope to hang the ship [a symbolic ark] in the kirk.'[13]

To understand the Old English *Æcerbot* rite, therefore, one need not systematically substitute pagan elements for Christian ones. One need not replace the church with a heathen temple, replace the blessing with a blood-sacrifice, replace the beggars with temple attendants, replace the Latin *dominus* with the Germanic dew-god, replace the names of the four evangelists with the names of four ancient deities, and replace the Virgin Mary with the primeval Earth Mother, as Sandman has done in his recent dissertation. Rather than inventing a wholly fabulous mythology and social setting for the rite, scholars might do it less violence if they accept it at its face value, as an expression of the piety and anxiety of eleventh-century Christian Englishmen. Having been brought face to face with famine, these Englishmen responded by calling on the assistance of the only magical power they thought they could trust: the God of the Covenant, patron of agriculture, the One who (in the words of an earlier poet) 'has control over both times and seasons' (*Beowulf* 1610b–11a).

Diehard neo-pagans may lament to see the Old English field blessing interpreted without reference to its supposed heathen mysteries. In attempting to account for key features of the eleventh-century text as we have it, I have not been concerned with certain enigmas of its prehistory. Chief among these is the source and meaning of the invocation *Erce, erce, erce, eorðan modor* ('Erce, erce, erce, mother of earth'). This line has defied interpretation by generations of scholars, and—if it is not simply a corruption of *Ecce, ecce, ecce, eorðe modor* ('Hearken, hearken, hearken, mother earth'), as seems possible—those persons may be correct who read the line as an invocation of some half-forgotten tellurian deity.[14] If so, the text provides evidence for a remarkable syncretism in late Anglo-Saxon England. In the present essay, I hope only to show that regardless of its possible pagan substrata, *Æcerbot* is a fascinating and instructive document of its time. Nothing like it has survived from the Middle Ages. When we read it with attention to its social and intellectual context, suddenly we can understand more clearly what the agricultural cycle meant in an age without massive shipments of petroleum-based fertilizer, without gigantic machines to break and plant the soil. In such an age the battle for survival was waged not just with the plough and sickle, but by spiritual means. Many persons today no longer share the devotional spirit that breathes through *Æcerbot*. Most of us today no longer believe in witchcraft. Still we can marvel at what it must have meant to live in an age when the labors of plowmen tilling the fields took place in a landscape made or marred by the struggle of invisible powers.

Yet we may ask: Did the rite work?

Many persons whose training in the sciences is more rigorous than mine will answer that the only way to know is by experiment. You will gather your sods and say your blessings, then wait to see what happens. I have a different answer. To me there can be no doubt: if the rite ever was enacted the way it is written, then there is no question of its not working. It could not help but work, almost regardless of the amount of annual rainfall. The reason for this is simple: the rite itself, for those who took part in it, was an act of communal re-creation. The rite would have been so dramatic a visual and auditory experience, from sunup to sundown, with the processions from the fields to the church and from the church to the fields, with the singing of masses and the chanting of prayers, that the attention of an entire community would have been riveted on the act of opening the fields. Once this attention was aroused and focused, then the long, hard, communal process of winning the year's food was well on its way.[15]

The virga *of Moses and the Old English* Exodus

THOMAS D. HILL

THE Old English poetic *Exodus* has long been admired as a dramatic and vigorous poem, but it is also notoriously difficult. I would like here to discuss a series of related images in the poem in order to elucidate some problems, and then to conclude with some reflections about the character and possible intellectual context of this extraordinary if cryptic poetry. To begin with the problems, the narrative structure of *Exodus* reaches its climax at the moment when the Israelites are hemmed in by the vastly superior armies of the Egyptians. Up to this point, God has protected them with signs and miracles, but here their situation seems utterly hopeless. With good reason, then, the Israelites are despondent until Moses tells them to look on as he will part the sea before them and thus free them from the danger of imminent destruction.

> hwæt! ge nú eagum   to on lociað,
> folca leofost,   faérwundra sum,
> hu ic sylfa sloh   ond þeos swiðre hand
> grene tacne   gársecges deop,
> yð úp færeð   ofstum wyrceð
> wæter ond wealfæsten,   wegas syndon dryge
> haswe herestræta,   holm gerymed,
> ealde staðolas . . . (278–85a).[1]

(Listen, you now see with [your own] eyes, dearest of peoples, a certain sudden wonder—how I myself and this mighty hand have struck with a green sign the depth of the ocean. The water moves up; hastily it makes, the water and walled place [*sometimes translated on the basis of an emendation,* 'the water into a walled place']. The paths

57

are dry, gray army roads, the ocean cleared away, ancient foundations. . . .)

Line 281, in which Moses speaks of the 'grene tacne' with which he will strike the sea to clear a passage, has attracted attention from editors and commentators; in fact the commentary on this line reflects almost paradigmatically the disagreements between those who interpret *Exodus* in terms of Christian-Latin allegory and those who insist upon a literal and 'Germanic' reading of the poem. E. B. Irving, a notable exponent of the latter point of view, discusses the phrase in his 'New Notes on the Old English *Exodus*' and comments: 'this [phrase] should be emended to *grēne tāne* "with a green branch," a much less affected phrase than *grēne tācne* "with a green symbol".'[2] This succinct and characteristically firm opinion has been challenged by J. P. Hermann, who argues that Moses' rod is described as a *tacen* in terms of the commonplace association of the rod of Moses and the Cross of Christ, and he suggests also that it is defined as 'green' because green is associated with charity in a variety of patristic texts.[3] I would agree with Irving that the phrase *grene tacne* is certainly difficult, and with Hermann in that it is very suggestive in this context; but the manuscript reading can be defended in terms of its literal meaning.

The phrase in question consists of two words and each raises a separate problem. Why is Moses' rod 'green,' and why is it in any sense a 'token' or 'sign'? In the Vulgate text of Exodus, Moses' rod is consistently referred to as a *virga*, and the most immediate answer to both questions is based upon the literal meaning of the Latin term *virga*. The modern reader of the Old English *Exodus* is perhaps most immediately puzzled by why Moses' rod should be green; but the answer is very simple. A *virga* is essentially a *green* branch and the various Latin dictionaries list this as the first meaning of the term. A glance at the extended meanings of the Latin word clarifies the relationship between the usual gloss of *virga* as 'rod' and this apparently more specialized sense of the word. A *virga* is a green branch, and also the rod of discipline for animals, slaves, and children. A thin dry stick would break if used for this purpose; a thicker stick (dry or green) might cause serious injury. A thin green rod can be used to strike a child or a slave and it will neither break nor cause serious harm. It might be asked whether the *Exodus* poet would have known this particular nuance of the term *virga*, but since Isidore of Seville etymologizes *virga* as deriving from *viriditate* no less than three times in the *Etymologiae*,[4] it is clear that the fact that a *virga* was a 'green' rod was readily accessible.

The second question, why a *virga* might be described as a *tacen*, can also be answered literally by a citation from Isidore, who remarks, 'hanc [i.e. a *virgam*] etiam philosophi ac reges et magistri et nuntii et legati utuntur' ('philosophers, kings, teachers, messengers and ambassadors make use of this [i.e. a *virga*].'⁵ Moses is of course simultaneously philosopher, teacher, and messenger; and though there was no king in Israel until Samuel annointed Saul, Moses surely possessed the power of a king. His *virga* is a sign of his authority in these various roles. The *virga* was, in fact, a common symbol of authority throughout the ancient world. Martine Dulaey, whose study of the symbolism of the *virga* in early Christian art is a very useful compilation of texts relevant to this question, remarks:

> In classical civilization, the *virga* has a variety of uses, and one fundamental meaning is apparent in all of them. The *virga* is first the instrument, then the symbol of power in the largest sense of the term, power over men and over animals, and, by extension, power over objects.
>
> Primarily, the *virga* is a weapon, an instrument of power which is used to flog people. It is by means of a *virga* that one pricked up and guided horses. By means of a rod, generally called a *ferula*, one beat disobedient slaves and tardy students.⁶

I would suggest then that the 'grene tacen' with which Moses parts the red sea is *grene* because it is a *virga*, a *green* rod; and that it is a *tacen* because it is a *sign* of authority. It is not 'affected' to call a *virga* a *tacen* because a *virga* is a sign, just as the riding crops which British army officers carry are a sign of their status. I am (and this perhaps betrays my prejudices) more sympathetic to Hermann's interpretation than to Irving's emendation of the phrase. But even if calling Moses' rod a 'green sign' is inevitably suggestive (given the usual associations both of Moses' rod and of 'green' in patristic commentary), the phrase also makes good literal sense. The phrase may suggest allegory, but it does not demand it.

In the light of this interpretation of line 281, we can understand more clearly a series of images in the Old English *Exodus* which reflect the fact that Moses' rod is not simply the instrument by which he works miracles, but also the rod of discipline. Thus in the opening lines of the poem Moses is defined in terms of both his relationship to God and his own natural abilities as a leader:

> he wæs leof gode,   leoda aldor,
> horsc ond hreðergleaw'   herges wisa,
> freom folctoga;   faraónes cyn,
> godes andsaca,   gyrdwíte band . . . (12–15).⁷

(He was dear to God, a prince of peoples, quick and wise, the leader

of the army, a brave people-prince. Pharoah's race, the enemies of
God, he constrained by rod-torment. . . .)

The striking figure in lines 14–15 to the effect that Moses 'bound' or
'constrained the race of Pharoah, the enemies of God, by rod-punishment'
has attracted some attention, but critics have done no more than to cite the
phrase (as Irving does)[8] as an instance of the poet's fondness for extravagant language. But if the image here is a striking one, it reflects traditional
usage. *Gyrdwite* is a *hapax legomenon,* but the elements *gyrd* and *wite* are
readily recognizable as 'rod' or 'staff' and 'punishment'; and in an age
when the rod was a common instrument for pedagogical and societal
discipline, the primary meaning of the compound must have been something like 'rod-punishment' or flogging. And if Moses' *virga* is a rod, the
plagae which he inflicts upon the Egyptians are 'stripes' or 'wounds' as
well as 'plagues' in our sense. For the sense 'plague' is a relatively late
development in the semantic evolution of the Latin term *plaga.* Given the
connotations of *virga* and *plagae* in classical civilization, it is perhaps not
too surprising to find an Old English poet speaking of how Moses
'flogged' the Egyptians into submission; but this image also is attested in
a text which the poet may well have known. According to Cassiodorus,
Origen's homilies on Exodus (in Rufinus' Latin translation) were the
authoritative commentary on that work;[9] these homilies were used by
Rabanus Maurus in his ninth century *Commentaria in Exodum,*[10] and in
at least one other instance Origen's homilies on Exodus have been shown
to provide a convincing explanation of a difficult line in the Old English
poem.[11] At any rate Origen's homilies on Exodus certainly influenced the
tradition of Biblical commentary. He describes Moses as coming to Egypt
'et *deferens virgam, qua castigat et verberat* Aegyptum decem plagis' ('and
bringing a rod with which he chastised and beat Egypt with ten plagues [*or*
blows],' italics mine).[12] Again, in a phrase which is conceptually quite
close to the Old English 'gyrdwite band,' Origen refers to the 'virga . . .
per quam Aegyptus subigitur et Pharao superatur' ('rod . . . by which
Egypt is subdued and Pharaoh is overcome').[13] And he often speaks of the
plagues with which Moses afflicted Egypt in terms of flogging: 'Nemo
ergo ita ineruditus divinae sit disciplinae, ut *flagella* divina perniciem
putet, ut *verbera* Domini poenalem credat interitum. Ecce etiam Pharao
durissimus; tamen proficit *verberatus.* Ante *verbera* Dominum nescit;
verberatus supplicari pro se Dominum rogat.' ('Let no one, therefore, be
so unaware of [the character of] divine discipline, that he think the divine
lashes a [simple] calamity [and] that he think the Lord's scourgings a
penal destruction. For behold Pharoah [is] most harsh: yet having been
flogged, he profits. Before the lashes, he does not know the Lord; having
been flogged, he asks [Moses] to pray to the Lord for him,' italics mine).[14]

From the currency of these images I would argue that the poet is deliberately echoing and adapting this kind of language in speaking of Moses subduing the enemies of God by *gyrdwite.*

The next image I would like to discuss has never occasioned any particular difficulty; but it is more meaningful if read in context as one of a series of images of flogging. The destruction of the Egyptians in the Red Sea is notoriously difficult in the Old English *Exodus,* and at one point the poet speaks of it in the following terms:

> laðe cyrmdon   (lyft up geswearc)
> fægum stæfnum,   flod blod gewód.
> randbyrig wæron rofene,   rodor swipode
> meredeaða mæst,   modige swulton (462–65).

(Hateful ones clamored, the heaven above darkened with the voices of those doomed to die. The blood pervaded the flood, the shield walls were broken * * *.)

Verses 464b–65a, 'rodor swipode / meredeaða mæst,' are usually translated 'the greatest of sea deaths lashed the heaven' and are taken as a reference to the violent storm which was traditionally thought to accompany the destruction of the Egyptians.[15] In all the other instances of this pattern of images the lash falls, as it were, on the Egyptians, and I wonder whether it might not be possible to take *rodor* as the subject rather than the object of *swipode* and then take *meredeaða mæst* as a parenthetical phrase describing the scope of the violence. One might then translate 464–65 'shield walls were broken; heaven lashed, greatest of sea deaths; proud ones died.' This is certainly less smooth syntactically than the usual translation, but this passage in the Old English *Exodus* is hardly characterized by smooth syntax. This suggestion is, of course, tentative. However one translates the lines in question, verse 464b is another instance of the imagery of flogging.

If these lines are relatively straightforward, the next passage of *Exodus* which I would like to examine is one of the most difficult and disputed passages in the poem. The poet is, again, describing the destruction of the Egyptians:

> gársecg wedde
> up ateah, on sleap.   egesan stodon,
> weollon wælbenna.   witrod gefeol
> heah of heofonum   handweorc godes,
> famigbosma   flodwearde sloh,
> unhieowan wæg,   alde méce,

> þæt ðy deaðdrepe   drihte swæfon,
> synfullra sweot,   sawlum lunnon . . . (490b–97).

(The ocean raged, drew itself up, glided on. Terrors were at hand, deadly wounds gushed. ★ ★ ★ . . . the unprotected path with an ancient sword, that at that deadly blow the troops slept, the band of sinful ones, they parted from their souls. . . .)

Irving in his edition and 'New Notes' follows earlier editors in taking *witrod* in line 493 as a variant form of an otherwise unattested compound noun★ *wigtrod* meaning 'battle-path.' He also argues that we should translate *gefeol* as a transitive verb meaning 'fell upon' and takes the phrase *handweorc godes* as the subject and *witrod* as the object of the sentence, thus translating 'High from the heavens the handiwork of God, foamy-bosomed, fell upon the war-track.'[16] This is a quite radical treatment of this passage. Emending *witrod* (in effect) to *wigtrod* involves an emendation *to* an otherwise unattested word and is suspect on these grounds alone. Even with the emendation there remain substantial syntactical difficulties. Old English *(ge)feallan* can be a transitive verb meaning 'fall upon' or 'attack,' but there is no morphological or other indication that *witrod* is the object of *gefeol*, and ordinarily *feallan*, like Modern English *fall*, is an intransitive verb. Again while the word order of Old English poetry is freer than that of the prose, we would have here (given this emendation and translation) object, verb, adverbial phrase, and then subject. This would represent unusually convoluted word order even for the *Exodus* poet, particularly since there is no (immediate) contextual reason for taking *witrod* as the object of *gefeoll*. The fact that Irving felt it necessary to provide a lengthy comment in his edition and to provide a translation in the 'New Notes' is at least some indication of the difficulties which this construction of the passage entails.[17]

I would propose (or rather would like to revive) a somewhat simpler interpretation. In his 1854 edition of the poem, Bouterwek took *witrod* as *vite-rod*, which he translates as *flagellum*, i.e. a 'punishment-rod.'[18] I do not think the emendation a necessary one,[19] but Bouterwek's interpretation of the compound is quite reasonable. Lines 492b–93a would thus mean 'the rod of punishment fell, high from the heavens.' One simple way of relating this sentence to its context would be to take it as a figurative equivalent of the narrative action of the next few lines: 'The rod of punishment fell, high from the heavens; the handwork of God [i.e. the sea], foamy-bosomed, struck those flood guards. . . .' The sea, the instrument by which God chastises the Egyptians, is here a 'rod of punishment,' an association which might seem odd or 'baroque' in itself but which accords with other similar images in the poem and derives from a well established tradition.

The final image I would like to discuss occurs in lines 499–500a, 'siððan hie on bogum brun yppinge / modewæga mæst.' These lines are obviously corrupt since there is no verb, and Irving in his 'New Notes' suggests that one might read them as 'siððan him on bogum bræc yrringa modewæga mæst' and translates 'the greatest of furious waves broke angrily on their backs.' Irving concludes by remarking 'Is the image here one of a scourge or a lash?'[20] This is obviously a radical emendation, but at the least, one can argue that given the currency of images of this character in *Exodus* and the phrase 'on bogum,' 'on [their] backs,' in line 499, it is quite possible that the image here was of a scourge or lash before it was virtually obliterated by scribal corruption.

I have been concerned with a specific pattern of imagery in *Exodus* rather than with the poem as a whole. But in working on these passages as well as on a variety of other problems in connection with a seminar on the poem, I have been struck by one feature of the poet's art which has, perhaps, been underestimated—the degree to which the difficulties in the poem are specifically verbal rather than conceptual. The pattern of imagery I have been concerned with here can serve as an example. Once one recognizes the implications of the term *virga* in its Biblical and classical context, the various images of flogging in the poem fall into place as traditional figures expressing the violence which Moses inflicted upon the Egyptians. The concept is really a very simple one. Or to cite another example, Fred Robinson's work on the poet's use of traditional Latin etymologies[21] illustrates the same feature of the poet's art—once one knows the etymology, the difficult phrase or odd epithet or apparently incongruous association is explained. *Exodus* as a poem strikes me as enigmatic but not complex. Its structure, as J. E. Cross, S. I. Tucker, and James W. Earl have shown,[22] reflects a common Christian understanding of the meaning of Exodus as a paradigm of Christian life, and the imagery of the poem (when we can comprehend it) derives from traditional Germanic diction on the one hand and relatively straightforward Latin and Christian sources on the other. *Exodus* is certainly a difficult poem, but the problems it presents are of a different kind than those which the reader of *Beowulf* must face.

Perhaps I can clarify my sense of the character of this poetry by an analogy. A good deal of attention has been devoted recently to 'Hisperic' or 'Hermeneutic' Latin poetry of the early middle ages.[23] I have been particularly struck by the argument of Michael Herren, the re-editor of the *Hisperica Famina*, that 'Hisperic Latin' is a specifically 'barbarian' phenomenon. To summarize his argument, when the barbarian Irish became competent in the Latin tradition, they were a bit disappointed because it was too classical, and they set out to devise a kind of Latin which was strange and rare in the same way that contemporary vernacular poetic language was. Early Germanic—specifically Old English—vernacular poetry is not as difficult as Celtic verse, but it is certainly obscure enough, and early medieval English scholars shared a taste for arcane and difficult Latin with their Irish and Continental contemporaries. I would extend Herren's argument to some degree and submit that this interest in a mysterious poetic language reflects barbarian taste, although 'barbarian' certainly does not mean 'crude' or 'unsophisticated' in this context. *The Book of Kells*, for example, is one of the great achievements of the human visual imagination, but it is nonetheless a 'barbarian' work in the sense in which I am using the term.

To return to the Old English *Exodus*, scholars have been reluctant to associate the difficult vernacular poetry of a poem such as *Exodus* with the difficult Latin of a poet such as Aldhelm, in part because of an unspoken assumption that such Latin poetry is furthest removed from vernacular culture. Herren's arguments challenge that assumption and permit us to reconsider—not so much the possibility of direct influence—as the possibility that 'hermeneutic' Latin and 'hermeneutic' Old English reflect a similar literary sensibility. And in one immediate respect this comparison is a fruitful one. I have suggested that *Exodus* is difficult verbally rather than conceptually and this generalization is emphatically true of Latin 'hermeneutic' poetry of this period. Once one recognizes the Greek borrowings and identifies the arcane vocabulary, the interpretation of these texts is relatively straightforward. Again the taste for extravagant 'baroque' verbal effect so evident in the Old English *Exodus* is also evident in the tradition of difficult Latin poetry. And defining *Exodus* as a monument of a specifically 'barbarian' Old English sensibility might also enable us to understand the strikingly Germanic character of this Biblical poem. The poet does not simply draw upon traditional Germanic diction, he revels in it and in several instances, at least, uses traditional images in a way which reflects a genuinely sophisticated command of German poetic idiom.[24] But, of course, if one defines *Exodus* as 'barbarian' poetry then the poet's interest in extravagant and sometimes obscure poetic language, his parade of seemingly esoteric Biblical learning, and his delight in traditional Germanic poetry, all reflect an essentially similar sensibility. In suggesting this definition of the art of the *Exodus* poet, I do not mean to imply that the poet was necessarily naive or was himself 'barbarian' in the pejorative sense of that term. Many of the identified authors of Latin hermeneutic texts were capable of writing classical as well as hermeneutic Latin, and *Exodus* might similarly be an extravagant set piece of an otherwise more conservative poet. But however the *Exodus* poet defined his achievement, the poem reflects a learned exuberance and a delight in the power of the word which derive from the tradition of vernacular poetry and vernacular learning, the 'barbarian' heritage of the Anglo-Saxon peoples.[25]

Cornell University

The Typological Structure of Andreas

JAMES W. EARL

THE oldest and most persistent critical approach to *Andreas* has been through its kinship with *Beowulf* and its adaptation of heroic poetics to a Christian subject.[1] The value of this approach, carefully carried out, should not be underestimated. I have chosen, however, to come at the poem from another direction—but one which need not contradict the results of an analysis of the poem's heroic aspects. I mean to study certain qualities of the poet's sources which he chose to preserve rather than change: the qualities of early medieval hagiography. The Old English poet was not insensible to these qualities, and we can show by careful comparison with his sources that he even heightened them from time to time. The student of hagiography knows that the saint's life is not just an entertaining story—this is painfully evident—but is a form of devotional literature with relatively precise aims and with conventional methods for exploring the truths of Christian history. Typology is the essence of Christian historical writing in general, and of the saint's life in particular. I would like to examine *Andreas* with regard to its hagiographic conventions and typological structure.

Several recent studies have pointed the way to a typological reading of *Andreas*. T. D. Hill has performed an elaborate reading of the poem's conclusion in terms of early Christian baptismal imagery, in a brief argument compelling enough that a new reading of the poem in those terms seems called for.[2] Penn Szittya began this task by analyzing the episode of the 'living stone' in lines 707–810 as an allegory of the foundation of the Celestial Church on earth, building his argument upon the imagery of the Harrowing of Hell in the poem.[3] These studies are representative of a wider movement in recent scholarship toward a reinterpretation of Old English poetic hagiography: Hill has provided a near-comprehensive interpretation of *Elene* as 'figural narrative,'[4] and

Joseph Wittig has devoted a similar study to *Juliana*;[5] and in an earlier article I have tried to explain why early medieval hagiography, especially that of Ireland and England, is particularly suited to such figural analysis.[6]

The present paper is intended to provide an analysis of *Andreas'* allegory in its hagiographic context, within which the studies of Hill, Szittya, and others can be brought together. The argument will focus on the typological relationships among the three major portions of the narrative: the captivity and liberation of Matthew from prison, which is the ostensible plot of the poem to line 1057; Andrew's conversation with Christ the ship's captain, which interrupts that first plot; and Andrew's passion and the conversion of the Mermedonians, which occupy the remainder of the poem. Not surprisingly, we will find that the poet's major concern is conversion, and that the unity of the poem depends upon the various traditional images of conversion in the early Church, especially the imagery of baptism, the Harrowing of Hell, and the Last Judgment. By analyzing these traditional images in the poem, we will see that the early episodes, Andrew's voyage and Matthew's liberation from prison, are very much part of this central conversion theme, serving as prophecy and figure for the ultimate conversion of the cannibals.

I. Allegory in the Poem

Hagiography as a genre begs for typological interpretation, and the story of Matthew and Andrew is no exception. There are several indications in *Andreas* itself that we are intended to read the story as a figural narrative; and since the allegorical nature of poems like this is still an issue among scholars, I will examine these details briefly before elaborating the allegory they point to.

First, the many inconsistencies and incongruities in the poem's literal narrative are earmarks of allegorical style. Where the poem makes no sense on the literal level, we are justified in seeking for consistent meaning on some other level. Some of the poem's incongruities have been discussed in this way before, and some have not. One of the most extraordinary of these latter will serve as an example: that is the sudden and inexplicable disappearance of Matthew and his nearly three hundred companions from Mermedonia and the poem, directly after they have been freed from prison. We are told only that 'Matthew led that company into God's keeping' (1044–45). Since the Greek and Old English prose versions of the tale *do* account for their disappearance, it is easy to assume that somehow a page has been lost in the early transmission of the poem; but there is no page missing at this point in our manuscript, and I will show that this detail, along with many such difficulties, can be understood easily and elegantly in an allegorical reading of the poem.

Second, and more immediately apparent perhaps as a call to allegory, are the implications of the 'living stone' episode, in which Christ brings to life a stone from the Temple; this stone then resurrects the Patriarchs, who preach Christ's coming to the Jews. It is Christ Himself who elicits from Andrew this bizarre version of His own mission, a tale which has no known apocryphal analogues and which clearly demands to be understood allegorically, as Szittya has shown. Since Andrew's strange and unique account of Christ's mission is accepted in the poem by Christ Himself without question, comment, or correction, we have to assume that the poet and his audience (or at least the original author and his audience) were well aware that Andrew's tale is not an account of literal history; in fact, we may conclude from the casual way in which the author deals with this small allegory, that he was familiar enough with this mode of narrative that he did not feel a need to call attention to it, or explicate it for his audience. Any Christian would realize immediately that the story is not a simple recounting of the Gospel story. The poet and his audience did not object to this deviation because they were accustomed to symbolic narratives of this type. We might also conclude that if the poet was willing to let Andrew tell *his* tale in this manner, it is possible that the larger narrative as well is not bound by the limitations of literality; it too may be an elaboration of Christian truths in such conventional symbols.

Third, and more striking even than the narrative incongruities of the poem or this short allegorical episode, is a sudden interruption of the narrative toward the end of the poem (lines 1478–91), a passage original in the Old English poem. Before the final miracle of the conversion of the Mermedonians, the poet addresses the reader directly and announces:

> Hwæt, ic hwile nu   haliges lare
> leoðgiddinga,   lof þæs þe worhte,
> wordum wemde,   wyrd undyrne.
> Ofer min gemet   mycel is to secganne,
> langsum leornung,   þaet he in life adreag,
> eall æfter orde;   þaet scell æglæwra
> mann on moldan   þonne ic me tælige
> findan on ferðe,   þæt fram fruman cunne
> eall þa earfeðo   þe he mid elne adreah
> grimra guða.   Hwæðre git sceolon
> lytlum sticcum   leoðworda dæl
> furður reccan;   þæt is fyrnsægen,
> hu he weorna feala   wita geðolode,
> heardra hilda,   in þære hæðenan byrig.

(Lo, for a time now I have told with words, in poetic song, the story of the saint, his famous fate and praise of what he did. To say all that he endured in life from the beginning is a long study, far beyond my measure; an earthly man wiser in the Law than I count myself will find in his heart that he knows from the beginning all the sufferings in grim battles which he bravely endured. However, we shall tell further some of the song in little segments; it is an old story, how he suffered a great many torments, hard battles, in that heathen city.)[7]

These lines are more than just a rhetorical disclaimer in the form of an *occupatio*. The poet here expresses a notion which should startle the modern reader: that a man wise in the Law will *already know* this tale in his heart. Strange as it is, the idea that the tale itself can be known through wisdom or piety, even without historical knowledge, is actually a *topos* in medieval hagiography. It is common for the hagiographer to point to the traditional nature of the saint's legend and to the legend's non-historical (or non-literal) basis. This is because the saint's life is ultimately devotional rather than historical in our sense of the word; it is more concerned with the truths which underlie Christian history, which motivate it and can be derived from it, than with the particulars of actual historical events.[8]

As an example of this *topos*, we might note the following 'disclaimer' inserted toward the end of the anonymous Anglo-Saxon *Life of St. Gregory*, written at Whitby in the early eighth century:

> . . . If any reader should know more about all the miracles of this kindly man or how they happened, we pray him, for Christ's sake, not to nibble with critical teeth at this work of ours which has been diligently twisted into shape by love rather than knowledge. . . . For 'the love of Christ constraineth us' to preserve the memory of his miracles according to this the measure of our feeble wit, and our God will provide us with instruction in this matter. So because we must always strive for universal truth, we have told the truth so far as in us lies.[9]

The resemblance of this passage to the lines from *Andreas* should be clear enough: in the midst of a digression in which the author protests the weakness of his own powers and the limits of his knowledge, he justifies himself by claiming that 'love' and 'God's instruction,' rather than knowledge, are both his sources and motives for composing the life. The *Andreas* poet's assertion that his story can be known through 'wisdom of the Law' when mere historical knowledge fails is a variation upon this conventional idea regarding the nature of hagiography itself.

Two more examples may make this point more compelling. Reginald of

Canterbury prefaces his Anglo-Latin *Life of St. Malchus* (c. 1100) with these lines:

> Malchus, whom it is sinful to believe was not just, holy, and beloved
>   of the Lord, was filled
> With the spirit of all the just, so that however many miracles we may
>   ascribe to Malchus
> Personally, we will not have deviated from the truth. In addition, we
>   do not deny
> That we have invented many things, as is the custom of versifiers.
>   But those who wish that we
> Credit their fictions will give credit to ours, and God will credit both
>   ours and theirs. Amen.[10]

Historical accuracy is not the hagiographers' greatest interest, nor is it their guide to truth. Perhaps the most bizarre testimony to this attitude toward the truth in hagiography is the tradition of writing the saint's life from no authority other than a visual portrait. The wisdom and devotion of the author is then the *sole* guarantee of what we would call accuracy. The most celebrated instance of this method is Agnellus of Ravenna's *Liber Pontificalis Ecclesiae Ravennatis* (ninth century). Agnellus openly explains:

> Where I could not uncover a story or determine what sort of life they
> led . . . I have, with the assistance of God through your prayers,
> made up a life for them. And I believe no deception is involved, for
> they were chaste and almsgiving preachers and procurers of men's
> souls for God. And if any among you should wonder how I was able
> to create the likeness I have drawn, you should know that a picture
> taught me. . . .[11]

The willingness of hagiographers to discuss their attitudes and techniques with such candor indicates their own understanding that these narratives have no necessary relationship with literal history, but are, rather, allegorical revelations of the spiritual truths implicit in the saint's very nature. Methods of composition are thus methods of interpreting spiritually the historical lives of the saints; and understanding these methods provides us with principles for interpreting their literary lives.[12]

The *Andreas* poet, like these other writers, declares his shortcomings unimportant; in his 'disclaimer' he identifies the real source and content of his tale as 'wisdom of the Law.' The final portion of the narrative, Andrew's *passio* itself, will be given to us only in bits and pieces (*'lytlum sticcum'*), which only this wisdom will make coherent sense of; in fact,

Andrew's life and the conversion of the cannibals are expressions of this wisdom. We are especially tempted to think so, because immediately after this passage we find an apostrophe to the stone on which God's Law itself is inscribed[13] and from which the flood of baptism and judgment flows which accomplishes the great conversion at the end of the poem. In the course of this essay we will see in more detail how these themes and images operate in the narrative; my purpose here has only been to point out that the poet is aware of the supraliteral nature of his story, and that he himself indicates the poem's allegorical nature both implicitly and explicitly.[14]

The fourth indication that we are to read *Andreas* allegorically is the most important for our analysis: that is the typological structure of the poem, built upon references and analogies to Scripture. The two portions in the poem which are most obviously structured in this way have already been dealt with by Hill and Szittya; here I will explore the larger structure of the tale within which these episodes play their parts.

II. The Typological Structure of the Poem

There is an arresting peculiarity in the overall structure of *Andreas*. The captivity and liberation of Matthew seem to be the sole concern of the poem's first thousand lines; but when that plot is resolved, Andrew's passion and the conversion of the Mermedonians occupy another eight hundred. The peculiarity of this structure might best be seen from Andrew's own point of view. At the beginning of the poem he is instructed to deliver his fellow apostle from prison. Once he accepts this mission, several hundred lines go by without reference to Matthew; during the long scene with Christ on the ship, the purpose of the journey is never mentioned. Instead, Christ turns the conversation to the subject of the Jews' refusal to accept Him. Only when Andrew has finally arrived in Mermedonia does Christ reveal to him (and to us) the larger mission implicit in the original assignment. Christ says,

> 'Ic adreah feala
> yrmþa ofer eorðan;   wolde ic eow on ðon
> þurh bliðne hige   bysne onstellan,
> swa on ellþeode   ywed wyrðeð.
> Manige syndon   in þysse mæran byrig,
> þara þe ðu gehweorfest   to heofonleohte
> þurh minne naman,   þeah hie morðres feala
> in fyrndagum   gefremed habban' (969b–76).

('I endured many torments on the earth; with kindly intent I would set this as a pattern for you, as it will be shown in this strange land.

71

There are many in this famous city whom you will turn to the heavenly light through my name, though they have sinned greatly in former times.')

Here Christ explicitly offers His own passion as a *bysen* (pattern) for Andrew's mission, establishing a clear typology for the narrative which follows. Once we grasp this relationship between Andrew's mission and Christ's, we may speculate on their analogies. For example, we might note Andrew's three-day passion, and we might interpret the role of the Mermedonians as we do that of the Jews in the Gospel story. Within this structure we might also see a parallel between the liberation of Matthew and his fellow prisoners, and Christ's Harrowing of Hell.

The dramatic surprise in these lines should not be missed: Christ explains that the revelation of his *bysen* in Mermedonia is to accomplish not just the liberation of the prisoners, as Andrew has originally been told, but also the conversion of their captors. It is the connection between these two missions I want to elucidate. Through Andrew's re-enactment of Christ's passion, we are told, many will be led *to heofonleoht*. Now in what way may it be said that Christ's passion allowed many to be led to the heavenly light? Most immediately, of course, Christ's passion was the occasion of the Harrowing of Hell, the release of all the just from the bondage of Satan and their entry into heaven: tropologically, it brought about the release of mankind from the bonds of sin and death, re-enacted in each person's baptism; and ultimately, it made possible the salvation of man at the end of time, when Satan will be bound again, the Jews will be converted, and Christ will lead the blessed to their heavenly reward. The story of the Harrowing is normally interpreted in terms of these other symbols; as an allegorical treatment of the doctrine of Redemption, the Harrowing is a powerful symbol, around which other narratives symbolic of Redemption tend to aggregate.

The relations between the Harrowing of Hell, baptism, and Judgment are well enough known that I need not go into them in detail. Let me just briefly call attention to the traditional baptism of catachumens on Holy Saturday, with its explicit associations with the crossing of the Red Sea, Christ's Descent, and the Final Judgment. The release from the bondage of Egypt to the Promised land, from the bondage of Hell to Heaven, from the bondage of sin to a life of grace in the Church, and from bondage in this world to the Kingdom of God—these are some of the best explored and most powerful typological structures in early Christian thought.[15]

Our interest in these structures is that just as in sacred history the Harrowing prefigures the Judgment, so in our poem the liberation of the prisoners prefigures the conversion and baptism of the Mermedonians. Andrew, fulfilling Christ's *bysen*, liberates the captives as Christ harrowed

Hell, and he accomplishes the conversion of his tormentors as Christ too will bring about the conversion of His tormentors, the Jews, before the establishment of the Kingdom of God at the Final Judgment.

Now if my suggestion that the conversion of the Mermedonians is typologically related to that of the Jews seems too far-fetched for the poem to support, we should recall the details of the conversion episode at the end of the poem: first the defeat of Satan in the prison, then the flood and fire (eschatological and baptismal images explicated by Hill); then the separation and destruction of the evil Mermedonians and the resurrection of the dead; all leading to the conversion and the final establishment of the Church in Mermedonia. Compare with this Augustine's summary discussion of the Judgment in the *City of God*:

> . . . In connection with that judgement we have learnt that those events are to come about: Elijah the Tishbite will come; Jews will accept the faith; Antichrist will persecute; Christ will judge; the dead will rise again; the good and the evil will be separated; the earth will be destroyed in flames and then will be renewed. All those events, we must believe, will come about; but in what way, and in what order they will come, actual experience will then teach us with a finality surpassing anything our human understanding is now capable of attaining.[16]

Given the suggestive parallel between the Mermedonians and the Jews in the poem and the welter of eschatological imagery at its conclusion, and given the importance of the conversion of the Jews in eschatological literature, we must ponder this association seriously.

I do not want to hesitate in this matter: our understanding of the poem's themes and structure depends heavily upon our understanding of the relationship of the Mermedonians to the Jews in the poem; the meaning and coherence of the story depend on it. Since this is an important point, and since the poet never explicitly makes this association, and since those not used to typological analysis of this sort may find the connection tenuous, I will dwell here a moment and marshall further evidence for this typology.

First, I would point out that Christ's *bysen* revealed to Andrew on the ship is precisely the story of the 'living stone' elicited from Andrew. The whole conversation between Christ and Andrew is focused on Christ's mission to the Jews. So the mission to the Mermedonians is explicitly *patterned upon* Christ's (and the apostles') mission to the Jews. If the Mermedonians are understood in this way, the long passage on the ship, which I will discuss as 'The Education of Andrew,' becomes an integral part of the developing themes and images of the poem; otherwise, the discussion of the Jews must seem arbitrary and unrelated to the rest of the poem, no matter how interesting it is in itself.

Second, we might note that the Mermedonians are described throughout the poem as *wærlogan*, 'covenant-breakers.' But what covenant? The word is used widely in Old English poetry of the fallen angels, devils, the Jews, and the damned; Wulfstan uses it for the English. What our poet means by it is clarified in the flood scene, when we discover that the very stone on which God inscribed the ten commandments is an *eald enta geweorc* ('ancient work of giants') among the Mermedonians; it is a foundation column under the city wall, where Andrew is imprisoned, and the new Church is built upon this column at the end of the poem (lines 1632–35). This is certainly a boldly conceived symbol calling attention to the relationship of the Mermedonians to the Jews.

In an unpublished study, 'A Figural Interpretation of the Pillars in the Old English *Andreas*,' David Riede notes that the many columns in Scripture are universally interpreted in early exegesis as the spiritual strength of the apostles; he understands this pillar, from which the water flows, in light of this exegesis and in light of John 7:8, 'Whoever believes in me, as the Scriptures say, from his breast shall flow fountains of living water.' This water is commonly interpreted as the preaching of the apostles and baptism. Riede then poses the obvious question: why do the waters of instruction and baptism in the poem flow from the pillar of the Old Law, rather than the New? He answers by citing Bede's discussion of the two pillars of the Temple, one of which attracts the Gentiles and the other of which attracts the Jews, *a luce scientiae legalis* ('by the light of wisdom of the Law').[17] Like other readers of the poem, Riede notes the parallel between the 'living stone' from the Temple which preaches to the Jews early in the poem, and the stone of the Old Law which converts the Mermedonians in the end.[18] His entire analysis points to a typological relationship between the Mermedonians and the Jews.[19]

A more direct explanation for the conversion of the Mermedonians by means of the Old Law comes from Augustine's discussion of the final conversion of the Jews in the *City of God*, where he explicates Malachi's verse 'Remember the Law of Moses thy servant':

Malachi thus admonishes his people to remember the Law of Moses, for he foresaw that for a long time yet they would not interpret it spiritually, as they ought to have done; and he continues, 'See, I shall send you Elijah the Tishbite, before the great and splendid Day of the Lord; and he will turn the heart of the father to the son and the heart of a man to his neighbour, so that in my coming I may not utterly shake the earth.' The belief that in the final period before the judgement this great and wonderful prophet Elijah will expound the

Law to the Jews, and that through his activity the Jews are destined to believe in our Christ, this is a very frequent subject in the conversation of believers, and a frequent thought in their hearts.[20]

The Jews are to be converted by having the Law of Moses expounded to them.

A third piece of evidence for the relationship of the Mermedonians to the Jews is an episode which appears in both the Greek and Old English prose versions of the story, though for reasons which I will explain it has not been included in *Andreas*. In these other versions, when the prisoners have been released Andrew instructs them,

'You shall find in the way a great fig-tree, and sit under the fig tree, and eat of its fruit, until I come to you; but if I delay coming there, you will find abundance of food for yourselves: for the fruit shall not fail from the fig-tree, but according as you eat it shall produce more fruit, and nourish you, as the Lord has said.'[21]

The image is a familiar one: the fruitless fig-tree of Matt. 21:18–22, Mark 11:12–14, and Luke 13:6–9 is understood by all commentators as an allegory of the Jews, specifically *Synagoga*. In Luke the episode is told as a parable in which the owner of the tree, finding no fruit on it for three years, tells the gardener to cut it down; but the gardener begs him to wait one more year. Ambrose interprets the image as God's attempt to save the Jews from their own destruction. The point of his exposition is that 'No one comes to Grace but he who knows the Law.'[22] Augustine uses the parable to explain the resistance of the Jews to the faith in his own day.[23] The fruitful tree of the Andrew story would seem then to be both a sign of the apostles' faith and a prophecy of the Jews' redemption. And it fits hand-in-glove with the story's imagery of hunger and food and the imagery of the Law.

A fourth indication of the relation of the Mermedonians to the Jews is the existence of at least two Irish analogues to our flood scene at the end of the poem. In both of these, the victims are a city full of Jews who scoff at the Eucharist and stab the Host, unwittingly re-enacting the crucifixion:

'Never was body without blood in it' say the Jews; to test it, the pure
   Body is wounded in the city where He received a poor welcome.
From God's Body when wounded came torrents of bright blood, like
   the strong waters of the Deluge; this is what all the pious tales
   relate.
Jesus' Body gradually filled the city with His blood; the Jews are

drowned in their dwellings by the Blood of the Just
One. . . .
God rises up to save the good Christian—wondrous deliverance!
The ground whereon he stood floated as a boat on the sea.[24]

Though the parallel with *Andreas* is only partial, it is striking; and
although the Irish texts are later than the original story of Andrew, we can
see that the outrageousness of Andrew's great miracle, like most miracles,
has become conventional to some degree; and here again the tale is
associated with the Jews (though not exactly their conversion!). But we
need not reach as far as these Irish poems to make the point; the whole
structure of *Andreas* suggests that we understand the conversion of the
Mermedonians as a figure for the conversion of the Jews.

We might say, then, to sketch the poem's typological structure in very
bold lines, that of the two objectives of Andrew's mission to Mermedonia
—to free the prisoners and to convert their captors—the first is described
in terms of the Harrowing of Hell, and the second in terms of the
conversion of the Jews. These two events are related to each other and to
Andrew's historical mission by the imagery of baptism, which involves
them both.[25] We might note in this regard the prominence in *Andreas* of
the rich imagery of the Exodus, which is the Old Testament type for all
these events: the cloud which hides the escaping prisoners, the opening
of the sea before Andrew, the water called forth from the rock, the tablets
of the Law, the earth swallowing the evil Mermedonians, and the eating
of manna.

Beyond typology, in more abstract theological terms the two episodes
are related by the general theme of conversion and the doctrine of
resurrection. Augustine again provides us with terms which unify these
diverse moments in history and in the life of the individual. In his
analysis of the Last Judgment he says:

... Even now men are being converted to the faith from the un-
belief in which the Devil held them in his power, . . . and this
'strong man' is obviously being bound in the case of every man who
is snatched away from him, as part of his property.[26]

Satan is bound, then, not only at the Harrowing and the Last Judgment,
but also upon the conversion of each soul at baptism. And in each instance
too there is a resurrection: when Christ harrows Hell the dead rise out of
their graves, anticipating the general resurrection before Judgment;[27] and
conversion to the faith is also described by Augustine as a resurrection,
the 'resurrection of the soul' which has been dead before God—'for souls
also have their own death, in the shape of irreligion and sin.'[28] His

summary statement of these notions should make clear the relevance of the doctrine to the structure of the poem:

> There are thus two rebirths . . . : one according to faith, which comes here and now through baptism, and the other in the body, a rebirth which will come . . . as a result of the great and last judgement. Similarly, there are two resurrections: the first, the resurrection of the soul, which is here and now, and prevents us from coming to the second death; and the second, which is not now, but is to come at the end of the world; this is not the resurrection of the soul but of the body.[29]

In the story of the conversion and baptism of the Mermedonians, *Andreas* concerns the first rebirth and the first resurrection, accomplished according to the *bysen* of sacred history, prefigured by Christ's passion and descent into Hell, which are in turn prefigured by the Exodus, and which prefigure in turn again the second rebirth and resurrection, the final Harrowing, the final conversion, and the final baptism, at the fulfillment of history.

So the two parts of the poem, the two missions of Andrew, are actually one, insofar as the deliverance of the prisoners is itself a figure for the conversion that follows.

It is interesting that *Elene* has a very similar structure, built upon the same typology. The conversion and baptism of Constantine introduces Elene's mission to find the true cross, which in turn results in the conversion of the Jews—literally!—which is an extraordinary distortion of history, of course, but one which makes sense as an exploration of the theme of conversion in the elastic language of the typological vision. We would certainly be at a loss to account for the conversion of the Jews in the fourth century in *Elene* without reference to this typology. Recall the conversion scene in the poem, when at the ninth hour, the hour of Christ's death and descent,[30] a dead man is resurrected by virtue of the cross; immediately Satan wheels in on the wind, complaining that he has been despoiled of his possessions by Christ, and he cries, 'O the Lord has bound me often in that narrow home!' (919–20), recalling Augustine's statement that Satan 'is obviously being bound in the case of every man who is snatched away from him, as part of his property.' The resurrection of the man is clearly and explicitly presented as a re-enactment of the Harrowing of Hell; moreover, it is presented as a figure for the conversion of the Jews, which actually and quite literally follows directly after. And in the end it is also a figure for the poet Cynewulf's conversion and salvation—and the reader's too.

Within the large structure I have suggested for *Andreas*, we now can begin to work out a detailed analysis. The allegory of conversion and salvation which I have sketched is contained in a tightly-knit narrative of three related episodes: the captivity and release of Matthew and his companions, the spiritual education of Andrew on the ship, and the conversion of the cannibals. Since this last has been dealt with by Hill, my own analysis will focus on the first two parts of the poem.

III. The Captivity of Matthew

The first important problem the poem presents to us is the significance of the Mermedonians' cannibalism, which provides the motive for most of the poem's action. Andrew does not bring to Mermedonia a remedy for the famine which has driven the people to cannibalism; they are saved by the conversion of their souls. Baptism is the remedy for the spiritual state which cannibalism symbolizes. John Casteen has shown that cannibalism serves a similar symbolic function in the Bible, at least in its medieval exegesis.[31] And cannibalism is only part of an elaborate pattern of food symbolism in *Andreas*.

David Hamilton has outlined for us the allegory of food and hunger in the poem, though he does not take the important step of casting his arguments into the traditional Christian vocabulary of spiritual hunger and spiritual nourishment, and for this reason his analysis of the images remains somewhat limited. When translated into the relevant theological and historical terms developed in Christian exegesis, the concepts he deals with are actually more inclusive than he argues. The conclusions he reaches about this aspect of the poem's allegory, however, are fundamentally correct:

> The Mermedonians are little more than a vehicle for the idea of spiritual hunger; their deprivation is unnaturally strained and can be understood only by recourse to an imposed, allegorical meaning. They embody spiritual privation, and their cannibalism, though basically a symptom of their inner nature, quickly becomes their total characterization.[32]

The use of food in Scripture as a metaphor for spiritual sustenance is widespread, as we should expect from the importance of ritual meals in both testaments. It begins with the fruit of the Garden, and includes the Paschal Lamb and the manna and water of the Exodus. The metaphor of food is common in the Psalms, the parallel structure of which can take on a new meaning for the reader of *Andreas*:

> He gives justice to the oppressed,
> He gives bread to the hungry.

> The Lord releases the prisoners,
> the Lord gives sight to the blind. (Psalm 146:7–8)

The food metaphor also ranges from the Banquet of Wisdom (Proverbs 9) to Christ's Last Supper, and from His instructions to the apostles to 'Feed my sheep' (John 21:15–17) to Paul's discussion of 'spiritual food' and 'spiritual drink' (I Corinthians 10:3–4) and Peter's 'pure spiritual milk' (I Peter 2:2).

As with most of this food imagery in the Bible, the traditions concerning spiritual hunger and nourishment most directly relevant to the story of *Andreas* are crystallized around the Eucharist. This is the spiritual food which is the alternative and corrective to the Mermedonians' privation; and much of the poem's imagery, from the manna on the ship to the water from the column, is eucharistic or is drawn from familiar figures for the eucharistic meal. Casteen has noted the 'false eucharist' of the Mermedonians in lines 1108–16, where one of the cannibals offers his own son to be killed and eaten.[33] This parody calls attention to the spiritual condition of the Mermedonians in terms of the Eucharist, which will be the means of their salvation.

Within the context of the commonplace vocabulary of spiritual nourishment, cannibalism clearly represents a displaced reliance upon man himself for spiritual sustenance. Interestingly, the *Andreas* poet uses the unique word *sylfætan* ('self-eaters,' 175b) for the cannibals. The word has always been glossed 'cannibals,' or 'those who eat their own kind,' though it should be apparent that in *Andreas*, where hunger and cannibalism represent spiritual conditions, it is an especially pointed term. Note the idea, developed by Augustine and Boethius, that the wicked man destroys himself and becomes nothing: 'For anyone who really is anything is assuredly this—a keeper, I mean, of God's commandments—since anyone who is not this is nothing, because he remains in the likeness of vanity, which is nothingness.'[34] In the *Consolation*, Philosophy addresses the wicked with words appropriate to the cannibals: 'Why do you whip yourselves to a frenzy, and ever seek your fate by self-destruction?'[35] The term *sylfætan*, in the context of the theme of spiritual hunger, describes those who derive nourishment from themselves rather than from God and who thereby destroy themselves. The Mermedonians are introduced as servants of the Devil, hell-bent on trying to satisfy their needs with human flesh and destroying themselves in the process.

The characterization of the cannibals as a *fordenera gedræg* ('throng of the damned'), as *deofles þegnas* ('devil's retinue'), and as *hæleþ hellfuse* ('men bent on hell') is clear enough; but the poet's description of the potion they use to transform their captives before eating them is notoriously confusing.

Syððan him geblendan   bitere tosomne
dryas þurh dwolcræft   drync unheorne,
se onwende gewit,   wera ingeþanc,
heortan on hreðre;   hyge wæs oncyrred,
þæt hie ne murndan   æfter mandreame,
hæleþ heorogrædige,   ac hie hig ond gærs
for meteleaste   meðe gedrehte (33–39).

(Then the magicians bitterly blended together with sorcery a horrible drink, which would change the mind and the inner thought of men, the heart in the breast; the mind was turned about, so that the bloodthirsty men did not care for the joys of men, but hay and grass tormented the weary ones because of a lack of food.)

Here the poet seems to confuse the condition of the captives with that of their captors, calling them *heorogrædige* and *meðe*, terms which are, according to Brooks himself, 'out of place here,' and 'more appropriate to the Mermedonians than to their captives.'[36] But there is a traditional Christian significance to the act of making men like beasts by means of a potion, and this significance obviates the most apparent difficulties of the passage.

Though Homer is seldom brought to bear on Old English poetry, in this case we are justified. *Andreas* is, after all, derived from the Greek legend of Andrew. The Greek Church had allegorized Homer just as the Latin Church had Virgil, and important details of the allegorized *Odyssey* made their way into Western Christian writings.[37] One of the most important and widespread of these Homeric allegories is that of Circe. Some of the vast lore surrounding her potion and the *moly* which preserves Odysseus from becoming a beast is at work in our poem. These traditions first of all influenced the original Greek legend of Matthew and Andrew, and were well known to the Anglo-Saxon poet as well in the form they had assumed in the West.

The essence of this allegory as it relates to our poem is this: Circe represents the demonic powers (Isidore calls her 'sorceress, poisoner, and priestess to demons'),[38] the powers which tempt men to turn away from God and thus become like beasts. The Greek Fathers identify Hermes with divine inspiration, the Gospels, or Christ; he delivers to Odysseus for his protection the plant *moly*, which has dark roots below and white flowers above. The plant neatly corresponds to the conception of man's nature which the allegory is exploring: he is partly of the darkness and partly of the light, he is part beast, but his soul tends towards God.[39]

It was Boethius who gave the allegory its fullest form in the West in the fourth book of the *Consolation*. In the course of her proof that evil men have no existence, Philosophy argues, 'anyone who abandons virtue ceases to be a man, since he cannot share in the divine nature, and instead becomes a beast.'[40] She then recounts the legend of Circe, who 'had power over the bodies of men, but could not change their hearts.' But, she goes on, 'poisons which can make [man] forget himself are more potent and deadly than Circe's because they corrupt the inner man. They do not harm the body, but they horribly wound the mind.' Boethius himself then sums up, 'although vicious men keep the appearance of their human bodies, they are nevertheless changed into beasts as far as the character of their souls is concerned.'[41]

This same tradition appears a century earlier in Hilary's *Life of St. Honoratus,* in a hagiographic form more nearly related to *Andreas.* Honoratus visits an island, where he first conquers 'the terrors of the solitude' and 'the army of serpents,' and then establishes a church and monastery. Christians flock there from every nation, and Hilary asks 'What barbarian ways did he not tame? And how often he changed, as it were, savage beasts into gentle doves!' Hilary goes on,

A variety of diseases of the soul were dispelled by his exhortations. Bitterness, moroseness and passion gave place to the liberty which Christ offers; and, after long and burdensome bondage in Egypt, there would come refreshing rest. Stupefying and amazing were the transformations; but they were not of men into beasts, changed (so the story goes) by the potions of Circe, but of beasts into men, changed by the sweetest of potions, the message of Christ, ministered to them by Honoratus.[42]

This story is especially interesting to us because the 'beasts' here are actually Christians, imprisoned by spiritual weaknesses, whom the saint releases from this 'bondage in Egypt' into the rest and freedom of Christ, by reversing Circe's magic. As in *Andreas,* the motif of the liberation of the beasts is not applied to the demonic powers inhabiting the island, but to the Christians held captive by them. In both cases, the liberation of the men from their bondage as beasts parallels the cleansing of the island and the establishment of the Church there.

Though one might assume from *Andreas* that the captives are actually changed into beasts, this is not so. They are blinded (which requires no exegesis) and they are given hay and grass to eat (a sign of insanity or possession),[43] but in neither the Greek nor the Old English version is a physical transformation mentioned. Rather, Matthew worries that he 'might behave like a dumb beast, out of despair.' The drug, which acts upon the spirit rather than the body, is the same as those 'diseases of the soul,' 'bitterness, moroseness, and passion,' of Hilary's work and the poison 'which corrupts the inner man' in Boethius' discussion. Within the framework of this imagery, it is hardly inappropriate for our poet to refer to the transformed captives as pejoratively as he does. Their hearts are turned away from God; and their weakness and despair highlight Matthew's unshakable faith and saintliness.

Matthew is not affected by the potion. As with the allegorized Odysseus in the writings of the Greek Fathers, the Word (Christ) grants him the light of God, without which man naturally becomes like a beast. The light is the light of heaven, the *heofonleoht* of line 974, which is won when the sufferings of this life are ended. The emphasis which the poet places on Matthew's heavenly salvation as the alternative to his transformation and destruction by the cannibals is an early indication of the poet's interest in the eschatological aspect of his story.[44] It is in the framework of the traditions growing out of the Circe legend, then, which become attached to the widespread imagery of spiritual nourishment, and are expressive of very common moral and theological ideas, that the *Andreas* poet develops the setting of his narrative.

IV. The Education of Andrew

When God finally decides to set in motion the machinery of Matthew's release, we are told:

> Þa wæs gemyndig   se ðe middangeard
> gestaðelode   strangum mihtum,
> hu he in ellþeodigum   yrmðum wunode
> belocen leoðubendum,   þe oft his lufan adreg
> for Ebreum   ond Israhelum,
> swylce he Iudea   galdorcræftum
> wiðstod stranglice (161–67a).

(Then He who established the middle-earth with his strong powers remembered how he dwelled in torments among strangers, locked in hateful bonds—He who often showed His love to the Hebrews and Israelites, as He resolutely resisted the magic arts of the Jews.)

Christ recalls His own passion at the hands of the Jews, which becomes the model for the suffering and deliverance of both saints in the poem.

Immediately afterward, when God assigns to Andrew the task of freeing his fellow apostle, Andrew replies:

> 'Hu mæg ic, dryhten min,   ofer deop gelad
> fore gefremman   on feorne weg
> swa hrædlice,   heofona scyppend,

> wuldres waldend,   swa ðu worde becwist?
>   . . . Ne synt me winas cuðe,
> eorlas elþeodige,   ne þær æniges wat
> hæleða gehygdo,   ne me herestræta
> ofer cald wæter   cuðe sindon' (190–93, 198b–201).

('How might I, my Lord, make a journey far away over the deep sea, as quickly as you command with your word, Creator of Heaven and Ruler of Glory? . . . The rulers and the foreign lords are not known to me, nor do I know the mind of any of those men, nor are the army-streets over the cold waters known to me.')

This absurdly inadequate reply, as God is to point out, amounts to a failure of faith. But in his failure, of course, Andrew has distinguished company. Jonah is the most obvious example of God's reluctant servant; and when Habacuc was called in Judea to rescue Daniel from the lion's den in Babylon, he replied much like Andrew: 'Domine, Babylonem non vidi, et lacum nescio' ('Lord, I have not seen Babylon, and know not the den,' Daniel 14:34). These two figures—the one called to rescue a fellow-prophet from captivity, the other to convert a city of unbelievers—reflect Andrew's position in the poem, and the parallels make the meaning of Andrew's story a little clearer, since both Old Testament episodes are common figures for the Harrowing of Hell, the Resurrection, and the Last Judgment.

After Andrew is chastised for his delay and hastens to fulfill his assigned mission, the poem takes an unexpected turn. More than seven hundred lines go by without reference to Matthew. During the long dialogue with Christ on the ship, the ostensible purpose of the journey is never mentioned. Rather, Christ guides the conversation carefully in another direction and gradually awakens Andrew to a larger vision of his mission to Mermedonia. We can see how Christ subtly manipulates the development of the encounter in the opening conversation, which we might paraphrase like this:

Andrew: Where are you from?
Christ: The wind blew us from Mermedonia.
A: Will you take us there? God will reward you.
C: But the Mermedonians kill strangers.
A: We still want to go.
C: Fine, then, if you can pay.
A: We have no money or food.
C: Why would you travel the sea without money or food? Life on the sea is hard.

A: Just because you have wealth and food you should not be proud. Christ said to welcome strangers and we are His servants. He told us, 'Go throughout the world and preach the faith, and I will provide for you.' Now will you help us?

C: Gladly.

Note that the question is never asked, Why do you want to go to Mermedonia? Instead, Christ tests Andrew with a less obvious question, Why would you assume such hardships without the comforts of money or food? Andrew passes the test; his explanation is actually a paraphrase of Matthew 10:9–10, in which Christ prohibited His disciples from carrying food or money while preaching to the Jews. He says, paraphrasing Christ:

> 'Bodiað æfter burgum   beorhtne geleafan
> ofer foldan fæðm;   ic eow freoðo healde.
> Ne ðurfan ge on þa fore   frætwe lædan,
> gold ne seolfor;   ic eow goda gehwæs
> on eowerne agenne dom   est ahwette' (335–39).

('Preach to the cities the bright faith over the expanse of the earth; I will protect you. On that journey you will not need to carry provisions, gold or silver. I will grant you favor in every good thing according to your wish.')

Compare the Gospel, 'Take no gold or silver or copper in your belts, no bag for your journey, nor two tunics, nor sandals, nor a staff.' The Old English prose version of the story is even clearer: Andrew quotes Christ, 'Næbbe ge mid eow hlaf ne feoh ne twifeald hrægl' ('Take not with you bread nor money nor two cloaks'). In fact, the entire tenth chapter of Matthew, which describes the mission of the apostles to the Jews, is a good description of the mission to Mermedonia:

'Behold, I send you out as sheep in the midst of wolves; so be wise as serpents and innocent as doves. Beware of men; for they will deliver you up to the councils, and flog you in their synagogues, and you will be dragged before governors and kings for my sake, to bear testimony before them and the Gentiles. . . . Brother will deliver up brother to death, and the father his child, and children will rise against parents and have them put to death; and you will be hated by all for my name's sake. But he who endures to the end will be saved' (Matthew 10:16–18, 21–22).

84

In both the original Greek and the Old English prose versions of the story, Matthew unambiguously cites the first verse of this passage as an explanation of his own sufferings in Mermedonia: 'Broþor Andreas, ac ne gehyrdest þu Drihten cweþende for þon þe "ic eow sende swa swa sceap on middum wulfum?" ' ('Brother Andrew, did you not hear the Lord saying indeed "I send you as sheep among wolves?" '). The corresponding passage in *Andreas* has been lost in the lacuna after line 1024.

With Andrew's reference to the mission to the Jews, the direction of the dialogue with Christ changes. From this point, the conversation focuses more and more sharply on the refusal of the Jews to accept Christ in spite of His miraculous ministry. The captain asks Andrew to tell Him about Christ and to calm his own disciples' minds as a storm rages around the ship; so Andrew tells how Christ quelled the storm on the Sea of Galilee— at which point the storm is calmed. Though Andrew has not been told that he is to pattern his mission after Christ's *bysen,* that typology is already at work. Christ begs for more instruction, in more specific terms, asking, 'How did it happen among men that the faithless Jews maliciously insulted the royal child who was born as a comfort for mankind?' (557–68). Then He asks 'Can you tell me whether your Lord worked miracles where the priests, scribes, and elders sat in council?' (603–09). Andrew's replies become more and more specific until he finally recounts the story of the 'living stone.' If we see this story in its context, we see that it is the capstone of a long argument about the Jews' refusal to recognize Christ. The whole episode fits into our poem because Andrew's mission itself is a sub-fulfillment of Christ's mission to the Jews; and within the typological framework of the poem the conversion of the Mermedonians is a prefiguration of the final gathering of the Jews into the faith. The relationship of the allegory of the living stone to the conversion of the Mermedonians is strengthened by Andrew's use of the stone at the end of the poem. As Christ addresses the *stan* of the Temple wall, so Andrew addresses the *stan* of the Old Law; both stones bear witness to Christ, and as stubbornly as the Jews disbelieved the evidence before their eyes, the Mermedonians hasten to accept it.

There is an obvious irony in Andrew's telling of the tale, of course, for we can hardly forget that as he recounts the Jews' refusal to recognize Christ, he himself does not recognize Him in the form of the captain. Andrew sees this irony when he finally realizes who the pilot was, and he assumes that his ignorance was a measure of his sinfulness. Indeed, Christ then explains that the whole charade was a lesson to correct Andrew's initial lack of faith.

The whole discussion on the ship, focused as it is on Christ's mission to the Jews and recalling too the hazardous mission of the disciples to the Jews, prepares Andrew for the bad news. For it is at this point that Christ explains that Andrew's mission is to be patterned on the *bysen* of His passion, and that the end result is to be the conversion of the Mermedonians.

But Andrew's spiritual education does not end here. Later, on the third day of his torments, he recalls how Christ said 'Why hast Thou forsaken me?' and he loses hope and asks to die. God strengthens him by showing him the fruits of his suffering—literally!—blossoming groves springing up where he had left his bloody tracks (1401–49). And at the end of the poem Andrew is corrected once more, when he hastens to leave his new church on the very day he founds it; but God appears to him and says 'Thou shalt not forsake that flock in so new a faith, but establish my name firmly in their hearts. Dwell in that city, protector of warriors, in the adorned halls, for the space of seven nights; then you may leave with my blessing' (1669–74). This last failure of Andrew is highlighted even more in the Greek and the Old English prose versions.

> Se eadiga Andreas þa wæs eft hwyrfende on Marmadonia ceastre and he cwæþ: 'Ic þe bletsige, min Drihten Hælend Crist, þu þe gehwyrfest ealle saula, for þon þu me ne forlete ut gangan mid minre hatheortan of þisse ceastre.'[45]

> (Then blessed Andrew turned back [*wæs hwyrfende*] to Mermedonia and said 'I thank you, my Lord Savior Christ, who convertest [*gehwyrfest,* turns about] all souls, because you did not let me leave this city in anger.')

We can see that Andrew is as much the converted as the convertor. The theme of Andrew's education is central to the entire tale. Just as the liberation of the prisoners is a figure for the conversion of the Mer-medonians, both are symbols of Andrew's own *hwyrft.* We find an analagous situation in *Elene,* where Elene herself (whom Hill interprets as a figure of *Ecclesia*) does not receive the gift of the Holy Spirit until after the conversion of the Jews at the end of the poem. The poem concerns her 'spiritual advancement,' as well as that of the Jews.[46]

V. *The Liberation of the Prisoners*

The symbolic nature of the liberation of the prisoners should by now be clear. I have already referred to Hilary's *Life of Honoratus,* in which the renewal of faith is described as a liberation, a reversal of Circe's magic, and freedom from Egyptian bondage. And Jean Leclercq has noted the use of the liberation motif as a common depiction of the spiritual freedom of the saint: 'The act which best symbolizes the achievement of inner freedom in hagiography, is that of liberating prisoners or the possessed . . . as in the

Life of St. Winnoc, in which it is said that he who so frees the captives re-enacts the mystery of the Exodus in which the Chosen People were freed.'[47] In *Andreas* too, the liberation of the prisoners (who are also possessed) functions in part as a symbol of Andrew's own interior spiritual state. And beneath this symbolism, of course, is the typology of the Harrowing of Hell, prefigured by the Exodus.

Christ's instructions to Andrew regarding Matthew's release are clearly meant to evoke the Harrowing:

> 'Þu hine secan scealt,
> leofne alysan   of laðra hete,
> and eal þæt mancynn   þe him mid wunige
> elþeodigra   inwitwrasnum,
> bealuwe gebundene;   him sceal bot hraðe
> weorþan in worulde   ond in wuldres lean,
> swa ic him sylfum ær   secgende wæs' (943b–49).

('You shall seek him and release the beloved one from the hatred of enemies, and all those people who dwell with him in the cruel bondage of foreigners, bound terribly; there shall quickly be a remedy for him in the world, and a reward in glory, as I said to him before.')

The earlier promise Christ refers to here is that of lines 102–06, in which God promised to reward Matthew's endurance with his salvation in 'radiant paradise, the brightest of glories, fairest of blessed homes.' In both of these passages, Matthew's release is described in eschatological terms perfectly appropriate to the Harrowing.

Andrew proceeds to the prison, where the seven gatekeepers fall dead, and with only a touch the gates fall open to the saint. As he leads the prisoners out, the poet says explicitly that Andrew leads the host 'into the Lord's keeping.'[48]

> Gewat þa Matheus   menigo lædan
> on gehyld Godes   swa him se halga bebead;
> weorod on wilsið   wolcnum beþehte,
> þe læs him scyldhatan   scyððan comon
> mid earhfare,   ealdgeniðlan.
> Þær þa modigan mid him   mæðel gehedan,
> treowgeþoftan,   ær hie on tu hweorfan;
> ægðer þara eorla   oðrum trymede
> heofonrices hyht,   helle witu
> wordum werede.   Swa ða wigend mid him,

87

> hæleð higerofe,   halgum stefnum,
> cempan coste,   cyning weorðadon,
> wyrda waldend,   þæs wuldres ne bið
> æfre mid eldum   ende befangen (1044–57).

(Then Matthew led the host into God's keeping, as the saint bade him; the troop on their desired journey was covered with clouds, lest the shield-enemies, the old enemies, should come to injure them with fllights of arrows. There the brave ones, the trusted companions, held council with each other before they separated; each of the men encouraged the other with hope of the heavenly kingdom, and warded off the torments of hell with words. Thus together the warriors, heroes bold in mind, excellent fighters, praised with hallowed voices the King, the Ruler of Fates, to whose glory an end shall never come.)

Lines 1046–48 provide a fascinating touch of traditional typology which supports our interpretation. God covers the escaping host with a cloud, an image obviously drawn from Exodus 14:19–20, where God hides the fleeing Israelites from the pursuing Egyptians by means of a cloud. The relation between the flight from Egypt and the Harrowing of Hell is too commonplace to require documentation here; I have dealt with it elsewhere, pointing out the imagery of the *descensus* in the Old English poem *Exodus*.[49]

Now we have finally arrived back at the puzzle I introduced at the beginning of this paper; for Matthew and the other two hundred and eighty-one prisoners are not mentioned again in the poem. It is this disappearance of the prisoners which is the most peculiar detail of the episode. The anomaly has not been explored or explained fully, perhaps, because of the common assumption that a folio has been lost at this point in the poem; there is certainly a lacuna at line 1024. The Greek and Old English prose versions relate at this point that Andrew sends the prisoners to wait for him under the fig tree, and Andrew's disciples and Matthew are swept off on a cloud to a mountain where Peter is teaching. The typology of this story is very interesting, but all this is missing from *Andreas*. No obvious lacuna, however, occurs where we would expect it in the narrative, which would be at line 1044.[50] If a page is missing, it may have contained some eighty lines of dialogue (and interesting dialogue, to judge from the other versions) between Andrew and Matthew after line 1024. The evidence of the MS seems to indicate that the poet purposefully eliminated that part of the story recounting the disappearance of the captives. They simply disappear, having passed 'into God's keeping.' And the point of this change is clear enough: such a resolution strengthens the analogy with the Harrowing of Hell and amplifies the tale's eschatological content.

As I announced in my introduction, the poet's major concern in *Andreas* is conversion—not only conversion in its most obvious sense, but also in its largest sense, the conversion of the world at the end of time, as well as its most personal sense, the strengthening of faith that is so familiar to us in poems like *The Dream of the Rood* and, more interestingly, in the four Cynewulfian signatures.[51] There is no end to the detailed image-by-image analysis of the poem which might be elaborated within the general framework I have laid out here. I have limited myself to just a few matters in those portions of the poem which have not been analyzed in such terms before. I do not think that the allegory I have described in any way limits our interpretation of the poem or conflicts with most interpretations already suggested. This understanding of the poem will conflict only with those which insist that the power of Old English poetry derives solely or mainly from its Germanic primitiveness in relation to the other Christian literature of the early Middle Ages. But such a view, for all its romantic attractiveness, is hardly tenable any longer, given the historical and literary researches of the last forty years. Clearly, the Germanic culture of England was profoundly (if unusually) Christianized, and the Christianity of England was profoundly Germanized. Rather than engaging in out-dated polemics, Old English scholars should be trying to analyze this fusion to discover how it was that at that time and place such a vigorous and unique culture was created from such an unlikely coupling. In any case, whereas most studies which focus on Christian literary conventions, allegory, or typology in poems like *Andreas* still conclude with an *apologia* for such an approach, I do not think that an elaborate defense need be made any longer for the investigation of common Christian ideas in Anglo-Saxon poetry.

Fordham University

Tradition and Design in Beowulf

THEODORE M. ANDERSSON

THE poets responsible for the earliest versions of medieval heroic legend appear not to have invented their stories, but to have fixed already existing oral stories in written form. So much holds true for French Carolingian epic and the scattered remnants of Germanic heroic poetry. By extension, it is generally assumed that there is a traditional core in *Beowulf*. If the stories of Count Roland and Sigurd the Dragonslayer were traditional, why should the story of *Beowulf* be less so? The folktale roots have been laid bare in an effort to recover the lost tradition, but folktale is not the immediate root of other heroic stories in the Germanic area and only serves to underscore the isolation of *Beowulf* in the context of this heroic literature. Dorothy Whitelock carefully argued the traditional status of Hygelac, but Hygelac is not the hero.[1] Larry Benson espoused a fairly thoroughgoing inventionist view and conferred traditional status only on the swimming contest with Breca, but this is a peripheral episode.[2] The central adventures of Beowulf's life continue to defy tradition. If we think that the poem is inherited because we know this to be generally true of medieval heroic poetry, we must look elsewhere for the traditional elements. They cannot be found in the exploits ascribed to the hero Beowulf.

In an interesting but not widely cited essay on 'Unity and Intention in Beowulf' P. G. Buchloh attempted to clarify the structure of the poem against the background of the heroic lay.[3] Buchloh advanced the idea that the Norse lays *Hamðismál, Atlakviða,* and *Hlǫðskviða* share a common narrative pattern involving a 'Journey,' an 'Arrival,' a 'Drinking Feast,' a 'Quarrel with Words,' and a 'Fight with Weapons.' (He adds that this pattern does not hold true for *Vǫlundarkviða* or the *Hildebrandslied,* while the *Finnsburg Fragment* and the *Brot af Sigurðarkviðu* are too incomplete to judge.) It takes very little reflection to grasp the application of this pattern to *Beowulf*. As Buchloh puts it (p. 102): 'After the introductory part (1–193) the Geats set out on their "Journey" to the Danes (194–228), and the ensuing "Arrival" has two stages, the meeting with the coast sentinel (229–319) and the "Arrival" proper (325–494). The Danes are feasting in their hall, and soon the "Quarrel" between Beowulf and Unferth arises. After the "Banquet" there follows the "Fight" with Grendel. This formal pattern, with a few variations, is repeated three times in *Beowulf*.'

The proposal is suggestive. In the absence of a known story about the adventures of Beowulf, it gives us some insight into the poet's point of departure in tradition and his elaboration of a pre-established narrative framework. The weakness lies in the incomplete correspondence of Buchloh's abstract pattern to the actual content of the extant lays. He reads the pattern from only three of these lays and even in those three the fit is imperfect. *Atlakviða*, for example, can be abstracted as follows: 1) introduction, 2) the messenger's journey, 3) arrival, 4) banquet, 5) invitation and consulation (but no 'Quarrel'), 6) departure of Gunnarr and Hǫgni, 7) journey, 8) the sighting of Atli's hall and a mention of sentinels, 9) Guðrún warns her brothers, 10) battle, 11) the slaying of Hǫgni, 12) Gunnarr's exultation, 13) the slaying of Gunnarr, 14) Guðrún's deceitful reception of Atli, 15) Atli's Thyestean banquet, 16) Guðrún's slaying of Atli, 17) the burning of the hall, 18) praise of Guðrún. It is clear that Buchloh's five-part structure does not adequately represent this narrative; there are two journeys, two arrivals, two banquets, but no quarrel, and there are important scenes for which Buchloh's pattern does not allow. The same strictures hold true for *Hamðismál* and *Hlǫðskviða*. *Hamðismál*, for example, contains an introduction, an incitation (Guðrún incites her sons Hamðir and Sǫrli to avenge their sister), a departure, the killing of Erpr by Hamðir and Sǫrli, the arrival at Jǫrmunrekkr's hall, a battle, the maiming of Jǫrmunrekkr, and the death of the brothers. Again, there is no quarrel (unless Guðrún's incitation or Jǫrmunrekkr's unanswered boasting is pressed into service) and no banquet except by implication in the mention of drinking vessels in stanzas 20 and 23.

What remains true in Buchloh's presentation is a certain similarity of characteristic scenes in the older heroic lay and *Beowulf*. I should therefore like to alter the emphasis in Buchloh's argument and stress not so much the overall structural correspondence, which seems to me partial, as the correspondence in scenic inventory. This altered perspective allows us to go beyond the three lays used by Buchloh and include the evidence provided by the other remnants of the Germanic heroic tradition. It will be seen that these sources are not less significant if we adopt looser terms and think of the typical scenes which the *Beowulf* poet may have inherited, in no particular order, from the older lay.

I begin by reviewing ten categories of scenes that account for much of the action in *Beowulf*:

1. Battle scenes in the open (Hygelac's raid, Ravenswood, the dragon).
2. Hall scenes of conviviality or celebration (mostly at Heorot).
3. Hall battles (Grendel and his mother at Heorot and Grendel's mother in her aquatic hall).
4. Journeys in quest of heroic confrontation (to Denmark and back, to the mere and back).
5. Sentinel scenes (the coastguard and Wulfgar).
6. Welcoming scenes (at Heorot or in Hygelac's hall).
7. The use of intermediaries (corresponding to the sentinel scenes in *Beowulf*, though not generally in heroic poetry).
8. The consultation of the hero with kings or queens (Beowulf with Hygelac, Hrothgar, or Wealhtheow).
9. Incitations or flytings (Unferth).
10. Leave-taking scenes (at Hygelac's court or Heorot).

If we call to mind the half dozen or so survivals of the heroic lay—the *Fight at Finnsburg*, the *Hildebrandslied*, *Atlakviða*, *Atlamál*, *Hamðismál*, *Hlǫðskviða*, and whatever constructs we surmise behind the Sigurd and Walter stories as well as vanished lays adumbrated in prose epitomes—we may quickly establish a very similar set of characteristic situations for this genre: (1) battle scenes (throughout), (2) hall scenes of (ominous) conviviality,[4] (3) hall battles,[5] (4) journeys in quest of heroic confrontation,[6] (5) sentinel scenes,[7] (6) welcoming scenes,[8] (7) the use of intermediaries,[9] (8) the consultation of heroes with kings or queens,[10] (9) incitations or flytings,[11] (10) leave-taking scenes.[12]

Almost every situation in *Beowulf* is in some way reminiscent of the ancestral form. Even the dynastic review at the outset of the poem can be seen as an expanded and itemized version of the invocation of antiquity traditionally used to preface the heroic lay. The similarity extends to the point of verbal echo since the 'in geardagum' of *Beowulf* has its counterpart in three Eddic lays: 'Ár var alda, þat er arar gullo,' 'Ár var, þatz Sigurðr sótti Giúca,' 'Atli sendi, ár til Gunnars' (where 'ár' may mean 'messenger' and not 'in days of yore').[13] The *Hildebrandslied* too vouches for tradition with the hearsay preface 'Ik gihorta ðat seggen,' and the convention persists down to the 'Uns ist in alten mæren wunders vil geseit' of redactions A and C of the *Nibelungenlied*.

As the poem progresses, Beowulf's interviews with royalty in Geatland (and later in Denmark) reenact the consultation scenes in *Atlakviða*, *Atlamál*, *Hamðismál*, and *Hlǫðskviða*. The journey abroad to meet the challenge characterizes these poems and, offstage, the *Hildebrandslied* as well. The formalities of the arrival at Heorot elaborate the use of lookouts and messengers in *Atlakviða, Atlamál, Hamðismál,* and *Hlǫðskviða,* a trend pursued with fond excess by the *Nibelungenlied* poet. The feasting and distribution of treasure in Heorot recreate the traditional milieu of heroic poetry. The exchange with Unferth is modeled on the Germanic flyting abundantly illustrated in the *Edda* and Saxo Grammaticus and surprisingly well maintained in the *Nibelungenlied.* The contest with Grendel takes place in the nocturnal hall setting familiar from the *Finnsburg Fragment,* the death of Sigurd in *Skamma,* or the attack on Ermanaric as described by Bragi.[14] The remainder of the poem only recapitulates these situations—more hall scenes, more converse at the banquet, more journeys, more battles. The point would seem to be that the *Beowulf* poet had at his disposal a certain inventory of conventional situations.

The more immediate question, and the question which has pre-occupied modern criticism almost to the exclusion of studies analyzing the traditional story elements, bears on the poet's organization of the scenes he inherited. How did he form his narrative and what is the broader purpose subtending the form that he chose? The supersession of the heroic lay entailed difficult new problems of 'design,' both in the sense of episodic arrangement and in the sense of an underlying intention. The dimensions of the formal problem have been clearly reflected in the critical response. In subordinating the old to the new and achieving a richer form, the poet produced a more complicated structure which has elicited comment ranging from claims of extreme ingenuity to the expression of some disgruntlement.[15] The massive scholarly tribute to *Beowulf* has obviously been taxed by an approach to the poem through its structure.

We all know that a good narrative poem should be well made, that is, susceptible of a clear and logical dissection, or in simpler terms still, possessed of a transparent plot and easy to summarize. In this respect, *Beowulf,* an eminently good poem, disappoints us. It is strangely built. It is full of temporal dilations, but it has a gaping hiatus between Beowulf's return to Geatland and his final adventure. It combines much haranguing with considerable narrative dearth; there are questions about the past and future left unanswered. The digressions are a problem in pertinence and it is hard to remember where they are inserted or in what order. The events of Swedish history in the second part are a tangle and even more difficult to retain. These anomalies of articulation are, we feel, at some level poetic deficiencies. And yet the poem is so extraordinarily satisfying that we have the nagging feeling that we are asking the wrong structural questions. The principle of goodness in the poem is clearly not narrative simplicity. It lies elsewhere.[16]

To some extent it is obvious where it lies, in elevated sentiment, rich language, elaborate courtesy, in the dramatic unfolding of achievement and failure. But there is another quality that sets *Beowulf* apart, along with Anglo-Saxon literature in general. It has to do with a persistent cultivation of mood and emotional resonance.[17] This is a quality which emerges clearly when Anglo-Saxon literature is considered in the larger Germanic context. It is not to be found until very late in the chilly verse and prose of medieval Scandinavia, nor in the bits and pieces of Old High German, nor even in the adjacent rhythms and idioms of the Old Saxon *Heliand*.

Beowulf is more remarkable in communicating an experience, or a series of experiences, than in telling a story. What holds the reader is not an orderly or even a dramatic progression of events, but the stylization of Beowulf in a series of encounters, the accomplished young man at Hrothgar's court, the high-spirited boy in the retrospective swimming contest with Breca, the complete warrior in the combats with Grendel and his mother, Hygelac's loyal retainer, the admirable ruler of the Geats, and the veteran spirit matched against the dragon in what is at once Beowulf's final victory and his crowning defeat. The heroic and personal postures in the poem are of course not so different from what we find in the lays and sagas of Germanic tradition, though the opponents are monstrous, but critics, especially since Tolkien's analysis in elegiac terms, have never been content to classify *Beowulf* as heroic poetry. Nor is the analogy to *Grettis saga* productive beyond the episodic correspondence. In the abstract, Grettir goes through the same experience, the rambunctious boy who comes of age, mellows, quells monsters, and succumbs in pathetic straits. But the similarity is only in the summary, not in the impact on the reader. The saga is full of extraneous adventures and the mood of Grettir's fate impinges on the story only now and then. The narrative economy of *Beowulf*, on the other hand, dispenses with distracting adventures and guides the reader more concentratedly and consistently into the recesses of the experience. The mood is always at the center of the poet's pre-occupation. Indeed, the mood becomes the substance of the work and when we explore the structure of the narrative, we should focus not on the sequence of events, but on the construction of atmosphere.

Much of the attractiveness of Buchloh's essay lies in the attempt to go beyond structural observations in order to analyze the *Beowulf* poet's 'intention.' The narrative amplification implies a meaning and this meaning can be found in the tension between a traditional form and a new purpose. On the one hand, Beowulf dies the traditional hero's death in defense of his kingdom, but on the other, his death turns out to be senseless because it exposes the kingdom to destruction. This result puts heroism in a questionable light and it establishes the poet as a detached spectator of heroic events. The discrepancy between heroic theme and authorial reserve is explained, reasonably enough, by the incongruity between the poet's native literary culture and his reinterpretation of this culture in epic and Christian terms. Buchloh speculates that his immediate aim may have been to support a kingship committed to the new faith and threatened by real or potential apostasies (p. 117): 'So, the *lar* of the *Beowulf* poet is that a king has to endeavour to become strong, the people have to endeavour to live in peace under his rule, but whether they may live in *frofor* and *dream* is not dependent on human endeavours, but lies alone in the hands of God, the *Metod*. If this *sententia* defines the basic attitude of the *Beowulf* poet towards his poem and towards his world, the discrepancy between the epic poet, who is detached from the heroic world he describes, and the Christian propagandist, who wishes to prove the validity of his principles, disappears.'

The sharp attitudinal distinction between *Beowulf* and Germanic heroic poetry may be open to some question. It could be argued that futility is always part and parcel of heroic grandeur and that some sort of social critique is always implicit in the heroic poem.[18] On the other hand, it is certainly true that the critique is formulated more insistently and more self-consciously by the *Beowulf* poet than by any of his predecessors in the heroic genre. As Buchloh points out elsewhere in his paper, futility lies at the very center of the work (p. 110): 'But the central theme, which is varied time and again, is that of the futility of all human efforts, and the almighty power of a good God.' The poet's mission may be viewed as an effort to extract meaning from the apparent meaninglessness of the heroic life. The emptiness of heroic posture is filled with the purposefulness of Christian aspiration. Beowulf's secular existence is a sequence of flickering successes capped by ultimate failure, but it is, after all, only a prelude to the vindication of the afterlife. The pessimism of the secular life is counterbalanced by the optimism of the spiritual life. Secular struggle has spiritual meaning and this is what distinguishes *Beowulf* from the antecedent lay with its grim finality, moderated only by a sort of academic glory bequeathed by the dying hero for the vicarious edification of his survivors.

The *Beowulf* poet, located between the spiritual limitations of the heroic lay and the new doctrine of salvation, resolves the conflict by putting the heroic life in perspective against the promise of a future reward. The structural problem confronting him is how to illustrate the futility of this life as a background for the permanence of the next. The raw material available to him was a stock of characteristic 'lay' scenes without spiritual implication, scenes which he proceeded to combine to form a new genre, the heroic biography. The most plausible model for this synthesis remains Virgilian epic. But the biographical dimensions of

Beowulf are limited. There are gaps in the hero's life and the scenic traditions taken over from the heroic lay were not well adapted to provide biographical continuity. Nor does the biographical model serve in itself to convey the message of futility, which is clearly the poet's concern. When it came to the infusion of his central theme, the *Beowulf* poet was obliged to go beyond his inherited scenic inventory and Virgil's epic form.

Buchloh reviews some of the techniques of amplification (pp. 106–07)—the descriptions of sight and sound, the emphasis on emotions, retrospection and anticipation, authorial commentary—but he understands them only in terms of the poet's new autonomy in relation to his story, an autonomy that allows him to analyze and evaluate from a greater distance. I should like to supplement this view with the observation that the epic elaborations and the arrangement of episodes serve to underline the message of futility. Descriptions, emotional portraiture, narrative digressions, commentary, and the movement backward and forward in time are designed for the most part to isolate a pattern of frustration in this life. The ordering and annotation of the traditional materials therefore contribute in and of themselves to the querying of the heroic career which Buchloh and others have commented on.

The organizing principle in operation throughout the poem is mutability. Brodeur, in his *Beowulf* book, wrote about the 'dramatic reversals' of the poem.[19] No sooner is one mood established than it is superseded by its opposite. Hope gives way to disappointment, joy to grief, and vice versa. It is not just a question of occasional tonalities; the main lines of the poem as a whole can be analyzed according to this alternation.

We are introduced to the Danish scene at the acme of accomplishment and optimism, the construction of Heorot and the expansive hall joys which it houses (lines 1–100). But this luminous tableau is darkened by Grendel's ravages (100–88). Hope mounts and the spirits of the Danes are raised by Beowulf's arrival and his confident promise of salvation (189–702), but the mood plummets once more at the sight of Hondscio disappearing into Grendel's maw (740–45). However, the setback is only momentary and Beowulf succeeds after all in rescuing the situation by routing Grendel (702–836). The relief experienced by all at the removal of this sinister force is celebrated with elaborate delight during the return from the mere and in Heorot (837–1250). But even in the midst of this celebration there are undertones of renewed woe. The success story of Sigemund, albeit a success story tempered by the reader's knowledge that not all dragon stories in the poem have a happy conclusion, is succeeded by the somber stories of Heremod and Finnsburg, illustrating the gloomy moral that promising beginnings can have sorry ends. The message is confirmed by the appearance of the unexpected distaff monster and the seizing of Æschere (1251–1320). Once more spirits droop, but briefly, for again Beowulf retrieves the situation by dispatching the monster mother in her watery haunts (1321–1590). The joy at Heorot soars (1591–1887) and persists in Beowulf's report to Hygelac (1888–2199), but here too there are counterbalancing resonances. The story of Thryth's conversion from vice to virtue is followed by the ominous implications of the Ingeld digression, intimations of doom that are borne out soon enough by the robbing of the hoard and the ravages of the dragon (2200–2323). From this point on triumph and despair merge as Beowulf encounters the new enemy (2324–2693), prevails and succumbs (2694–2820), and is consigned to the funeral pyre (2821–3182). The larger lines of the development may be tabulated as follows:

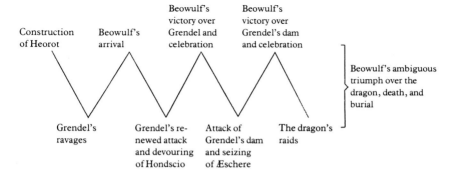

This is the larger pattern, a rising and falling of hope and fear, success and failure, joy and grief, in short, the rhythm of a mutable world. It might be argued that the pattern is implicit in the story and would exist in any narrative in which victory and defeat are interwoven. What is peculiar to *Beowulf* is the cultivation of the pattern in every segment of the poem, the smallest as well as the largest, and the explicit reminders throughout that good yields to bad or the reverse.

We observe the pattern already in the prefatory matter, the enumeration of the Danish dynasty. Scyld Scefing is 'found destitute' (7a), but by a compensation of fate becomes a great king.[20] His son, the older Beowulf or Beow, is sent by God 'as a comfort to his people' (14a) and reverses their suffering. So much is positive, but we are reminded that life ends in grief no matter how glorious the career. Scyld dies and the people mourn: 'him wæs geomor sefa / murnende mod' (49b–50a). A king is alternately a consolation and an affliction to his people, an idea which is not far from the theme of the poem as a whole. It prepares us for the accession of Hrothgar and the mixed fortunes of his reign. His success culminates in the construction of Heorot, a scene of feasting and liberality, but hardly has this height been attained than the fall is anticipated with a mysterious reference to 'the hostile flames of hateful fire' (82b–83a). On the heels of this forecast come Grendel's depredations and the recision of hall joy. The poet specifies the ensuing grief with unremitting variation:

> Þa wæs æfter wiste   wop up ahafen,
> micel morgensweg.   Mære þeoden,
> æþeling ærgod,   unbliðe sæt,
> þolode ðryðswyð   þegnsorge dreah . . . (128–31).

(Then in the wake of feasting voices were raised in lamentation, a great clamor in the morning. The glorious ruler, the excellent prince, sat joyless, suffered and endured great sorrow for his thanes. . . .)

The perception of woe is urged repeatedly, as is the remorseless reign of terror initiated by Grendel (136b, 156a, 159b). Denmark has fallen from a peak of glory into a chasm of misery at the moment of Beowulf's appearance. The juxtaposition of Beowulf 'the mightiest of mankind' (196) to the Danish 'suffering harsh, hateful, and long-lasting' (191b–92a) sounds in itself the theme of release and the message becomes explicit when Beowulf addresses the Danish coast guard with a promise of 'relief' (280a), 'remedy' (281b), and the cooling of 'seething cares' (282). In short, his mission is the reversal of fortune. This section reduces to the following outline:

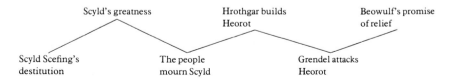

Scyld's greatness   Hrothgar builds Heorot   Beowulf's promise of relief

Scyld Scefing's destitution   The people mourn Scyld   Grendel attacks Heorot

Reversal is consequently the theme of the welcoming ceremonies at Heorot. Hrothgar declares that help has often appeared imminent when his warriors have vowed action over their ale cups, but the following morning the hall was again awash with the blood of murdered retainers. The period prior to Beowulf's arrival has therefore been a time of dashed hopes, a pattern which the new development promises to change. A sequence of slender and increasingly wistful hopes is replaced by a great and justified hope. This new mood is signalled by a feast during which everyone celebrates, as it were, in advance. The high spirits culminate in the flyting with Unferth, which concludes with Beowulf's rejoinder that Grendel would not have prevailed had Unferth been as fierce as he claims.

Thus the debate with Unferth reemphasizes the idea that fragile remedies and false promises have yielded to a real delivery. The prospect is greeted with an outpouring of joy. The Danes rise from the nether regions of despair to a state of high expectation. The gist of the story up to this point has not been a detailed narrative of how Beowulf got to Denmark, and why, but rather an analysis of the Danish mood and how it is altered by Beowulf's presence. It is a history of sensations—grief, hopelessness, fear, joylessness and their opposites, good cheer, hope, release, confidence.

All of this changes once again with Grendel's invasion of the hall. He is a studied antithesis to the evening's celebration. He bears God's anger (711b), is deprived of joy (721a), and advances with a wrathful spirit (726a). Unlike the hall laughter of the evening's festivities, Grendel's anger is laughter distorted:

> Þa his mod ahlog;
> mynte þæt he gedælde,   ær þon dæg cwome,
> atol aglæca   anra gehwylces
> lif wið lice,   þa him alumpen wæs
> wistfylle wen (730b–34a).

(Then his spirit laughed; the horrid monster thought to separate the life of every man from its body—he had an expectation of feasting.)

But the reader is immediately reminded that Grendel's fortunes are also labile (734b–36a): 'Fate did not decree that he should partake of more of mankind beyond that night.' The monster gulps down just one more hall-thane, then Beowulf prevails as Grendel discovers that his earlier strength is, unexpectedly, of no service to him. Beowulf's triumph appears to terminate the preceding vacillations of fortune with an air of finality and the stage is set for another celebration at Heorot.

The victory is celebrated first by an equestrian entertainment. As the troop gallops back from the mere, or perhaps at intervals in the gallop, a singer recites the tale of Sigemund's unbroken successes. But a cautionary note intrudes on this heroic elation when the singer turns to Heremod's career, which, despite great expectations—'many a wise man had trust in him as a relief from afflictions' (908b–09)—ended in crime. Case and counter-case. If the digressions are pertinent and heroes past are to be associated with heroes present, Heremod is an image of what Beowulf might become, a specious 'relief from afflictions' who ends badly.[21] The juxtaposition of the two lays is an implicit anticipation of Hrothgar's sermon; the impermanent and questionable nature of success is mixed into the careless strains of triumph.

The celebration continues in the same vein at Heorot. Hrothgar pronounces a congratulatory speech in which he greets the unexpected release from his woes, but in the midst of this expansive good feeling we are reminded that Heorot is not restored forever and that the hall-dwellers will eventually be engulfed in Hrothulf's treachery (1018b–19). The danger of strife and betrayal that always lurks in the meadhall is reinforced by the story of Finnsburg, in which Hildeburh laments 'the murderous misfortune of her kinsmen, where before she had had the greatest joy of this world' (1079–80a). The plunge from joy to sorrow in Finnsburg and the sight of slaughter in the morning look backward and forward to the carnage of Grendel and his mother in Heorot. As the respite was brief and delusive in Finnsburg, so it has been and will be in Heorot. The atmosphere of fragile hilarity and Heorot's vulnerability are restated when, after a renewal of joy and convivial clamor (1160b–62a), Wealhtheow comes to Hrothulf, then to Hrethric and Hrothmund, whom he is fated to betray, and, sensing what lies ahead, appeals to Beowulf for his protection. At the conclusion of the feast, the juxtaposition of festive harmony and impending disaster is summarized one final time (1232b–34a): 'There was the best of feasts, men drank wine. They did not know their fate, the destiny determined of old. . . .' Once more in outline:

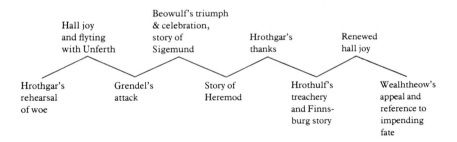

Now we turn to Grendel's aggrieved mother and destiny is fulfilled, again in the form of a sudden and unexpected reversal of fortune, a veering from respite to affliction (1280b–81a): 'The men were soon overtaken by change.' The new fiend seizes and carries off Æschere—'cearu wæs geniwod' (1303b), and Hrothgar commemorates the loss in the same words—'Sorh is geniwod' (1322b). It is as if joy can have only one natural consequence, the renewal of sorrow. But the reverse is equally true and Beowulf confronts the challenge by countermanding the word 'sorrow'—'Ne sorga,' he says (1384a) and intones the much-quoted sentiments about gaining glory before death, sentiments which have regularly been invoked to validate our notion of the fatalistic Germanic mentality, but which, in the context of the poem's mood, are another example of ambivalent enthusiasm in a gulf of underlying despondency. Beowulf promises relief, but he does so in the larger framework of rising and falling fortunes and with a consciousness that success is always tinged by the reversal that inevitably follows, in this case the ultimate reversal of death.

The ambivalence is reformulated as Beowulf arms and prepares to dive into the mere. He addresses Hrothgar on the provisions to be observed in the event of his death, so that the shadow of defeat rests on the probability of victory and confidence is mitigated by an allowance for failure. Uneasiness is characteristic of the poem throughout. Emotionally it is not single-ply, the light and dark layers blend. Whether they do so to cancel or accentuate each other is a matter of the reader's perspective.

The battle with Grendel's mother is itself described as a mounting and plunging of fortunes. Beowulf grasps Hrunting only to discover that for the first time this much-tested sword has no bite. The blade fails, but not the boldness, and he resorts to 'the power of his hand-grip' (1534a) to throw down his antagonist. She counters with what is technically known as a 'reverse' in wrestling and pins him. Only his armor saves him from the point of the knife. The climactic reversal occurs under divine auspices; God makes our hero aware of the sword among the accoutrements in the hall and he seizes it to sever the monster's head. For good measure he beheads the lifeless Grendel as well, a wanton gesture of triumph tempered by a painful flashback to Grendel's depredations in Heorot, where he devoured fifteen of Hrothgar's 'hearth-companions' (1580b).

The final extermination of monsters should be an occasion for some crowning revelry, but the poet shrinks back again. Instead of a hymn of release, we are now given a view of Beowulf's companions on the shore despairing of the outcome and fully expecting that Beowulf has succumbed. Only when Beowulf breaks the surface is the illusion of bereavement dispelled and the meters peal joy once again. The emphasis is as much on the unexpected conquest of woe as on the real achievement. In *Beowulf* victory is always extracted from defeat, a tension which makes it more valuable than foregone success. Defeat yawns under every victory and underscores the frailty of success as one of the larger themes in the poem. Even Beowulf's report at Heorot adheres to this rhythm, rehearsing how the battle would have been lost but for God's intervention.

After the slaying of Grendel's mother, the measure of success is full. Beowulf has accomplished his vow and cleansed Heorot, which stood at the beginning of the poem as the culmination of Danish hall-joy and which is once again free for the feasting. How is this splendid outcome greeted? Not by songs, merriment, drinking, or joyful converse, but by

Hrothgar's somber sermon. Heremod is invoked, as after the first victory, and Beowulf is warned how pride grows and the soul succumbs:

> Nu is þines mægnes blæd
> ane hwile;   eft sona bið,
> þæt þec adl oððe ecg   eafoþes getwæfeð,
> oððe fyres feng,   oððe flodes wylm,
> oððe gripe meces,   oððe gares fliht,
> oððe atol yldo;   oððe eagena bearhtm
> forsiteð ond forsworceð;   semninga bið,
> þæt ðec, dryhtguma,   dead oferswyðeð (1761b–68).

(Now your might flourishes for a time. Only too soon will sickness or blade deprive you of strength, or the grip of fire, or the surging of water, or the onslaught of the sword, or the flight of the spear, or relentless old age; or the brightness of eye will dim and darken; soon it will be, warrior, that death will overpower you.)

This may seem like a cold congratulatory message, but it is perfectly characteristic of the *Beowulf* poet, for whom the underside is always uppermost. Hrothgar goes on to verify the truth of what he says by reviewing the history of his own fall from glory. His words are a prudent containment of the momentary triumph and a telling anticipation of Beowulf's later career.

The same rhythm of sorrow and relief obtains on Beowulf's return to Geatland. This section is prefaced by another digression, the story of Thryth's reform from a vicious beginning to a generous end. Whatever the exact relevance of the account, it illustrates that the most startling changes are possible. Surprise is the theme of Beowulf's interview with Hygelac, who greets the returning hero with amazement and delight because he had not expected him to survive the encounter. Beowulf then launches into a report of the 'multitude of sorrows' (2003b–04) and 'persistent misery' (2005a) created at the Danish court by Grendel's ravages and the joy brought by his own victory—never had he seen 'under the vault of heaven greater mead-mirth of hall-sitters' (2015–16a). But here as always in the poem, joy is not allowed to prosper and Beowulf cannot forebear a comment on the ephemeral nature of this 'mead-mirth.' He relates the marriage plans for Freawaru and Ingeld and the hope of settling the feud between Danes and Heathobards, but the prognosis is not sanguine. The vicissitudes of the Danish court are not over and lie as much in the future as in the past. This section of the narrative yields the following synopsis:

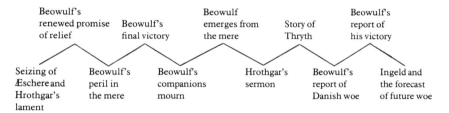

Beowulf's renewed promise of relief		Beowulf's final victory		Beowulf emerges from the mere		Story of Thryth		Beowulf's report of his victory
Seizing of Æschere and Hrothgar's lament	Beowulf's peril in the mere		Beowulf's companions mourn		Hrothgar's sermon		Beowulf's report of Danish woe	Ingeld and the forecast of future woe

Beowulf's relation of his contests adheres to the same oscillating line: Grendel's bloody visitations followed by Beowulf's reprisals, the monster's mournful departure followed by the 'song and glee' (2105a) of the celebration, the unhappy retaliation of Grendel's mother followed by Beowulf's final triumph. The poet supplements Beowulf's version with his own summary, which is similarly structured as a series of contrasts. Beowulf is given a gift of both horses and treasure, a gesture that constitutes proper behavior toward a kinsman as contrasted to the weaving of 'nets of malice' (2167a) and the plotting of death. He in turn conducts himself bravely and with discretion, behavior contrasting to drunkenness and the slaying of 'hearth-companions' (2180a). At this point the narrator raises the mysterious matter of Beowulf's inauspicious youth and recaps his whole career with the words (2188b–89): 'The glorious man recovered from each of his afflictions.' Since the Thryth digression leads into this segment of the narrative, we may imagine that she is paradigmatic for Beowulf's career—a bad beginning and a glorious recovery.

This reading would be well and good if it covered Beowulf's total career, but the larger reversal from bad to good in the monster segment is subject to another reversal from weal to woe in the dragon segment. The dragon brooding over his treasure is an apt emblem of the latent menace that broods over the history of kings and heroes. The menace can be activated at any time by minor causes, in this case the intrusion of a thief, who removes a precious cup from the dragon's hoard. The dragon awakens from his sloth and the fiery ravages begin. But like his monstrous kin in Denmark, the dragon too is subject to reversals (2322b–23): 'He relied on his cave, his prowess, and his wall; his expectation deceived him.' Beowulf is doomed along with the dragon and the battle is prefaced by clear pronouncements of the outcome (2341b–43, 2397–2400, 2419b–20, 2423b–24). The mood is reinforced by Beowulf's recalling of Herebeald's death at the hands of his brother Hæthcyn, the Old Man's Lament, the wars of the Swedes and the Geats, and Hygelac's death.

The battle itself is a sequence of bitter disappointments: the shield protects Beowulf for a shorter time than it should, for the first time in his life he does not prevail, the sword blade fails ('swa hyt no sceolde,'

103

2585b), 'he who once had ruled a people suffered distress, enveloped in fire' (2594b–95). But the final reversal is in Beowulf's favor. It becomes clear in his dying words:

> Ic ðas leode heold
> fiftig wintra;   næs se folccyning,
> ymbesittendra   ænig ðara,
> þe mec guðwinum   gretan dorste,
> egesan ðeon.   Ic on earde bad
> mælgesceafta,   heold min tela,
> ne sohte searoniðas,   ne me swor fela
> aða on unriht.   Ic ðæs ealles mæg
> feorhbennum seoc   gefean habban;
> forðam me witan ne ðearf   Waldend fira
> morðorbealo maga,   þonne min sceaceð
> lif of lice (2732b–43a).

(I ruled this people for fifty winters; no king of any neighboring people dared attack me with warriors, threaten me with terror. On earth I awaited my destiny, bore myself well, sought no treacherous quarrels, nor swore unrightful oaths. Though sick with mortal wounds, I may have joy of all this. Therefore the Ruler of men need not reproach me for the murder of kinsmen when life slips from my body.)

In other words, Beowulf has lived in a way that allows him to die with satisfaction, with 'joy of all this.' He has remembered that he will die and lived accordingly so that he need not fear the judgment of the Ruler of men. His life has been mindful of death. Everything in it has been a momentary release from anguish, but the final release is secure.

The drift of the poet's thematic design should now be clear. *Beowulf* is a kind of *memento mori* dwelling insistently on the transitoriness of earthly things. It works in a way quite analogous to the verse epistle of consolation addressed by the *Beowulf* poet's contemporary Alcuin to the afflicted brethren of Lindisfarne after the viking raid of 793.[22] Alcuin uses both the life of universal history and the life of the individual to illustrate the scourge of fortune. Kingdoms fall—witness the fate of Babylon, Persia, Rome, Jerusalem, Africa, Spain, and Italy. 'This general ill,' Alcuin suggests wanly, 'relieves individual woes' (line 71). But the individual also succumbs, as Alcuin is not slow to visualize in one of those clinical descriptions of old age in which the *memento mori* excels. The only refuge in this secular wasteland is the hope of heaven.

Your [Christ's] people await another life in the kingdom of heaven,
  Where sweet peace prevails and no battles are fought.
As fire tempers gold, tribulation cleanses the just
  So that a purer soul will rise to heaven (87–90).

And again:

Thus almighty God will test holy men with cruel
  Lashes, only to bestow joyful rewards in heaven (95–96).

Alcuin's technique and message are not unlike those of the *Beowulf* poet, who is deeply preoccupied with the ephemeral nature of history and the hero. *Beowulf* is a poem essentially about mutability. The structure is not some elaborate scheme of internal correspondences, but a simple wave pattern of hope and despair redeemed only by the promise of permanent release. The traditional episodes of heroic poetry are organized according to the notion that life is unstable and is lent stability only by trust in the hereafter.

The result of this process is a larger, quasi-epic narrative illustrating the mutability of the heroic life. The poet drew his settings from the scenic repertory of the older heroic lay, but he strung these traditional scenes together with a moralizing commentary in the form of digressions, flashbacks, anticipations, authorial remarks, reflective speeches, and a persistent emphasis on unexpected reversals—all tending to underscore the peaks and valleys of human experience. In working toward an epic form, he did not transcend his tradition by creating new types of scenes, but only by introducing multiple occurrences of the old types, and of course by dilating the individual scenes. The scenery itself is traditional. What is new is the way in which the poet combines and adapts the inherited scenes. He tells us clearly enough that he knows the heroic lay because he includes references to it in his digressions. But his aim is to supersede the old form, to find a broader conception which subsumes the old one. The short lays become parenthetical *exempla* to serve his new purpose. He surpasses the limitations of the antecedent form, the quick succession of six or eight deeply but roughly etched scenes in which the action exhausts itself without probing the implications. His poem may be viewed as a study of the unstated implications in the anterior lay. It questions the nature of heroic success and failure by playing them off against each other in constant alternation.

Ups and downs are of course the narrative skeleton of any medieval battle sequence. The hero even in romance takes a teeth-rattling blow on the helmet, sags to one knee, and loses consciousness for a split second before he finally prevails. What distinguishes *Beowulf* is that the rise and fall of expectations is so much a part of the poetic fabric and is so consistently fixed in the reader's perception of the action by the use of explicit outbursts of joy and woe, harangues, personal discomfitures, and personal resolutions. The affiliation with heroic poetry may be justified for the poem in the revised sense that it pits the heroic temperament not against a hostile world, but against a mutable world. Traditional heroism confronts a stable spirit with stable misfortune—it is limited because it pits one mentality against one contingency. *Beowulf* pits a scale of emotions against a scale of conditions, good and bad. The outlook is richer and more supple.

In the final encounter with the dragon the peaks and valleys of experience tend to collapse into a uniform mournfulness over a life committed to heroism, but confined by the decrees of mortality. The power of youth is reduced to the moral stance of old age. In one sense Beowulf's record of prowess becomes meaningless. But in a larger sense, his struggle with mutability acquires a sanction unknown to pre-Christian heroic poetry because it is crowned with the certainty of divine approval. For the vivid single catastrophe of the heroic lay, into which the hero plunges without reflection or hope, the *Beowulf* poet has substituted a long life seasoned by contemplative moments and dignified by the promise of salvation. The warrior king who has borne himself well through the vagaries of fortune, so insistently illustrated by the poet's narrative rhythm, has earned the traditional hero's good name and the Christian hero's future reward.

Stanford University

The Middle of Things: Narrative Patterns in the Iliad, Roland and Beowulf

PHILLIP DAMON

CURRENT notions about narrative structure have been enriched or, depending on one's view of the matter, confused by the contagiously abstract methodologies associated with the work of Claude Lévi-Strauss, his collaborators, and his successors. Lévi-Strauss' 'paradigmatic' brand of structural analysis was first presented to the scholarly public in the form of an essay called 'The Structural Study of Myth,' which undertook to interpret the story of Oedipus by eliciting from its various states a non-linear pattern of motifs which was alleged, contrary to appearances, to have as its theme the Athenians' intellectual uneasiness over the tradition that their ancestors were born from the earth.[1] His methods, subsequently refined and elaborated, reached a spectacular maturity in the four volumes of *Mythologiques*: *Cooked and Raw, From Honey to Ashes, The Origin of Table Manners,* and *The Naked Man.* His riper formulations are highly resistant to summary, but I will risk defining the Straussian paradigm as a set of anecdotal polarities or binary oppositions which have a thematically proportional relation to each other and in this relation bear meanings of fundamental cultural significance. In the Shimsian Indian myth which he calls 'The Tale of Asdiwal,' he isolates a series of oppositions such as Low and High, Earth and Heaven, Man and Woman, Mountain-Hunting and Sea-Hunting, Land and Water, Matrilocal and Patrilocal Residence.[2] All of these narrative ratios have as their proportional feature the fact that the hero tries to mediate between them, to resolve the oppositions, and fails each time. In a complicated virtuoso argument, these failures are shown (or at least said) to be reducible to the Shimsians' own unsuccessful social effort to reconcile, via the institution of cross-cousin marriage, the competing claims of the maternal and paternal lines in matters of inheritance and precedence. This socio-economic theme, which is not explicitly rendered at the linear or cause-and-effect level of the narrative, emerges (or is asserted to emerge) at the deeper, more disembodied level of the non-linear paradigm.

My willingness to treat an extraordinary intellectual performance with such injurious brevity should prove that I have no special interest in defending the interpretation itself. It and others like it have in fact been subjected to much ostensibly damaging empirical criticism which Lévi-Strauss has tended to answer by elegant demonstrations that empirical criticism is irrelevant. What I shall call the paradigmatic style of structural analysis appeals to me more as an aid to reflection or focus of attention than as part of a general theory of culture. It is possible to disbelieve, as many have disbelieved, his sometimes quite reductive and always astonishing interpretations and still take an exploratory interest in the general conception of narrative structure on which they are founded. My own interest has been heightened by the loose affinities which his paradigms bear to certain rhetorical patterns which are generally agreed to be operative in Homer and which have also been detected in the medieval French epic. These are the so-called 'pedimental' or 'geometric' arrangements of action which have been studied in the *Iliad* and *Odyssey* by Myres, Shepherd, and Whitman, and in the *chanson de geste* by Fern Farnham and John Niles.[3] The term 'pedimental' is intended to suggest an analogy with the ordering of pictorial detail within the pediment of a Greek temple, where the most important image will be placed centrally at the apex of the triangle and the subordinate images will be grouped symmetrically around it, two by two. Homer often structures sequences of action in this way. The sequence's critical incident will be emphatically situated at the center, and the others will be deployed around it in balancing, contrasting, or otherwise interacting pairs. The interactions between the members of a pair will commonly have thematic force, as Professor Whitman has shown so well. I plan to extract a pedimental sequence from the *Iliad* and the *Roland* and to analyze it from a paradigmatic point of view. I shall, that is to say, regard their paired incidents as sets of ratios and try to show that these ratios constitute a thematic statement. I shall then apply my findings to a consideration of some venerable problems in *Beowulf*.

The structural center of the *Iliad*, unlike that of the *Odyssey*, has never attracted much attention, so I shall need to begin by saying that there is one and by providing a few rough lines of demarcation. In the ninth book, Phoenix tells the story of Meleager, who left the battle at Calydon and had to be entreated to return. Johannes Kakrides, the Homerist and folklorist, has shown that the entreaty of the recalcitrant hero was a traditional motif and that the process of persuasion had a fixed order.[4] The hero is first besought by persons with no special claim on his affections, then by his parents and/or friends, and then, after he has rejected all appeals, he is entreated and finally persuaded by his wife. So with Meleager. He first rejects the appeal of the elders, then of his parents, and then of his close friends. Finally,

> . . . as the chamber was under close assault, the Kouretes
> were mounting along the towers and set fire to the great city.
> And then at last his wife, the fair-girdled bride, supplicated
> Meleagros, in tears, and rehearsed in their numbers before him
> all the sorrows that come to men when their city is taken. . . .
> And the heart, as he listened to all this evil, was stirred within him,
> and he rose, and went, and closed his body in shining armour.[5]

Everyone knows how closely Meleager's situation resembles that of Achilles during the Embassy scene of the ninth book. Achilles is entreated in precisely the same way Meleager was. The first appeal comes from Odysseus, whom Achilles clearly dislikes. The second comes from Phoenix, the old tutor who calls Achilles son and whom Achilles calls father. The third comes from Ajax, the blunt, honest warrior whom Achilles seems to recognize as a comrade and friend. He refuses them all, and the final, successful appeal does not occur until the beginning of the sixteenth book, when the situation of the Greek camp markedly resembles that of Calydon at the moment when Meleager's wife won him over. The Trojans have mounted the Greek wall and are, for the first time, 'crashing against the ships with burning fire.' It is then that Patroclus, 'weeping warm tears,' describes the disaster to Achilles in poignant detail and Achilles relents in his fashion and sends his men, his friend, and his armor back into the battle. The Embassy scene does not formally end until the first fifty lines of the sixteenth book, when Patroclus takes the role of Meleager's wife and brings this traditional motif to its traditional conclusion. The gradually increasing pressure on the defenders, which Phoenix describes in two lines, fills six books in Homer's story—from the tenth through the fifteenth book. These books, framed by the beginning and end of the Embassy, describe the siege of the Greek camp and the gathering Trojan offensive which almost drives the invaders into the sea. They occupy, with almost mechanical precision, the center of the *Iliad*—the fulchral area between the parts of the poem which might be called, in very general terms, the absence of the hero and the return of the hero.

A traditionally salient episode in the literature of sieges is the breaching of the city's fortifications. At the end of the twelfth book—the very mid-point of the six central books—Hector dramatically breaks down the

Greek gates and leads a charge through them. Around this central event we find a characteristically pedimental pattern which ostentatiously contrasts Hector's conduct with that of a Trojan ally named Asios, who cuts a very considerable figure during the offensive but is mentioned nowhere else in the poem and seems to enter the action here primarily to provide a foil for Hector. The massed Trojan assault begins with Poulydamas giving, as usual, advice to Hector. Poulydamas comes closer than any other hero in the *Iliad* to achieving the status of a personification—the embodiment of prudence, the very voice of practical wisdom. His prudence is not, however, an unequivocal virtue. In the twelfth book, for instance, he sees what he regards as a cautionary sign from Zeus and urges Hector to retreat. Hector rejects his advice, and the larger context makes it plain that he is right to do so. Zeus wants Hector to reach the ships and would not be sending signs to make him give up the assault. Excessive prudence, as Hector pointedly suggests, is hard to distinguish from cowardice. Poulydamas loses this argument, but he is at least allowed to make the point that excessive bravery is equally hard to distinguish from rashness, and the justice of this point is elaborately emphasized by the pedimentally enforced contrast between Hector and Asios. As a prelude to the offensive, Poulydamas advises Hector to stop his men from making individual chariot sorties against the Greek fortifications and to draw them up in a tight infantry formation. Hector willingly obeys this advice, but Asios alone rejects it and, keeping to his chariot, leads a wild, uncoordinated attack on the left side of the Greek wall. As he runs into stiff opposition and openly expresses his dismay, we move to Hector advancing in good order and battering down the gate at the center of the wall. Then back to the left side of the wall and the disastrous end of Asios' charge, his extended death scene, and the bodies of his men piled around him. Then once again to Hector, who is now inside the wall, listening to and agreeing with prudent tactical advice offered by Poulydamas. The poem's center—the part framed by the extended embassy scene—may be represented by this diagram:

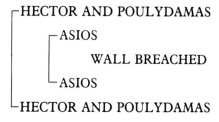

MELEE

  HECTOR AND POULYDAMAS

    ASIOS

      WALL BREACHED

    ASIOS

  HECTOR AND POULYDAMAS

MELEE

The victorious consequences of Hector's prudence are framed by the beginning and the end of Asios' defeat and by the two scenes in which Hector, unlike Asios, listens to sound advice.

This careful and indeed rather contrived symmetry is a good specimen of Homer's pedimental technique, and it suggests that Asios' presence here is designed to establish at the middle of the action a version of that great commonplace of heroic literature, the relation between *sapientia* and *fortitudo*. This commonplace was one of Curtius' major exhibits, and he showed how often it manifests itself in a contrast between the warrior whose bravery is directed by prudential considerations and one whose bravery is not.[6] If we take Asios' reckless courage and Hector's careful attention to wise counsel as a narrative ratio in search of a proportion, we may detect paradigmatic possibilities in the two large blocks of action to either side of the center. To one side we have the deeds accomplished by Diomedes and Ajax during the absence of Achilles and Patroclus. To the other we have the deeds accomplished by Achilles and Patroclus after their respective returns to the battlefield. Homer's active interest in enforcing thematic contrasts between the earlier and later *aristeiai* has often been mentioned. These contrasts are sometimes quite precise and specific, although I shall have to keep to generalities. Throughout the *aristeia* of Diomedes and the complicated engagements between Ajax and Hector, there is a running emphasis on obedience to good advice, attention to cautious second thoughts, a reflective sensitivity to the relation between ends and means. The exploits of Patroclus and Achilles, on the other hand, have as their burden imprudence, unnecessary risk, disregarded counsel, and headlong abandon regardless of consequences. Whitman's account of Diomedes as a foil to Achilles—a superlative young hero without Achilles' tragic complexity—is a convincing one; and Diomedes' punctilious, rather sententious concessions to prudence stand in marked, detailed contrast to Achilles' frantic, self-destructive sweep through the Trojan army toward Hector. We have, then, at the poem's center a compendious and explicit ratio in the form of a contrast between Hector and Asios. This ratio moves along the same axis as the larger and more diffuse contrasts which are deployed around the center. This is the nuclear aspect of a narrative paradigm which has a considerable amount of generality within the European epic tradition. Hector is to Asios as Diomedes is to Achilles or, to choose the painfully obvious example, as Oliver is to Roland.

Most analyses of the structure of the *Chanson de Roland*, among them those of Le Gentil and Rychner,[7] have distinguished four major parts: the treason of Ganelon, the Battle of Roncesvalles, the punishment of the pagans with or without the Baligant episode, the trial and punishment of Ganelon. Fern Farnham has proposed, and given important reasons for

doing so, a modification of these analyses which makes the death of
Roland a fifth, central part around which Roncesvalles is symmetrically
balanced against the defeat of the pagan army and Ganelon's treason is
balanced against his punishment. She is rather worried about the
asymmetrical narrowness of what she calls the central panel, and I think
that she has in fact missed the true dimensions of the poem's structural
center. If we want a well-framed, symmetrically poised scene which
operates axially between Charlemagne's disaster at Roncesvalles and his
victorious revenge, we will not begin at the onset of Roland's agony but
somewhat earlier, at laisse 128, when the Saracens' fifth and most
destructive charge has left sixty alive out of four thousand, and for the first
time Roland stops dealing blows long enough to look around, reflect, and
ask himself what he has done.

> When Count Roland sees the slaughter of his knights he calls to his
> companion, Oliver: 'Fair Sir, dear companion, in God's name what
> do you think now, seeing so many good vassals lying on the ground?
> We may well mourn for sweet fair France, which is despoiled of such
> noble knights as these! Oh King, my friend, I grieve that you are not
> here.'[8]

At this point, the emphasis shifts from the battle itself to the reactions and
fates of the principals. The wisdom of Oliver's advice to blow the horn and
the consequences of Roland's folly are now blindingly clear; and the two
of them now come together at the last, in bitterness and magnanimity, to
say their farewells and die. The fifty laisses from 128 to 178 are, I take it,
the poem's center—the part which is framed by the two battles and around
which disaster and triumph, betrayal and vindication are deployed. And
this center is, of course, dominated ethically by Oliver's famous distinction: 'Knightly courage used with prudence is one thing and folly is
another; and tempered judgment is more to be valued than the rashness of
arrogance. The French are dead because of your heedlessness.'

The central contrast between *sapientia* and *fortitudo* is both more
obvious and more complicated than in the *Iliad,* where Asios is simply
rash and Hector's prudence is the unproblematical norm. Scholarly
opinion varies on this point, but it may be almost safe to say that while
Oliver's judgment is undoubtedly correct, the poem tends to raise
questions about whether this kind of correct judgment is the only
standard by which Roland's rashness is to be measured and understood.
The earthquake, the darkness at noon, the sacramental aspects of Roland's
preparation for death, Gabriel's descent to accept the offered glove—all
these have seemed to many to introduce overtones of the willed self-
sacrifice which Saint Paul called 'foolishness to the Greeks'—an act

whose meaning belongs among the mysteries of faith and is thus inaccessible to the ordinary canons of judgment. This religious transvaluation of the heroic contrast between prudence and folly might be defined as a ratio between human judgment and God's judgment, and this ratio has its paradigmatic dimension. The *Roland*'s version of Poulydamas is Naimes, the counsellor whose wisdom is the stipulated datum, to whom Charlemagne says, 'You are a wise man.' It is Naimes who, at the beginning of the action, says of Ganelon's plea for peace with the Saracens, 'There is wisdom in what he says,' and carries Charlemagne and the Franks along with him. The only dissent comes from Roland, whose competence in such matters is called into question by his own best friend. But Roland's intransigence is right and Naimes' wisdom is wrong. At the end of the poem we see Gabriel giving Charlemagne essentially the same advice that Roland had given him when he handed him an apple and said, 'I present you with the crowns of all kings.' For Roland, there will be no stopping until the Emperor is universally triumphant; and God, for reasons that may well differ from Roland's, agrees. In the final laisse, we see Charlemagne as we saw him at the beginning, victorious but weary, ready to rest. This time it is God who summons him to new battles and lets him know that for the Church Militant there is no rest, ever. Earlier Charlemagne had listened to Naimes' wisdom. Now, he will listen perforce to God, who seems to speak much the same language as Roland. At Ganelon's trial the Franks are once more on the side of prudence. Their arguments for acquitting the defendant are as plausible as Naimes' arguments for peace had been.

> 'It would be best to leave things as they are. Let us abandon the trial and ask the King to allow Ganelon to go free this time. Then let him serve the Emperor with love and faith in the future. Roland is dead; you will never see him again, and no gold and no riches will bring him back. Any man who . . . would put it to the combat is a fool' (Merwin trans., p. 103).

But, as the Virgilian saying goes, 'It seemed otherwise to God.' Thierry takes the fool's role, urges trial by combat, and God expresses his disagreement with the Franks through Thierry's victory. The ratio between Oliver's prudence and Roland's folly, explored discursively at the poem's center, is proportionate to the ratio between Naimes' initial advice which the Franks call wisdom and Thierry's terminal advice which they call folly.

I have naturally been interested by Robert Kaske's analysis of the theme of *sapientia* and *fortitudo* in *Beowulf* and by his observation that this theme is discursively explored at what may reasonably be called the poem's center.[9] This is the part which lies between Beowulf's victories over Grendel and his mother and his last, fatal fight with the dragon. It includes the farewell interview with Hrothgar, the return to Hygelac's court, and the summary account of Beowulf's long reign. Klaeber refers to it as 'a slender bridge,' which is fair enough if one is thinking in terms of linear sequence. From the paradigmatic viewpoint, however, it looks somewhat sturdier. The center is seamed with references to a combination of fortitude and wisdom as the heroic ideal. Beowulf is more or less continuously praised for possessing both qualities, and he is urged to retain them. Hrothgar gives this advice a peculiarly Germanic turn in his account of the ruler who exemplifies the ideal at the beginning of his reign but later deserts the ways of wisdom and meets an evil end. It is not, he says, that wisdom will prevent disaster, for the wise fall along with the brave. The function of *sapientia* is not to guard against the blows of fate but to make them a little more bearable. The man who meets his troubles armed only with fortitude is miserable indeed. Beowulf's experiences at Hrothgar's court have as their background the decay and imminent destruction of the Scylding dynasty and Danish power. As Professor Kaske points out, Hrothgar's problems seem related to a deeply meditative approach to affairs which cannot translate itself into effective action: *sapientia* without much admixture of *fortitudo*. Hygelac is, on the other hand, all *fortitudo*, the architect of a rash expansionist policy which has brought on the Geats a crippling defeat at the hands of the Frisians and contributed to the dangerous enmity of the Swedes. Beowulf's death has as its context a lament for a doomed nation, its strength sapped and its alliances ruined by displays of courage ungoverned by wisdom. The heroic imbalance in the characters of Hygelac and Hrothgar are plainly related to the fates of their people. Both deviations from the heroic norm have brought disaster, but Hrothgar's analysis of *sapientia* seems justified in the end. The aura of tragic nobility and elevated pathos which hangs over his destiny is missing from the adventurous and bloody history of Hygelac. As in the *Iliad* and the *Roland*, the emphatic central distinction between strength and wisdom is deployed outward into a similar distinction working within or against the broader action of the poem.

Most comparative approaches to the structure of epic poems have employed a syntagmatic or Proppian model of analysis in order to establish formal connections. This method tries to produce a typology or metastructure by comparing linear patterns, sequentially arranged strings of episodes. It is a valid and useful procedure, but I am inclined to hope that my non-linear paradigm also constitutes a genuine point of comparison and additional evidence for the continuity of technique and theme within the European epic tradition. I accept the proposition, 'Comparaison n'est pas raison,' but I am nevertheless tempted to elicit an interpretive focus for *Beowulf* from my sense of the way the contrast between wisdom and bravery operates elsewhere. My impression is that in the *Iliad* and the *Roland* this contrast tends to complicate our judgment of the hero's great, suicidal gesture—to make it harder rather than easier to grasp its ethical and spiritual bearings. Unfortunately, an account of this impression in the *Iliad* would require an essay which it is impracticable to produce at this moment. A brief comment on the *Roland* may, however, give a general sense of what I mean. Oliver is right about Roland's lack of measure, and the fact that God is also right does not make him any the less so. Seen from the steady viewpoint of the poem's most reliable moralist, Roland's blind self-assertiveness has needlessly destroyed the rear guard. 'Woe is us, Roland, that we ever saw your bravery.' Nothing that Roland says or does in the poem contradicts this estimate of his character and his performance. Only after the damage has been done do we find that, under the aspect of eternity, Roland's flaws and folly have served the mysterious working of God's providence. Roland is powerfully vindicated at the end, but his vindication points to the spiritual ambiguities of experience rather than to its moral certainties.

The meaning of Roland's last, fatal battle is, in short, problematical, and one will not get at it by trying to decide whether his conduct at Roncesvalles was exemplary or defective. The poem, properly understood, informs us that it was paradoxically but significantly both. The paradox seems to me roughly similar to the complexities which attend Beowulf's last fight. The poem clearly leaves open the possibility of starkly alternative responses to the aged hero's determination to fight the dragon alone and without the support of his comrades. This is shown by the number of mutually exclusive judgments which have been passed on it. His fatal gesture has been viewed as the disastrously rash act of a brave but spiritually somewhat decayed old king whose pride has overcome the prudence of his younger days. Margaret Goldsmith speaks of Beowulf's 'deterioration' and views his display of courage as 'a sympton of arrogant self-confidence' which may ultimately be pardoned by God but which is in itself both foolish and sinful.[10] The gesture has also been understood as the culminating triumph of a virtuous sage whose youthful wisdom has ripened with experience. Professor Kaske refers to the fight with the dragon as 'a brilliant device for presenting in a single action not only Beowulf's final display of kingly *fortitudo,* but also his development and his ultimate preservation of personal and kingly *sapientia.*'[11] Both these responses being possible, the analogy of the *Roland* suggests to me that it might be critically more valuable to maintain the tension between them than to force a choice or try to bring them into some kind of harmony.

I do not see how a neutral reading of the text can avoid the conclusion that lines 2345–49a of *Beowulf* imply a serious miscalculation based to a perceptible degree on excessive self confidence:

> Oferhogode ða hringa fengel,
> þaet he þone wid-flogan weorode gesohte,
> sidan herge; no he him þa sæcce ondred,
> ne him þæs wyrmes wig for wiht dyde
> eafoð ond ellen. . . .
>
> (Then the ring-giver scorned to approach
> the dragon with troops, with a full army;
> he did not fear a fight with the serpent;
> its strength and fire seemed nothing at all
> to the strong old king. . . .)[12]

The precise connotations of *oferhogode* are not determinable, but they may not lie too far from the *ofermod* which, in *The Battle of Maldon*, inspired Byrhtnoth to let the Vikings ford the river and destroy his army. The messenger's lament makes it plain that Beowulf's courage has been even more calamitous than Byrhtnoth's. But there are also indications in the text that divine providence had shaped the fight, that Beowulf was the man whom the True King of Victories had chosen to open the dragon's hoard, and that He was with him both before and after the decision to fight *ana mid ecge* ('alone with the sword,' 2876a). Unlike some students of the poem, I am unable to determine with certainty from the text how long it was required for Beowulf to come *on ðæs Waldendes wære* ('into the Lord's keeping,' 3109), but I see no obstacle to the assumption that he went directly to glory. A feasible inference is that, motives and consequences notwithstanding, God approved. I suggest that the thematic contours of the poem's conclusion are rather like the last act of Roncesvalles and (to assert what I have not shown) the end of the *Iliad*: a bleak picture of the desolation wrought by an extravagant feat of pure fortitude which is heavily nuanaced by indications that the hero will not, for reasons that transcend his own intentions, abide our question about his wisdom.

University of California, Berkeley

Beowulf *and Traditional Narrative Song: The Potential and Limits of Comparison*

JOHN MILES FOLEY

IN the twenty-five years since Francis P. Magoun's introduction of the Parry-Lord oral theory into Old English poetry, and especially since the appearance of Albert B. Lord's *The Singer of Tales* in 1960, we have come to understand *Beowulf* and other poems in new and interesting ways.[1] Discussions of oral traditional structure, founded comparatively in analyses of Serbo-Croatian and ancient Greek oral song,[2] have illuminated many aspects of Anglo-Saxon poetry, from the level of the verse or line to that of the typical scene or theme.[3] That our progress in charting the traditional structure of *Beowulf* is largely the legacy of investigations carried out in these two poetries has, however, proved to be a mixed blessing. On the one hand, the art of the Homeric ἀοιδός and Yugoslav *guslar* has had and will continue to have much to teach us about the fundamental dynamics and aesthetics of Old English poetry; without their examples most of what we know about the traditional nature of *Beowulf* might well remain unknown. And yet the comparison has not been without its liabilities: reasonable doubts have arisen over the reliability of the formulaic test for orality and over the make-up and very existence of themes in Old English.[4] At the same time, scholars have had difficulty agreeing on definitions for various compositional units, mainly because of an untenable assumption made in 'translating' the concepts originally developed in Greek and Serbo-Croatian to the Old English *Beowulf*. Most simply put, the assumption is that oral traditional units, both formulas and themes, have a single archetypal shape and a single uniform dynamics in all traditions, and that these units will therefore answer to essentially the same definitions regardless of linguistic and prosodic idiosyncrasies.[5]

This unrealistic view has led in some cases to reduction rather than true comparison, and it has obscured the relationship of Old English verse to the larger context of oral traditional literature as a whole.

The major thrust of this paper will be to try to clarify that relationship by illustrating in modest scope what I take to be a reasonable caveat—that in comparing traditional and possibly oral materials, we must be equally as concerned about real or apparent differences as about real or apparent similarities, and with what these differences can tell us about oral literature as a whole. I will first consider some fundamental aspects of the Old English formula from the viewpoint of comparative metrics; although the demonstration must be brief, it will concentrate on the extent to which the metrical bases of Homeric Greek, Serbo-Croatian, and Anglo-Saxon poetry compare or differ and how the verbal formulas they shape compare or differ. Second, I will add some notes on the form and dynamics of larger narrative units, or themes, in *Beowulf* and selections from Yugoslav oral narrative, concentrating on the tradition-dependent aspects of the narrative multiforms. Finally, a short description of a Serbo-Croatian 'song amalgam'—that is, two epic poems in the process of becoming one—will illustrate how traditional song is formulaic at the level of what Lord has called 'story pattern'[6] and will suggest amalgamation as one source of narrative inconsistencies of the type found in Homer and in *Beowulf*.

When Milman Parry developed his definition of the formula, 'a group of words which is regularly employed under the same metrical conditions to express a given essential idea,'[7] he meant it to serve for one traditional compositional unit and one only—the Homeric formula. As Parry understood the process of formula generation, the verbal utterance took its shape from the hexameter. Gregory Nagy has since that time argued convincingly that, from the diachronic point of view, formula generates meter and not vice versa.[8] But even if the habitual groupings of words produced the abstract pattern over time, later on (as Nagy himself suggests) the abstract pattern came to govern the deployment of phraseology, particularly in the synchronic medium of performance. Michael Nagler has demonstrated the spontaneity of traditional verse-making at many levels and has observed 'that there may be formulas that are not made up of word groups at all, and, more generally, that considerations other than the present concept of word end may contribute to feelings of rhythmical subdivision within the epic hexameter.'[9] His original notions about the 'traditional phrase' have done much to free Homeric studies of the not infrequent charges of mechanism and over-determinacy.[10] In his recent *The Winged Word*, Berkley Peabody has rigorously described the generativity of the hexameter and its 'colonic composition.'[11] In short, to a greater or lesser degree depending upon particular viewpoint and rhetorical position, we must still consider the metrical foundation as a crucial part of the formula-making process.

To take this premise one step further, we must understand the Homeric formula in terms of the Homeric hexameter. This much is surely obvious enough, but the next step is apparently not so simple, for it has been violated over and over again in oral literature studies. It is basically this: to understand the formula in any traditional poetry, including Old English, we must look to the metrical structure of that tradition and that tradition alone. Trying to construe the Old English multiform phrase in terms of the Greek line must necessarily be a Pyrrhic task: all we can 'prove' is that Old English is, is not, or is to a certain degree Greek. But unless we are willing to take the particular, tradition-dependent characteristics of each prosody into account, carefully noting the features most important to formula generation, we are doomed to such tautologies.

For the present purpose I will concentrate on two specific measurements, *syllabicity* and *internal structure*, to contrast the three poetic lines in question. That is, the comparison of the Homeric hexameter, Serbo-Croatian epic decasyllable, and Old English alliterative line will try to judge to what extent each is (1) syllabically regular and (2) structured by formal demarcations (caesurae, bridges, diaeresis) within the line. Skeletal diagrams of each meter appear below.

	1		2		3		4		5		6	
Hexameter	— ∪∪		— ∪∪		— ∪∪		— ∪∪		— ∪∪		— ∪	

	1	2	3	4		5	6	7	8	9	10
Decasyllable	s	s	s	s	*MC*	s	s	s	s	s	s

Alliterative line	ś ś	|	ś ś

Though we are limited here to the briefest of suggestions, we can note the considerable degree to which the hexameter is dependent upon both syllable-count and formal demarcations. Though the line may theoretically consist of from twelve to seventeen syllables through dactylic-spondaic substitution, in practice most lines are fifteen to sixteen syllables in length.[12] The complex network of caesurae and diaeresis yields four sub-units, or cola, per hexameter; these word-units are, as Peabody has shown, at the foundation of oral composition in the ancient Greek epos.[13] The colon is also an essential sub-division of the Serbo-Croatian decasyllable (*epski deseterac*), where it is consistently defined by syllable count. Roman Jakobson's 'metrical constants' for the *deseterac* include regular syllabic extent and placement of main caesura (marked *MC* in the diagram above), a network of bridges which disallows word-break at certain positions, and a 'quantitative close';[14] he notes in addition that the line rhythm tends toward a trochaic pentameter.[15] In short, both poetic lines exhibit regular syllabicity and rather complex internal structure, especially with respect to the formation of the metrical colon, a unit which may be said to *encapsulate* utterance. Since both metrical filters impose rather severe restrictions on the verbal components they shape, it is not difficult to imagine how phraseology could be hypostatized or fossilized over time to an appreciable degree—perhaps to the degree we name 'formula.'

But the Old English alliterative line, specifically the meter of *Beowulf*, depends much less on syllabicity and internal structure than do its counterparts.[16] Individual lines vary in count from eight to fifteen syllables (excluding the hypermetrical lines), a difference of nearly 100 percent. Though editors have long recognized a verse or half-line structure,[17] this segment cannot be termed a colon, for it is too variable both in syllabic count and stress position to perform the encapsulating function observed in the largely quantitative Greek and Yugoslav meters. What does remain constant from one line of *Beowulf* to the next, almost all critics agree, is the occurrence of four heaviest stresses per line (along with a variable number of secondarily stressed positions) and alliteration between verses. Beyond these regularities, any attempt to catalog line rhythm must resort to a series of abstract generative patterns in order to rationalize variance caused by resolution and syllabic proliferation within a pattern. Under the metrical conditions of Old English verse, the stress maximum and the secondary stress maximum (hereafter SM and SSM)— and *not* the colon—serve as the fundamental consistency in the shape of the line. Instead of word-units or quanta, in which variance is tolerated to differing degrees but always according to certain basic and rather demanding rules, we encounter in the alliterative line a series of maximal points relative to what surrounds them. In other words, the primary site for consistency and patterning is in Old English not the colon of syllabic extent and internal structure but the *stress maximum position* and *secondary stress maximum* position. The SM and SSM have a finite length; each consists of the root of either a single, uncompounded word or an element of a compound—in other words, each is usually a single morpheme.[18] Any longer, more complex utterance immediately becomes subject to the generative system of metrical variation, and cannot maintain the consistency of verbalization typical of colonic composition. In understanding the verbal formula in *Beowulf*, then, we would do better to conceive of a lexical core or kernel at a stressed position and of a looser (and therefore more variable) aggregation of material forming a shell.[19] The result will then agree with what has been observed in Old English: a lower percentage of classically defined formulas and a higher index of variability among systems.

But there is another factor to be taken into account. As I have shown elsewhere,[20] *Beowulf* displays a level of purely metrical formula. Fully 94 percent of the poem is founded upon one of three templates which I have identified and analyzed using computer techniques,[21] patterns of potentials which form a small subset of the possibilities inherent in the alliterative line. This template may be defined as a 'rhythmic underlay, one whole poetic line in length, with verse (half-line) substitution, which pre-determines the structure of its verbal counterpart the formula' ('Formula and Theme,' p. 219; italics deleted). Below the level of verbalization, then, there lies a suprasegmental latticework, a set of rhythmical predispositions from which the lexical reality of the verbal formula takes its shape. These patterns are syllabically very flexible, as in view of the properties of the line they must be, and prescribe only the relative positioning of SM's and SSM's. In other words, they sharpen the morphemic focus of the alliterative line and help to define the much looser surrounding structure as well. But their contribution is finally to sequence and to relative position rather than to bound phraseology;[22] they *align* rather than *encapsulate*. Overall, as the following diagram illustrates, the formula in *Beowulf* is best viewed as a generative process which begins with the metrical template and which extends upward to a lexical component.

VERBAL ISSUE (half-line)
   Members of a formulaic system
      gégnŭm gángăn (314a)
      Gréndĕl góngăn (711a)
      góld gĕgángăn (2536a)

   Metrically related phraseology
      þrým gĕfrŭnŏn (2b)
      hýrăn scóldĕ (10b)
      gómbăn gýldăn (11a)
      æftĕr cénnĕd (12b)
      géong ĭn géardŭm (13a)

METRICAL TEMPLATE (half-line)

   ś   š̆   ś   š̆

In future studies it will be useful to examine this process from a number of perspectives; for the moment we must be content with a functional definition of the verbal formula. I offer the following as a first approximation: *a verbal formula in Old English poetry is a recurrent substitutable phrase one half-line in length which results from the intersection of two compositional parameters—a morphemic focus at positions of metrical stress and a limited number of metrical formulas.*[23] The first parameter denominates an emphasis on the stressed core of the phrase, while the second speaks to the relative position of stressed elements. This conception has the advantages of (1) indicating in general terms the way in which the diction is generated and maintained; (2) being quite specific about the stressed position as the fundamental site for repetition; and (3) eliminating the need for the unwieldy and often inexact distinction between formula and system. A verbal formula is part of a process—at times the process yields one product and at times another, according to the distribution of maximum and secondary stresses, the influence of the underlying metrical template, and the demands of the narrative. At no time does the formula become simply an artefact; at no time does it lose its identity as a multiform.[24]

Turning now to the level of the theme, I will first juxtapose a number of versions of the narrative multiform that Lord has called 'Shouting in Prison,'[25] the typical scene found at or very near the beginning of most return songs in the Serbo-Croatian tradition. My examples are drawn from return songs by the *guslar* Mujo Kukuruzović from the region of Stolac, a singer collected by Parry and Lord in 1933–35.[26] The Kukuruzović material is taken from two songs called by the collectors 'The Captivity of Alagić Alija' (texts *6618* and 1868)[27] and 'The Captivity of Ograšćić Alija' (*6617* and 1287a). As we shall see later on, they are two variants of the same generic song. By collating these texts, we can to a limited extent gauge thematic variance from performance to performance and song to song within a singer's repertoire and study the variorum identity of the theme.

To begin, I offer a brief recapitulation of the action of 'Shouting in Prison' in Kukuruzović's songs. As the song opens, whether with a proem (*pripjev*)[28] or not, either Alagić Alija (AA) or Ograšćić Alija (OA) is crying out loudly in lamentation (motif #1). The banica reports his shouting to her husband the ban and, explaining that the noise has kept their son from nursing, demands that the prisoner be either released or hanged (motif #2). The ban refuses on the grounds that AA/OA had before his capture wreaked havoc in Christian territory, and he fears a repetition; after the hero dies, the ban says, he will grind up his bones for cannon fodder (motif #3). The banica then replies that she will kill their son unless some action is taken, noting that the ban is too old to father another heir. When she repeats her demands, he suggests that she enter the prison herself and personally conduct the bargaining for release (motif #4).

The breakdown into motifs is a convenient first step in penetrating the wholeness of the theme.[29] Though there is no opportunity in the present format to justify these divisions exhaustively, I note in passing that a great many themes in Serbo-Croatian epic seem to subdivide along dialogue axes, with a change of speaker indicating a new sub-unit, and that I have generally employed this criterion in marking motif boundaries. Narrowing the focus, then, I propose to examine rather closely #1 and #3 in 'Shouting in Prison' with a view to (a) their narrative sequences, (b) the extent and kind of verbal correspondence among instances, and (c) the consistency or texture of (a) and (b) from motif to motif. Much of this analysis will review what Lord has said about the theme as 'a repeated narrative element together with its verbal expression, that portion of a poem, an aggregate of specific verses, that tells a certain repeated part of the narrative, measureable in terms of lines and even words and word combinations.'[30] It will also form the background for considering the 'sea voyage' multiform in *Beowulf*.

A. THE CAPTIVITY OF ALAGIĆ
ALIJA *6618*. 20–28

α_1 Pocmilijo sužanj u zindana—
       Ako cmili, nevolja mu bila.

β_1 Čij' l' je sužanj? Čija li tavnica?
       To je sužanj Alagić Alija,
       A tavnica bana karlovskoga.

γ Pa je jadan Turčin pocmilijo,
       Od dnev' do dnev' za neđelju dana,
       Za neđelju bijelije dana.
       Vazda Turčin u tavnici cmili.

(The captive was shouting in prison—
If he was shouting, he had some
    misfortune.

Whose prisoner was he? Whose
    prison was it?
The prisoner was Alagič Alija,
And the prison that of the ban
    of Karlovo.

C. THE CAPTIVITY OF OGRAŠČIĆ
ALIJA *1287a*.12–20

α_1 Pocmilijo sužanj u zindana—
       Ako cmili, nevolja mu bila.

β_2 Nije lahko ni dvadeset dana,
       Ja kamoli dvadeset godina,
       Prez promjene u lednu zindanu.
       Niti znade kad mu ljeto prođe,
       Niti znade kad mu zima dođe.

γ Pa je jadan Turčin pocmilijo.
       Sužanj cmili za neđelju dana.

(The captive was shouting in prison—
If he was shouting, he had some
    misfortune.

It is not easy to be incarcerated for
    twenty days,
Not to mention twenty years,
To exist without change in a cold
    prison.
One knows neither when spring
    arrives
Nor when winter comes.

And so the wretched Turk was
  shouting,
Day after day for a full week,
For a week of white days.
The Turk shouted continually in
  prison.)

And so the wretched Turk was
  shouting.
The prisoner shouted for a full week.)

B. THE CAPTIVITY OF ALAGIĆ
ALIJA 1868.1–6

D. THE CAPTIVITY OF OGRAŠĆIĆ
ALIJA 6617.1–8

α_2 Šta no nešto u Zadarju cmili?

α_2 Što no nešto u Janjoku cmili?

β_3 Da je vila u gori bi bila?
    Da je guja u kamen' bi bila?
    Nit' je vila, nit' je šar'a guja,
    Nego jadan Alagić Alija.

β_3 Da je bila u gori bi bila?
    Da je guja u kamenu bila?
    Nit' je vila, nit' je šarna guja,
    Nego jadan sužanj nevoljniče,
    Nevoljniče Ograšćić Alija.

γ Turčin cmili tri bijela dana.

γ Turčin cmili tri bijela dana.

(Who was that shouting something in
  Zadar?

Could it have been a mountain
  nymph?
Could it have been a snake under a
  stone?
It was neither a nymph nor a spotted
  snake,
But the wretched Alagić Alija.

(Who was that shouting something in
  Janok?

Could it have been a mountain
  nymph?
Could it have been a snake under a
  stone?
It was neither a nymph nor a spotted
  snake,
But the wretched, unwilling captive,
The unwilling Ograšćić Alija.

The Turk shouted for three white
  days.)

The Turk shouted for three white
  days.)

Motif #1, the four occurrences of which are given above, follows the
proem in texts A and C. While the *pripjev* is itself optional for most
singers (here, for instance, it precedes one version of AA and one of OA; it
is also lacking in one version of OA and one of AA), its appearance
apparently does condition what follows, at least in Kukuruzović's songs.
For, as indicated in the textual comparison, the presence of the proem
leads to a certain song beginning (α_1) and its absence to another (α_2).
Briefly stated, Kukuruzović follows the *pripjev* with a declarative statement about the shouting (A.20–21 and C.12–13); on the other hand, when
motif #1 starts the song, it takes the form of a series of rhetorical
questions (B.1ff. and D.1ff.), the answers to which establish the hero's

identity. A quick examination of the texts reveals that motif #1 is itself composed of three units, labeled α, β, and γ. The β section depends on α and is thus influenced by the occurrence or non-occurrence of the *pripjev*, but the γ section seems to be an independent unit which lexically echoes α and completes a small ring structure.

The density of verbal correspondence is greatest between texts B and D, where only a place-name substitution (*Zadar/Janok*) and what Robert Austerlitz has called a 'terrace'[31] keep the motif instances from being identical. Texts A and C, which begin with *pripjevi*, diverge widely in β and also exhibit a good deal of difference in γ. The point is that verbal correspondence, which takes the form of whole-line and colon repetition in the Serbo-Croatian tradition, is not uniform in density either from instance to instance within the motif or from one part of a motif to the next. While the abstract pattern α-β-γ remains constant over the four texts, the actual verbalization of that pattern can take different shapes, depending in this case on the way in which the song begins.

As the textual comparison indicates, motif #3 subdivides into four units: (δ) introduction and address, (ϵ) AA/OA's heroic deeds, (ζ) the ban's promise, and (η) grinding the bones.

A. 46–67

δ A bane joj 'vako progovara:
 'Gospojice meni mila bila,
 Ni dosad mi nisi mrska bila.

ϵ A znadeš li u zočas ti bilo
 Dok j' Alija bijo na Turćiji?
 Dosta nam je jada učinijo—
 I majaka jadni' ostavijo,
 I sestara u crno zavijo.
 Stotinu je kula zapalijo,
 Krajem mora i krajem limana,
 I sad svaka omeđina sama.

ζ Kad sam njega ufatijo živa,
 Bacijo ga u moju tamnicu.
 Tad sam Bogu jemin učinijo
 Da mu neću na tavnicu saći
 Dok mu duša u kostinam' tuče.

η hA mu duša iz kostiju iziđe,[32]
 Njegove ću kosti pokupiti.
 Pa ću kosti ložit' u odžaku.
 Pa ću kosti u dibeku tući.
 Palić i moru na širinu—
 Nek od vraga ne ostaje traga!'

C. 31–50

δ 'Gospojice meni mila bila,
 Ni dosad mi nisi mrska bila.

ζ Kad sam njega živa ufatijo,

 Ja sam Bogu jemin učinijo
 Da mu neću na tamnicu sići
 Dok mu duša u kostima tuče.

η Kad mu duša is kostiju pođe,
 Njegove ću kosti pokupiti.
 Ložiću u mome odžaku.[33]
 Pa ću kosti u dibeku tući.
 Palić i moru na širinu—
 Šenluk činit' iz moji' topova.

ϵ A znadeš li dugo jadna bila
Dok j' Alija bijo na Turćiji?
Dosta nam je jada načinijo—
I majaka jadni' ostavijo,
I sestara u crno zavijo.
Stotinu je kula zapalijo,
Krajem mora i krajem limana,
I sad svaka omeđina sama.'

(But the ban spoke to her in this way:
'My dear lady,
Up to now you have not been difficult.

But do you recall how it was
When Alija was free in his Turkish
   homeland?
He caused us misery enough—
He left mothers grieving
And dressed sisters in black.
He set fire to a hundred towers,
At the edge of the sea and the edge
   of the lake,
And now all our borders are
   unguarded.

When I captured him alive,
I threw him into my prison.
Then I promised God
That I will not go down into the
   prison
While his spirit enlivens his bones.[34]

But when his spirit leaves his bones,
I will gather them up,
Heat them in a chimney,
Grind them in a mortar,
And shoot them into the expanse of
   the sea—
Let there be no trace left of the devil!')

('My dear lady,
Up to now you have not been difficult.

When I captured him alive,

I promised God
That I will not go down into the
   prison
While his spirit enlivens his bones.

But when his spirit leaves his bones,
I will gather them up,
Heat them in my chimney,
Grind them in a mortar,
And shoot them into the expanse of
   the sea—
I will fire a salute from my canon.

But do you recall that you were long
   miserable
While Alija was free in his Turkish
   homeland?
He caused us misery enough—
He left mothers grieving
And dressed sisters in black,
He set fire to a hundred towers,
At the edge of the sea and the edge
   of the lake,
And now all our borders are
   unguarded.')

B. 28–44

δ   A bane joj reče lakrdiju:
     'Gospojice meni mila bila,

ε   A znadeš li Alagić Alija
     Kad je bilo na zemlji turćiji?
     Sedam nam je džada zastavijo—
     Tri su s mora, četiri sa suha.

     Stotinu je kula zapalijo,
     Krajem mora i krajem limana,
     I sad svaka omeđina sama.

ζ   Pa sam Bogu jemin učinijo—
     Kad sam njega živa ufatijo,
     Bacijo ga u moju tamnicu—
     Da mu neću u tamnicu sići
     Dok ja čujem da je u vjer' duša.'

D. 23–39

δ   A bane joj sjede besjediti:
     'Gospojice meni mila bila,
     Ni dosad mi nisi mrska bila.

ε   A znadeš li u zočas ti bilo
     Dok je Alija bijo na Turćiji?[35]
     Dosta nam je jada učinijo—

     I majaka jadni' ostavijo,
     I sestara u crno zavijo.

ζ   Pa sam Bogu jemin učinijo

     Da mu neću na tavnicu saći
     Dok mu duša u kostinam' tuče.

η   hA mu duša iz kostiju iziđe,
     Njegove ću kosti pokupiti.
     Pa ću kosti ložit' u odžaku.
     Pa ću kosti u dibeku tući.
     Palić i moru na širinu—
     Nek od vraga ne ostaje traga!'

(And the ban spoke a word to her:
'My dear lady,

But do you recall Alagić Alija
When he was in Turkish territory?
He took over seven roads—
Three from the sea, four from dry
   land.

He set fire to a hundred towers,
At the edge of the sea and the edge
   of the lake,
And now all our borders are
   unguarded.

And so I promised God—
When I captured him alive,
I threw him into my prison—
That I will not go down into the
   prison
While I hear his spirit lives.')

(And the ban began to address her:
'My dear lady,
Up to now you have not been difficult.

But do you recall how it was then
While Alija was in his Turkish
   homeland?
He caused us misery enough—

He left mothers grieving
And dressed sisters in black.

And so I promised God

That I will not go down into the
   prison
While his spirit enlivens his bones.

127

But when his spirit leaves his bones,
I will gather them up,
Heat them in a chimney,
Grind them in a mortar,
And shoot them into the expanse of
   the sea—
Let there be no trace left of the devil!')

The first of these units, δ, is quite stable, the *bila* rhyme[36] contributing to the preservation of the couplet. Element ϵ, which details the destruction caused by the Turkish hero, is moveable, occurring at the end of the motif in text C. Variation in the verbalization of ϵ takes the form of added or deleted whole lines rather than formulaic substitution. This integral or quantum variation is typical of narrative passages which enumerate items, such as the hero's *accoutrements* in an arming theme. In less catalog-like units, formulaic substitution is more common.

Unit ζ consists of an optional condition ('When I captured him alive') and result, usually followed[37] by the ban's pledge to maintain AA/OA's imprisonment until the captive's death. Here again the verbal correspondence is almost complete. The last unit, η, which occurs in all texts except β, is verbalized very consistently, with limited variance in the first, third, and final lines of the sequence. The first two of these lines vary only in the choice and morphology of related or identical verbs, and the last is a whole-line formula often associated with cannon firing in celebration. Once again we can discern a clear overall motif pattern, with integral units ordered in a logical configuration: even the 'displacement' of ϵ in C maintains narrative sense in using the history of the hero's exploit as an explanation for the proposed desecration of his bones. The degree of verbal correspondence, however, varies from unit to unit within the motif, and is to some extent dependent upon the texture of the narrative.

To sum up the brief survey of 'Shouting in Prison,' we note that the two basic features described by Lord as characteristic of the theme do in fact apply. Both *narrative sequence*, illustrated here in the analysis of theme into motifs and even smaller logical parts, and *verbal correspondence* give the multiform typical scene its definition. It is also important to note some other points uncovered in our examination. First, as might be expected given the colon structure underlying formula generation, the verbal agreement between instances is largely in terms of whole lines or cola. The entire line and the caesura-bound hemistich (either the four- or six-syllable colon) are thus the data of the theme. Second, though the narrative sequence seems to remain almost absolutely constant and to oversee the thematic progress of the story, in rare cases (e.g., #3, ϵ) a unit can be transposed, provided that the narrative logic is maintained. Third, verbal correspondence is not of uniform density throughout the theme or from instance to instance; certain motifs are much more stable formulaically than others.[38] Of course, many more individual formulaic relatives would be discovered if the referent were enlarged to whole song texts, but we are speaking here of the formulaic texture of certain narrative structures within songs rather than of single formulas with relation to entire texts. Fourth, variation in verbalization of the theme can take a number of forms, among them what may be termed 'formulaic variance,' in which lines and part-lines recombine and permute according to systemic principles, and 'ornamentation,' in which a non-narrative, paratactic gloss not necessary in itself but rather complementary to a necessary element is included.[39] Though incomplete, this sketch of the theme in Kukuruzović's return song may help to open up the dynamics of the narrative multiform, to relieve it of too strict a definition or conception, and perhaps to make comparison a more realistic undertaking.

For the Old English theme is equally dynamic, though in its own, tradition-dependent way. Its texture is also uneven, with certain sections exhibiting one level of verbal correspondence and other sections differing. Though we do not have the *embarras de richesse* of multiple texts which the Serbo-Croatian material offers, let us examine a well-known typical scene—the sea voyage—as it occurs in *Beowulf*.[40] The two sea voyages may be rationalized by the motif structure shown below.

Occurrence #1 (lines 205–303a)

A. Beowulf leads his men to the ship (205–09)
B. The ship waits, moored (210–11a)

C. His men board the ship, carrying treasure (211b–15a)

D. Departure, voyage on the sea, arrival (215b–25)

E₁. Mooring the ship (226a)
   W. Armor (226b–27a)
     Z. Prayer of thanks (227b–28)
   X. The coast-guard approaches; he and Beowulf confer (229–300)
E₂. Mooring the ship (301b–03a)

Occurrence #2 (lines 1880b–1919)

A₁. Beowulf [leads his men] to the ship (1880b–82a)
B. The ship waits, moored (1882b–83)
   V. Excursus on Hrothgar's treasure (1884–87)
A₂. [Beowulf] leads his men to the ship (1888–89a)
   W. Armor (1889b–90a)
   X₁. The coast-guard approaches (1890b–95)
C. His men board the ship, carrying treasure (1896–99)
   X₂. The boat-guard is rewarded (1900–03a)[41]
D. Departure, voyage on the sea, arrival (1903b–13)
   X*. Beowulf and his men approach the harbor-guard (1914–16)[42]
E₁. Mooring the ship (1917–19)

The basic narrative structure of the sea voyage may thus be represented as a sequence of five elements: (A) Beowulf leads his men to the ship; (B) the ship waits, moored; (C) his men board the ship; (D) departure, voyage on the sea, arrival; (E) they moor the ship. Within this structure are interwoven particularizing elements. The W-motif, 'Armor,' variable in position, seems to serve as the prerequisite for the X-motif, 'The coast-guard approaches'; where the latter first occurs, the former closely precedes it. In Occ. #1 W introduces X within the E element, and in #2 W is followed by X_1 before the C element. In narrative terms, this means that 'Armor' and its consequent can be developed during the mooring of the ship (#1) or before Beowulf's men carry the treasure on board (#2), depending on the story demands.

The X-motif, most Protean of any of the elements, deserves close attention. It concerns an encounter with the guard of whatever coast one lands on or is in the process of leaving, and is applied to at least two distinct characters and situations in *Beowulf*.[43] In Occ. #1 the story line calls for an expansion of X into a lengthy exchange between the coast-guard and Beowulf. Working within the traditional idiom, the *scop* thus accomplishes two things concurrently: he both fulfills the thematic conditions and suits the structure to its narrative environment. Beowulf identifies his people and purpose, points of information vital to what follows, and the identification proceeds naturally (that is, traditionally) out of the sea voyage multiform. This same potential for modification or variation shows up in a different way in #2, where X occurs three times $(X_1, X_2, X^\star)$. The symbol $X^\star$ denotes a reversal of the more usual action of the X-motif. In all other instances, the coast-guard approaches the Geats; in #1 he comes to challenge their disembarkation, and in X_1–X_2 (#2) he again moves to greet them, though this time in a friendly manner, as the *litotes* (1892–95) indicates. The harbor-guard of $X^\star$, on the other hand, has been watching for Beowulf and his men for a long time. He has remained at the shore, waiting for the returning heroes to approach him. This reversal in the direction of encounter is particularized and context-sensitive, but it springs from the same traditional form, the motif X.

The major motifs A–E also reveal a certain amount of adaptation to context, though they vary in structural stability. Element A, for example, splits in Occ. #2, enclosing a number of details within the capsule A_1–A_2.[44] One dimension of the division is clear: A_1 mentions nothing about Beowulf's companions (thus the brackets in my schema), and we can see that in Occ. #1 A includes both the hero and his men. A_2 thus fills out the element, if we may speak in such terms, by describing the embarkation of Beowulf's men. Motifs B, C, and D are quite stable within the sea voyage sequence, especially the last of them, which is tightly organized around a three-part series of departure, voyage, and arrival. Two specific features further structure the action of the D motif: (1) the 'go until one sees the destination' commonplace[45] and (2) the notation of wind and the ship's sail. The splitting of E in Occ. #1, like that of A in #2, presents evidence of the pliability of traditional elements; again the recurrent structure is adapted to the narrative context.

Taken together, the two instances of the sea voyage in *Beowulf* collectively exhibit a discernible and dynamic *narrative sequence,* an action pattern not dissimilar in nature to that found in the Serbo-Croatian material. In applying the first of Lord's criteria for the theme to what we have in *Beowulf,* we seem to have a close fit: with the exception of the Old English poet's somewhat greater flexibility in motif development (which may well be the product of our necessarily limited textual sample),[46] there is considerable similarity between the Old English and Serbo-Croatian themes in terms of narrative sequence. But what of the second criterion, *verbal correspondence?* Are we likely to observe the same close fit across traditions along the axis of actual verbalization?

To answer these questions we must recall what was said earlier about the tradition-dependent nature of the formula in *Beowulf.* With that principle in mind, it is possible to predict another directly related tradition-dependency—the nature of thematic data. First, we cannot expect a large proportion of whole-line or half-line formulas as verbal correspondence in Old English poetry, since that expectation presupposes a colonic formula. And, as we have seen, Old English prosody tends away from colonic phraseology. Second, and more positively, what we *can* expect as thematic data are highly variable half-lines which may have in common only their stressed cores. As I have demonstrated elsewhere,[47] verbal correspondence may appear to take the form of single morphs, roots of words whose systemic context is metrically (and therefore lexically and syntactically) highly variable. This does not preclude formulaic content (e.g. *sīdfæþmed scip/sīdfæþme scip* [302b/1917b]), but simply makes it more likely that single words will constitute thematic resonance in the verbal dimension. I do not believe that, given the metrical background and the density of morphemic redundancy, one can explain away these data as words which are likely to occur in such a description. As noted above, lexical items at positions of metrical stress are the products of a process, and that process, which does not characteristically yield colonic phraseology, should be understood on its own tradition-dependent terms. Following is a tabulation of morphs which help to define the sea voyage in *Beowulf.*

A:A$_1$,A$_2$—none
B:B—none
C:C—*sande/sande* (213a/1896a), *nacan/naca* (214a/1896b), *stefn/-stefna* (212a/1897b), *bearm/mæst* (214a/1898b; see below)

D:D—*Gewāt/Gewāt* (217a/1903b), *wæg/wēg* (217a/1907a), *winde/wind* (217b/
1907b), *wudu/-wudu* (216b/1906b), *-sīð/sīðes* (216a/1908a), *sǣ-/sǣ-* (223a/
1908b), *bundenne/bunden* (216b/1910a), *brim-/brim-* (222a/1910b), *sund/
sund-* (223b/1906b), *flota fāmīheals/flēat fāmigheals* (218a/1909a), *-clifu/
clifu* (222a/1911a), *-næssas/næssas* (223a/1912a), *up/up* (224b/1912b)
E₁,E₂:E—*sǣldon/sāle/sāle/sǣlde* (226a/302a/1906a/1917a), *sīdfæþmed scip/
sīdfæþme scip* (302b/1917b), *on ancre fæst/oncerbendum fæst* (303a/1918a),
-wudu/wudu (226a/1919a)
W:W—*syrcan/-syrcan* (226b/1890a)
X:X—*weard/-weard/-wearde/-weard* (229b/1890b/1900a/1914b).

In addition, there exists in *Beowulf* a tradition-dependent, local
resonance of morphs which may be called *responsion*. Rather than being
attached to a certain narrative event or pattern and echoing traditionally
against other occurrences of the event or pattern, these words respond to
proximate partners, lexical relatives usually no more than about twenty
lines away.[48] Responsional pairs appear to comprise a kind of 'local theme'
engendered by a lexical focus at stress positions and the variational style;
in *Beowulf* they often make connections on a non-narrative level, connections that would otherwise not obtain.[49] Though there is no opportunity
at present to do more than suggest the presence of responsion and to list
the occurrences in the sea-voyage theme (see the table below), I would
suggest its crucial importance to the poetics of *Beowulf*. For example,
many rhetorical figures thought by some critics to be direct borrowings
from Latin authors can be derived from the interaction between responsion and other aspects of Germanic verse form.[50]

Occ. #1

sund-/sund/sund	208a/213a/223b
secg/secgas	208b/213b
lēoda/lēode	205b/225a
land-/land	209b/221b
-wudu/-wudu	208a/226a
beorge/beorgas	211a/222b
gewāt/Gewāt/Gewiton	210a/217a/301a
flota/flota	210b/301b
ȳðum/ȳþ-	210b/228a
stefn/-stefna	212a/220a
stigon/stigon	212a/225b
wundon/wunden	212b/220a
gūð-/gūð-	215a/227a
-searo/-searu	215a/232a
bǣron/beran	213b/231a
beorhte/beorhte	214b/231b
līðende/liden/-lāde	221a/223b/228a
gesāwon/geseah	221b/229a
-fȳsed/fūs-	217b/232a

-holm/holm-	217a/230a
-clifu/-clifu	222a/230a
sældon/sāle	226a/302a

Occ. #2

gold-/golde	1881a/1900b
Cwōm/-cuman	1888a/1894a
sǣ-/sǣ-/sǣ-	1882b/1896b/1908b
ancre/oncer-	1883b/1918a
-genga/gange/-genga	1882b/1884a/1908b
rād/rād	1883b/1893b
naca/nacan	1896b/1903b
-stefna/-stefna	1897b/1910a
mæst/mæste	1898b/1905a
sande/sande	1896a/1917a
māðmum/māþme	1898a/1902b
Land-/land/lande	1890b/1904b/1913b
ȳðum/ȳðe/ȳþa	1907b/1909b/1918b
sāle/sælde	1906a/1917a
fæst/fæst	1906a/1918a
Hrōðgāres/Hrōðgāres	1884b/1899a
gifu/ofgeaf	1884b/1904b
wynnum/wyn-	1887a/1919a
hring/hringed-	1889b/1897b
fōron/fōr	1895b/1908b
scipe/scip	1895a/1917b
-weard/-wearde/-weard	1890b/1900a/1914b
bunden/bunden-/-bendum	1900b/1910a/1918a

If the sea voyage theme and the theme of 'Shouting in Prison' resemble one another quite closely on the level of narrative sequence, they diverge considerably with respect to verbal correspondence. To be sure, there are hard lexical data (of similarly uneven distribution) for both traditional themes, but these data take tradition-dependent form. The Old English correspondence manifests itself mostly in morphs in positions of metrical stress, with a less strictly defined (and therefore more variable) environment. Occasionally a half-line formula—understood in the classical colonic sense—occurs, but relatively infrequently. The Serbo-Croatian correspondence, on the other hand, consists of lines and cola, the bound, encapsulated phrases determined by a syllabic and consistently demarcated metric. Neither the sea voyage nor 'Shouting in Prison' is less a theme for its similarity to or difference from its counterpart; rather each theme is actualized in a form governed by the prosody of the tradition involved. Small wonder, then, that their narrative sequences (that is, their extra-prosodic dimensions) should resemble one another, or that their modes of verbalization should vary.

In turning to the final section of my paper, that which treats the 'story pattern' level of multiformity, it will be necessary to concentrate solely on the Serbo-Croatian evidence. This narrowing of the sample is not only an attempt at brevity but also a response to an obvious but too often over-looked problem in comparative oral studies: we simply have no multiple epic texts in either Homeric Greek or Old English. The demonstration will therefore proceed from the same four song texts by Kukuruzović that were used to examine the theme—two versions of 'The Captivity of Alagić Alija' (*6618*, 1868) and two of 'The Captivity of Ograšćić Alija' (*1287a*, *6617*).

Part I of both generic songs may be described as what Lord has called a 'return song' pattern, a sequence of five elements: *A* (Absence), *D* (Devastation), *R* (Return), *Rt* (Retribution), and *W* (Wedding).[51] Numerous songs follow this sequence rather closely. They usually begin with some evidence of a withdrawn or absent hero (*A*) and of the hero's suffering at the hands of a captor far away from his homeland (*D*). After a bargain is struck for release, the hero returns (*R*) and takes revenge (*Rt*) upon those disloyal to him during the period of his absence. The song customarily closes with the hero's marriage of his betrothed or 're-marriage' of his wife (*W*).[52] We have already analyzed one of the themes which expresses *A* and *D*, and can add at this point that Part I of both songs follows the sequence out, with one significant exception.[53] Since AA's and OA's wives are unfaithful to them, the return song cannot proceed to its usual coda in *W*, but ends unresolved in what we may term *W⁻*: the hero takes revenge on his wife by slaying her and dropping her body at his mother's feet. AA/OA then abandons his Turkish homeland and, pledging further revenge, rides off to join the enemy Christian forces in an attack on his own people.[54] The paradigm of return is formally complete, but the song, having veered off in another narrative direction, goes on.

To place this turn of events in its proper perspective, let us consider first what happens in the second part of the epic. The Turkish hero's journey ends at a Christian encampment where the bans are planning their attack. Eventually AA/OA's original loyalty re-emerges and he rushes off to warn his countrymen of the impending danger. But in the meantime the attack gets underway, and the story shifts away from AA/OA to the battle; in fact, AA/OA soon disappears from the action entirely. Perceiving their desperate situation, the Turkish forces launch a counter-attack which succeeds overall, but during which a Turkish maiden and heroes are captured by the ban of Janok. The rest of the plot line involves the rescue of these prisoners by means of a complex plan involving the usual elements of disguise and deceit, and both epics end with the maiden and heroes returning to their homeland. In schematic terms, the pattern of Part II of AA/OA runs as follows: Attack (*At*) to Counter-Attack (*CAt*) to capture and its consequent Absence (A) to Devastation (D) and finally to Return (R).

$$At \rightarrow CAt \rightarrow A \rightarrow D \rightarrow R$$

In fact, the return of the Turkish maiden to her proper locale amounts to a kind of W element, since that rescue and return reverse the rite of bride-stealing which was earlier actualized perversely in her capture by the ban.

Stepping back a bit and taking a wide-angle view of the entire epic structure, we can see a double cycle return pattern at the foundation of the story. The first of these, which follows the A–E sequence closely and in a familiar way, ends with the death of AA/OA's unfaithful wife. In fact, her very lack of fidelity stands as the condition for continuance; it is because of her treachery that AA/OA seeks further retribution (Rt) by deserting his people.[55] In logical terms, W ends the story, while W^- offers a bridge to the second part of the narrative. It is interesting to note that precisely at this juncture, immediately after W^-, Kukoruzović makes an 'error.' In text *6618*, he begins to tell the second section of OA rather than AA, a natural slip given the generic near-identity of the two songs. He catches himself after a few misguided verses and returns to the original story line.[56] Text *1868*, however, is a hybrid: here Kukuruzović never re-aligns himself after the slip but continues on with the 'wrong' story. These two instances of what may be called 'generic override,' one much more extensive than the other, help to establish the two-part structure of the song.

One more piece of evidence needs to be adduced. In a conversation[57] with Parry and Lord's native assistant Nikola, Kukuruzović included as part of his repertoire of thirty-eight songs a *pjesma* described by Nikola as '*Pije vino mlad janočki bane,* | *A do njega Takulija bane,*' or 'The young ban of Janok was drinking wine, | And next to him Takulija ban.' Now since we know that *guslari* assign no titles to their songs but habitually describe them by giving the first line or two, we can safely posit that the song in question opens with these verses. Remarkably, these very same lines also constitute the beginning of what I have identified as Part II of 'The Captivity of Ograščić Alija'; and Part II, we will recall, shifts focus rather abruptly away from the Turkish hero and onto the Christian attack. The necessary conclusion is clear: at least in the case of the 'Ograščić Alija' and probably in the case of the 'Alagić Alija' as well, what we have is a *song amalgam*, a combination made by stitching two songs together. Further, we seem to have caught the amalgamation in progress; the material exists in the *guslar's* repertoire both as a fused whole and as individual parts.

The demonstration of a song amalgam has a number of implications for the comparative study of the Homeric epics and of *Beowulf*. Ideas about 'parts' of narratives need not suggest either *Liedertheorie* or the written strata of the Analysts; quite traditional processes can account for story line development. In addition, though there is no time to go into detail, the OA/AA amalgam reveals a number of narrative inconsistencies, such as the sudden disappearance of the original hero from Part II mentioned above. Many such supposed 'blemishes' can be traced to the overlap induced by song combination, so that we need not see the *guslar* 'nodding.' The instability of the epic after the unfaithful wife's demise (*W-*) and these narrative inconsistencies, together with the existence of OA, Part II as a song by itself in Kukuruzović's repertoire, suggest a relatively recent amalgam, though of course we cannot be sure. What we should take note of, however, is the comparative backdrop afforded by this example. Distinctive tales, such as Beowulf's account of his adventures before Hygelac, for example, may at some point have existed apart from the main frame of the monster-fights.[58] And if we find narrative inconsistencies in Homer and *Beowulf*, we should consider the possibility that they arose from an amalgamation of stories which once existed (and perhaps still did exist at the time of the composition of our *Beowulf*) as individual tales. In this light Grendel's curious and magical *glof* may become somewhat less enigmatic.

I will not attempt to summarize in any detailed manner the conclusions of this paper, but will simply point to a principle which the first two of its sections try to illustrate: the principle of *tradition-dependence*. Now that we have extended the oral theory to a great number of literatures and have in the process uncovered striking similarities in their compositional make-up, it is time to close the ranks a bit and to inquire about the *differences* among traditional poetries. Only when we know how a given literature conditions formula, theme, and story pattern—and know it with precision—can we consider the oral theory applied with rigor and to best advantage. With this kind of real comparative information in hand, we can approach *Beowulf* both by analogy and on its own terms, seeking the truest and most suggestive of comparisons while remaining attentive to the unique nature of the Old English traditional aesthetic.[59]

University of Missouri

Interlocking Mythic Patterns
in Beowulf

ALBERT B. LORD

THERE are two discrete narrative patterns that are found fairly widely in Indo-European epic or story tradition, the possible presence of which I should like to explore in *Beowulf*. The first of these involves three stages. (a) A powerful figure is not present or, for various reasons, is powerless in a situation of danger to his people. (b) During the period of his absence, or of his inability or unwillingness to act effectively, things go very badly for those around him, and many of his friends are killed. Finally, (c) the powerful figure returns or his power is restored, whereupon he puts things to right again. The first element in the pattern is sometimes preceded by a quarrel, which motivates either the absence of the powerful figure or his loss of power.

Readers of the *Iliad* will recognize, of course, that this is the often remarked pattern of the main part of the poem with (a) the withdrawal of Achilles from battle because of his quarrel with Agamemnon, (b) the ensuing difficulties of the Achaeans and the death of Patroclus, which motivates (c) the return of Achilles to the battle and the victory of the Achaeans that follows.[1] Its other classical example is in the *Odyssey*, where (a) Odysseus' absence causes (b) the nefarious activities of Penelope's suitors, which are put a stop to by (c) the return of Odysseus. There are numerous examples of the pattern in oral traditional Slavic epic, both Russian and South Slavic.[2] Its existence in Germanic is attested by *King Horn*. Its occurrence in at least three traditions belonging to the Indo-European realm seems to indicate it as prevalent and possibly as originating in Indo-European. One should not be surprised to find it, or at least vestiges of it, in *Beowulf*, since one of the pattern's characteristic elements is a long period of devastation. That in itself qualifies the *Beowulf* poem for consideration.

For the first element (a), Hrothgar is powerless against Grendel. The resulting difficulties (b) over a long time—twelve years—are clear, and need not be elaborated on. With the advent of Beowulf (c), Hrothgar's surrogate, the difficulties begin to be overcome, although they cost Beowulf the death of his companion Hondscio. Beowulf maims and drives away the monster Grendel, and the ancient joy and peace return to Heorot.

One is tempted to view the absence of Beowulf himself at the beginning of the poem as the proper first element of the pattern. It may be so vestigially. If that is true, then the lack of a leader is indicated in two ways in *Beowulf*: i.e., Beowulf's absence and Hrothgar's impotence.

This pattern, or the continuance of its central period of difficulty, is repeated with the coming of Grendel's dam, whose elimination of Æschere duplicates and deepens the pattern, because Æschere is emphatically identified as Hrothgar's favorite counsellor (see 1708–09, 1323b–29). Hondscio's relationship to Beowulf is 'unmarked,' and in the early part of the poem he is not even named. In contrast, Æschere is mentioned by name and 'marked' in his appearance in this episode. I have sometimes wondered whether the telling of the Grendel episode in Beowulf's recapitulation of the event (lines 2000–2100) actually represents the incident in its form before it was combined with that of Grendel's dam. In that case, Hondscio's name would have occurred in the early part of the poem. At any rate, Hondscio and/or Æschere are killed, and after the death of the second, Beowulf again appears to remove the difficulties and once again restore peace and joy to Heorot.

The pattern does, then, seem to occur in *Beowulf*, and it is possible that the deaths of Hondscio and Æschere can be interpreted as vestiges of the death of the substitute. They, together, are Beowulf's Patroclus or Enkidu (Gilgamesh's companion). This interpretation would remove what to me has been a puzzling difficulty in the Grendel episode, namely the death of Hondscio while Beowulf looks on. The death of Æschere causes no such difficulty because Beowulf was not in Heorot at the time of the second attack.

One should also remark that the pattern of absence, devastation, and return often, and, indeed, originally or ideally, includes elements of disguise, deceptive story, mocking or testing, and recognition, as in the seasonal pattern in the Homeric Hymn to Demeter.[3] All these elements are associated with the hero's return and with the establishment of his identity. They are all to be found in the classic example of the pattern in Homer's *Odyssey*. They are present in more modern oral epic traditions, e.g. in the Turkic epics and in Slavic return poems, both Russian and South Slavic, to mention only two out of the numerous modern cultures still preserving their traditional narrative traditionally. The challenge of Unferth, beginning 'Are you that Beowulf who?' (lines 506–28), fits into this pattern as an element of mocking or testing.[4] Whether or not this episode is an example of a traditional Germanic flyting, as Professor Clover argues in a forthcoming essay,[5] a challenge of the hero suits the pattern and is appropriate where it is in *Beowulf*. In other words, the flyting might be used in the Germanic version of the pattern where the mocking or testing appears in the basic Indo-European tradition, to which Slavic and ancient Greek belong. Be that as it may, mocking in the context of determining identity, feigned or otherwise, is a part of the complex of the return pattern, and I would like to suggest that it may occur here in that complex in *Beowulf*.

Let me turn now to an investigation of the second pattern that was mentioned at the beginning. Stories with this pattern tell of the encounter of the hero and a companion, or companions, with first a male monster, which he overcomes, and then a female monster, or a divine temptress who wants to keep him in the 'other' world. His escape from the one and his rejection of the offers of the other involve breaking a taboo and/or insulting a deity, and as a result one or more of his companions is killed. The hero, then, with a question in his mind concerning his own mortality or immortality, goes on a journey in which he learns the answer to that question.

The Homeric example of this is in the wanderings of Odysseus. The hero blinds the Cyclops Polyphemus, thus offending Poseidon, and with Apollo's help he defies the powers of Circe, who wishes to detain him in the 'other' world. In the Polyphemus episode Odysseus loses some unnamed companions, but in the second incident, that with Circe, he loses a named and otherwise 'marked' (the youngest) companion, Elpenor. After this, Odysseus goes to the land of the dead and there learns when death will come to him.

This second pattern, then, also contains a death at a climactic point. In it a hero, often of unusual birth, with a companion or companions, encounters a monster of cannibal propensities who kills one or more of the hero's companions, but he overcomes the monster sometimes by seriously maiming him. That episode constitutes the first element in the pattern. We have seen it in the encounter of Odysseus and his companions with Polyphemus (and it is duplicated in the episode with the Laestrygonians) but it fits the Humbaba episode in *Gilgamesh* also, so far as we can tell, although some details are not clear. In that episode the hero of the epic, Gilgamesh, who is part god and part man, and his mortal companion, Enkidu, penetrate into the apparently sacred Cedar Forest where they overcome and kill the monster Humbaba. These elements correspond to the Grendel episode in *Beowulf*, of course.

Following the episode with a male monster, the hero comes into conflict with a female figure who wishes to keep him with her in her world but whom he thwarts. His companion or companions are also involved in this episode, but they are not immediately or literally killed in it. I have in mind the incident of Odysseus and Circe in the *Odyssey* and of Gilgamesh and Ishtar in the *Gilgamesh* epic. In the latter, Gilgamesh, returning in glory from his conquest of Humbaba, is seen by the goddess Ishtar. She falls in love with him and wants him to be her lover. He refuses and she calls on her father to send the Bull of Heaven against the two heroes. They slay the Bull, and Enkidu throws a haunch of the animal at the goddess, who is furious. Finally the gods in assembly decree that one of the two must die, and the choice falls on the mortal Enkidu. The episode with Grendel's dam in *Beowulf* fits in the sequence in this pattern, but there are clearly points of divergence, particularly in that Grendel's dam is killed, whereas Ishtar and Circe are only frustrated.

The third element in this pattern is the climactic one to which the first two have been leading. It is the death of one of the hero's companions, a death that is caused by the actions of the hero and his companions in elements one and two. It is clearest in *Gilgamesh* where Enkidu's death is caused by the breaking of taboos or the insulting of the gods by the two protagonists in killing Humbaba and thwarting Ishtar. This third element is vestigial in the *Odyssey* in the death of Elpenor, which occurs at the proper position in the story to fit into the pattern. It is preceded by the episodes of Polyphemus and Circe; it is followed by a journey during which the hero's ultimate destiny, death, is discovered.

The element of death is certainly not clear *at this point* in *Beowulf*. One may see it vestigially in the deaths of Hondscio and Æschere, but these do not occur in the expected place. That answer may be correct, yet in the Scandinavian analogues usually cited for these episodes, e.g. the incident of the she-troll and the giant at Sandhaugar in the *Grettis saga*, the same positioning of a death before each of the fights is to be found. The stories in those analogues are complete in themselves and do not go on to a sequel, as in *Beowulf* and in my two main sources for the pattern, i.e., the *Odyssey* and the *Gilgamesh* epic.

Whether we accept Hondscio and Æschere as possible vestiges that have been misplaced or simply as pointing forward to a death not present, or whether we simply note the absence in *Beowulf* of this crucial element, this absence (or vestige) must somehow be explained. To do so is not difficult, as a matter of fact, and the explanation leads us, I believe, to a clearer indication not only of the presence but, more significantly, of the importance of this pattern in that poem.

There is an essential difference between the adversaries in the ancient examples and those in the Germanic ones in *Beowulf* and in the sagas. In the former the adversaries are 'sacred,' and therefore the opposition to them by the hero is tantamount to sacrilege. Although the details are not

clear, it is apparent that when Gilgamesh and Enkidu slay Humbaba in the
Cedar Forest they have incurred some degree of guilt. This guilt is, of
course, crystal clear in the incident with Ishtar and the Bull of Heaven.
Death for one of the two heroes must follow, and the gods choose Enkidu,
the mortal companion of the partly divine Gilgamesh, as the one who
must die. The death of the companion is motivated by the guilt of the pair.
In the case of the *Odyssey* the fact that Odysseus had offended the god
Poseidon by blinding his son, however justified the hero's actions might
be, is made abundantly clear in the song. That Odysseus in the episode
with Circe has thwarted her wishes to turn him into a swine and to keep
him with her forever is also apparent. But the death of Elpenor is no
longer evident as the result of Odysseus' deeds, partly, of course, because
his punishment for the maiming of Polyphemus was already realized in
his eventual wanderings and shipwreck. The pattern is weakened but it is
still there, for Odysseus goes to the land of the dead and there learns,
among other things, that death will at some time come to him quietly
from the sea.

The loss (or perhaps better the absence) in Germanic tradition of the
sense of guilt in breaking taboos and insulting the gods, explains the
breaking of the pattern at this moment in *Beowulf* by the omission of a
special death, or at best by its vestigial survival earlier in the poem. The
hero not only does not incur any guilt in the Germanic reinterpretation of
the pattern, but, quite the opposite, he gains great glory by overcoming
the evil chaos caused by Grendel and Grendel's dam.

The pattern may be seen to be resumed, however, in the return journey
of Beowulf to his homeland, although this is on another level of reality.
We are given not the prophecy of death, as in the *Odyssey*, but its actu-
ality.

We see then in these three cases of the pattern (1) a clear working out
of it in *Gilgamesh*, replete with guilt that causes death; (2) a form in the
Odyssey that still holds a strong element of guilt, but death as the result is,
while clearly present, only vestigial, since the hero's guilt is punished
otherwise, and (3) a form in *Beowulf* in which guilt has become virtue and
the pattern is broken, leaving either a gap or at best an enigmatic and
unclear vestige.

The interlocking of these two patterns from the deep past of the story,
modulating from the hopeful eternal return of the cyclical myth of annual
renewal, through the death of the substitute, to the eventual acceptance of
man's mortality, provides a mythic base both for the triumph of Beowulf
over the evil generations of Cain and for the inevitable death of the hero in
old age, still fighting against destructive forces.

But Beowulf's last deed and his last words held hope within
them:

Albert B. Lord

Dyde him of healse   hring gyldenne
þioden þristhydig,   þegne gesealde,
geongum garwigan,   goldfahne helm,
beah ond byrnan,   het hyne brucan well—;
'þu eart endelaf   usses cynnes,
Wægmundinga;   ealle wyrd forsweop
mine magas   to metodsceafte,
eorlas on elne;   ic him æfter sceal.'
þæt wæs þam gomelan   gingæste word
breostgehygdum,   ær he bæl cure,
hate heaðowylmas;   him of hræðre gewat
sawol secean   soðfæstra dom (2809–20).[6]

(Then the prince, bold of mind, detached
his golden collar and gave it to Wiglaf,
the young spear-warrior, and also his helmet
adorned with gold, his ring and his corslet,
and enjoined him to use them well;
'You are the last survivor of our family,
the Wægmundings; fate has swept
all my kinsmen, those courageous warriors,
to their doom. I must follow them.'
    Those were the warrior's last words
before he succumbed to the raging flames
on the pyre; his soul migrated from his breast
to meet the judgement of righteous men.)

Harvard University

Beowulf *in the Context of Myth*

MICHAEL N. NAGLER

IF we differentiate myth, which deals with 'first things' and tends to use a nearly worldwide repertoire of themes and symbols, from the relatively local and more restricted phenomenon of legend, then the mythic aspect of *Beowulf* has received short shrift. Old English scholars have made great strides in situating this isolated literary heirloom in its historical context as a specimen of Germanic legend, but they have not, to my knowledge, had a great deal to say concerning its connections with Indo-European or more universal mythology.

It was the classical scholar Joseph Fontenrose who first called attention to *Beowulf* as a tripartite exposition of the widespread Indo-European and Near-Eastern combat myth. As he says in *Python,* 'the more one looks at Grendel's dam, the more she looks like Tiamat.'[1] Fontenrose's exhaustive yet sensitive study delineates clearly what we might call the onto-logical or cosmogonic concern of that great myth: the eternal struggle between chaos and order, figured as a clash between death, cold, and darkness on the one hand, and life and light on the other. In *Beowulf* the myth takes the specific form of a clash between the 'daemonic' forces of nature and the lightly Christianized sky-god who orders, tempers, and after all has created nature. I would like to carry this line of discussion further in two rather different directions. First, I want to show how deeply the level of organization that we call myth has reproduced itself in the level that we call literature, giving shape to such literary features of the poem as its imagery, pace, vocabulary, and syntax. Then, returning to the myth itself, I want to speculate a bit about its psychological rather than cosmogonic significance, and here I may have a rather new line of inter-pretation to suggest. In the interests of brevity I will concentrate on the central combat of *Beowulf,* and in particular on the climax of that combat and a few surrounding details.

Let me begin with a comparison. When epics, especially 'primary' or oral epics, follow the same myth they seem to show parallelism not only in theme, plot, and the larger framework of narrative organization, but often in the most surprising and unpredictable details. This is because no one narrative rendition can work all the symbolic elements of the myth into the discursive logic of a single story line—the myth is just too big. Therefore the epic singers did two things: they retold the same myth repeatedly within the same performance, and they developed each repetition (not counting bare allusions to the myth) with a fresh set of images and other details that were a traditional part of the myth's infinite variety, but that were not necessarily connected to the logical requirements of the poet's surface narrative. In this sense, the singers of tales did not feel that they were tied down to the rationalistic demands of their own particular story line, with its chain of causes and effects that served to keep the narrative moving but did not necessarily express what they were really trying to say.[2]

So it was with the *Beowulf* poet, and so had it been centuries before him with the poet of the *Odyssey*. Therefore we need not be at a loss if some apparently arbitrary details of the combat between Odysseus and Polyphemus resonate suggestively with similar details in Beowulf's fight with Grendel's dam, even if those details appear in their immediate context for different reasons. For example: Polyphemus devours two of Odysseus' men and beds down with his flock for the night, rolling a stone across the entrance to his cave to trap the hero and the rest of his crew inside. Odysseus recalls:

> Now I wanted, by one impulse of my valiant heart
> To go up to him with drawn sword and palpate the brute
> For the spot where the heart-sac cradles his liver
> And stab him through the chest; but another impulse checked me:
> For that way would the lot of us have perished there and then.
> In no wise would we have been able to roll the massive stone
> From the high cave mouth he had blocked with it (*Od.* 9.299–305).

Instead of killing Polyphemus with his sword, Odysseus spies an olive stake lying in the back of the cave and uses the stake to blind Polyphemus and make good his escape with the Cyclops' sheep, as we all recall. Now if you believe that the reason which Odysseus gives for his not using his sword is the 'real' reason, you will believe anything the poet tells you, which means you will be a very good listener but a poor scholar of myth. Let us try for the moment to be both. Grendel's mother seizes Beowulf and drags him into her underwater lair. There he strikes her fiercely with his sword, the one he borrowed from Unferth, but for some unaccountable reason—the poet mentions twice that this has never happened before (1406b–61, 1525b–28)—it fails. Fortunately, after a serious *contretemps*, the hero spots an ancient giant-weapon among the gear hanging on the wall (1662), and with this sword he easily dispatches her and makes off with his own life and the hilt of the sword.

Clearly each poet was dealing with the same theme, but each had to make a story out of it in his own way. The theme is that when the hero descends from the realm of the sky-god to do battle with the demon of darkness, whatever (relatively) ordinary, earthly weapons he brings with him are of no avail. Reduced to desperation, he must have recourse to the demon's own weapon—or rather, as I will explain in a moment, to a weapon that is in the demon's possession. Putting the factitious explanation for the non-use of his sword offered by Odysseus, who of all people could have contrived a way to get out of the cave if he really wanted to, alongside the mysterious impotence of Hrunting, to which the *Beowulf* poet draws attention without offering an explanation, we can appreciate the extent to which the chronologically earlier poem is composed in a more sophisticated and in this case literally rationalizing style.[3] This difference in degree of rationalization only makes more intriguing the fact that both poets are preserving the same story.

The thematic fact that the demonic adversary himself or herself is not using the fatal weapon also makes its appearance in both poems, also worked into the story in different ways and on different levels of rationalization. The olivewood stake is being stored by Polyphemus 'til he might carry it' (9.320); the old giant-sword is greater than any other man *ætberan meahte* 'might carry' (1561b). Even the grammar seems to reflect the theme of present disuse, of potentiality, in both contexts, but the rationalism of the Greek story obscures the interesting question of why the weapon isn't being used by the demon, while in *Beowulf* that question is once again thrown into high relief without being answered.

The question can be answered by a further comparison. The earlier of the two great primary epics of ancient India, the *Rāmāyaṇa*, comes to its climax when the great hero Rama slays the arch-demon Ravana. This he does after much travail and many near-fatal setbacks, when his brother and thousands of followers have been killed (most of them several times). He overcomes Ravana at last with a superweapon called the *pāśupatāstra*, 'the arrow of Shiva,' which the gods have given him for that very purpose. The hero has this weapon in his quiver all along, but he 'forgets' to use it until he is reminded of its purpose by his charioteer Matali (just as he conveniently forgets that he himself is an incarnation of the Lord of the sky, Vishnu; compare *Beowulf* 1553b–56 and 1661–64). Clearly this is parallel to the eleventh-hour discovery of the fatal weapons in *Beowulf* and in the *Odyssey*; but there is more. A closer parallel to the plot structure of the

Danish expedition in *Beowulf* occurs in the *Bāla Kāṇḍa* or 'youth section' at the beginning of the *Rāmāyaṇa*, where Rama and his brother do a tour of the various forest-ashrams ('hermitages') in the company of a sage who has borrowed the young heroes for that purpose from their father. The peace and quiet of these ashrams is being upset by demons who periodically disrupt and desecrate the sacrifices of the pious brahmins, and Rama and his brother destroy these demons with ease. Though the ashrams are in the forest, geographically remote from civilization, they represent order under attack by the forces of irreligion, so that when the Grendels are stung to jealous fury by the recitation of creation mythology in the hall of Heorot and must be quelled by an itinerant culture hero, the episode is quite similar in its conception and execution.[4] It is on this trip to the forest-ashrams that Rama encounters his first version of the Shiva-weapon, a bow so gigantic that five hundred stalwarts must labor to roll it out for him in its iron case. To show his prowess (and of course his identity) Rama lifts the great bow with one hand, strings it effortlessly and—here is the most revealing parallel—breaks it. The bow of Shiva, like the sword in the possession of the Grendel clan, has never been used by any other man and will never be used again, even by this one.

If this weapon does not belong to the hero and is not used by his adversary, whose is it? It is the weapon of the sky-god, which the chaos-demon has stolen. That is why the 'gigantic' sword has written on its hilt, the only part that survives, the beginning of that primordial conflict when God destroyed with flood the insolent race of giants . . . *þæt wæs fremde þeod/ecean Dryhtne* ('that was a race alien to the eternal Lord').[5]

I will return to these portentous words at the conclusion of this paper; but clearly the runic inscription on the hilt is no mere decoration. It tells us iconographically just what this weapon is: God's instrument for quelling the forces of disorder. God punished this rebellious race at the beginning, when the rise of fratricidal violence spewed evil into the world, and he did so with water (106–14).[6] Now, at the end, when he exterminates at least one line of that monstrous progeny, the death weapon retells the story of that beginning, as it was and always will be. When Rama's missile returns to his quiver it is *kṛtakarma*, 'its work is done'; and similarly with this sword. Its purpose is to destroy the Grendel race, and when that purpose is accomplished it melts away. But not entirely; the poet obviously feels that this battle is only one episode in an unending struggle that began with the introduction of evil into the world, in primordial times. As God served the giants with flood, and as he serves Grendel's dam with his sword (a sword which is wielded for him by Beowulf and engraved with the magically potent story of that emblematic victory *in illo tempore*), he serves the powers of cold and darkness in every season, as we are told by the simile at lines 1607b–11, and indeed in another way at every morning, another point to which we must soon return.

From the point of view of the individual hero this victory over Grendel's dam is a definitive, unique event, and its uniqueness is symbolized perfectly in the disappearance of the blade. But the poet also knows that it is an archetype, and that is symbolized by the permanence of the hilt.[7]

The apparent reference to the Old Testament in the inscription on the hilt has caused some unnecessary confusion, largely because of the old debate concerning what element in *Beowulf* is pagan and what represents a Christianity without its special ethical or normative values. It will take a subtle theologian to explain the difference between paganism and Christianity stripped of its ethical values. Certainly the *Beowulf* poet was not interested in the difference. For him the Indo-European creation myth, with its story of a titanic race which rose up against the sky-god and was quelled (as is related for example in Hesiod, *Theogony* 617ff), meant the same thing as the Old Testament creation story with its deluge and its obscure giants and rebellious angels. Both levels of mythology in his cultural tradition pointed to man's heroic capacity to overcome disorder in himself, exemplified in Christ's struggle and resurrection in the service of God. That power which sustained order in the world of nature had established order in the beginning of time and was even now sustaining order in man as a personal, a religious, and a social being. The *engla dryhten* subsumed the traditions of the *eorla dryhten* without a hitch.

It is not in the least necessary to assume that the poet had reasoned this all out consciously, as we are now attempting to do. He does not need to be given a place between, say, St. Augustine and Otto of Freising as an interpreter of the Old Testament reference to giants. But the exegetical tradition of the Fathers had entered somehow the stream of his consciousness and helped him to see and to present both his racial, Indo-European inheritance and the conglomerate of relatively learned and relatively recent inheritances as so many successive idioms within a coherent tradition. It was this integrative genius which gave him much of his power as a poetic artist and much of his cultural value to his society; and the only gift which could explain his capacity to see an underlying unity running through these various cultural idioms was his capacity to see what they all meant.

Beowulf uses the sword of the giants just once. Then it ceases to be a sword and becomes a treasure, in fact *the* treasure worth rescuing from the mere of the Grendels, along with Grendel's head:

> Ne nom he in þæm wicum,   Weder-Geata leod,
> maðmæhta ma,   þeh he þær monige geseah,

buton þone hafelan   ond þa hilt somod
since fage . . . (1612–15a).

(The prince of the Weder-Geats took from the dwelling no more
treasures—though he saw many there—than that head and that hilt,
gleaming with jewels. . . .)

If I am correct about the mythical origins of this sword-treasure, then its
restoration to the land of the living, solemnly described at 1677–86, is as
crucial to the underlying story as the victory over Grendel's dam itself. As
an emblem, or rather talisman, we may believe that the presence of the
runic inscription will help Hrothgar establish order in the world just as it
helped Beowulf slay Grendel's dam in the hellish fen whence he re-
possessed this precious thing. For Hrothgar, whose feebleness had
almost brought about the decay of his kingdom, the hilt is not just
symbolic, it is potent. Not through violence—it is no longer a weapon—
but through its blazon of moral authority it will help him restore order to
his beleaguered world. No wonder the aged king gazes on it with such awe
(1687) and launches into a panegyric of Beowulf and on the power of God
to overcome the disruptive vices.

But why the ghastly head along with the hilt? Fontenrose has shown
that the sword, the head, and the unexplained light which shines forth
when the Grendel line is quelled are so many different tokens of the same
thing. The Old Iranians called it $X^v ar\partial nah$, their Indic cousins *amṛta*
(cognate with Greek *ambrosia*), and in a less mythopoeic age the
demented air force general in *Dr. Strangelove* called it his 'vital essence.'
In pre-neurotic times, it was the elixir which orders and illuminates the
materia of life. [8]

The symbolism of light shining unexpectedly in the darkness is carried
to an extreme, one might say an archetypal extreme, in one passage in the
Odyssey. The connection between Odysseus' misadventure on Thrinakia,
where his men attack the cattle of the sun, and the misadventure in
Polyphemus' cave, where they make off with the flock of that very 'solar'
individual, is almost explicitly drawn for Odysseus by the seer Teiresias
(11.100–09).[9] Not to dwell here on the complexities of the Thrinakian
myth, as soon as Helios learns of the attack upon his herds he threatens to
'go down into Hades and shine among the dead' (12.383). Zeus hastily
appeases him, of course, but at least on the level of imagery, the sun has
briefly descended into the nether darkness and has been rescued for
gods and men (12.385–86).

It is clear that Homer, as a poet, strongly felt the potent ambivalencies
between sight and blindness, darkness and light, cold night and victorious morning, and he reproduced them in what we would consider the

strictly literary aspects of his narrative art. To mention one example from the fight with Polyphemus, Homer describes the preparations for the blinding of the Cyclops—his equivalent to the decapitation of the Grendels—with the usual sensuous vividness of the great oral poet. We see the sleeping giant, the brilliantly imagined glow of the stake in the fire, Odysseus working with his men 'like a shipwright' (9.371ff). But with the *blinding* of Polyphemus (at about line 9.390) all the visual imagery shuts off and we are left with sounds and groping. Any great narrator might have done this, perhaps, but considering the prominence of the themes of light and darkness in the myth, it is hard not to see a direct continuity between those traditional motifs and the concerns of Homer's art.

It was no different with the composer of *Beowulf*. The head, the light, and the precious sword, we learn from Fontenrose, are the controlling themes of the myth. They are no less the controlling images of the poet's description of the climactic moment in it:

> He gefeng þa fetelhilt,   freca Scyldinga
> hreoh ond heorogrim,   hringmæl gebrægd
> aldres orwena,   yrringa sloh,
> þæt hire wið halse   heard grapode,
> banhringas bræc;   bil eal ðurhwod
> fægne flæschoman;   heo on flet gecrong,
> sweord wæs swatig,   secg weorce gefeh.
> Lixte se leoma,   leoht inne stod,
> efne swa of hefene   hadre scineð
> rodores candel (1563–72a).

(Then the warrior of the Scyldings, fierce and bent on slaughter, seized the linked hilt, he drew the blade, desperate for his life; in anger he struck so that it hit her neck hard and severed the vertebrae. The sword struck clear through her doomed flesh. She fell to the floor; the sword was bloody; the man rejoiced in his deed. A radiance shone; the hall was filled with light, just as the sky's candle shines from heaven in brilliance.)

Note how the pace of the description focuses down by what Alain Renoir has called 'progressive magnification' to the death-blow and four separate images of its victorious result, each given in a single verse:

> heo on flet gecrong,
> sweord wæs swatig,   secg weorce gefeh.
> Lixte se leoma. . . .

149

This psychologically vivid moment is presented in two pairs of verses that embody first the objective and then the subjective viewpoint on the hero's victory. Each pair in turn describes the state of the respective antagonist, whether defeat or victory, in the first verse, then gives what may seem to be a naturalistic detail, the kind of thing that would register on the mind in such a crisis, but that is also a pregnant mythological symbol. No mere 'objective correlative' of the first verse, though partly that, it greatly expands and as it were universalizes its meaning.[10] To repunctuate and paraphrase on this level of meaning: 'The demon fell (i.e. "her" weapon was bloodied): the hero rejoiced (i.e. God's light shone forth).' The bloody sword and the shining light draw their evocative power both from the deep background of the tradition—for as we have seen they are archetypal images—and from the surrounding context which precedes and follows this moment of the narration.

It is significant that line 1570 delivers two statements of the same symbol: *Lixte se leoma . . . leoht inne stod*. First of all, this repetition begins to relax the pace of the narration. The climactic four-verse unit preceding it gave four separate and complete predications for one mythological fact, 'hero defeats demon.' With line 1570 we begin to return to the normal leisurely style of description by interlocking cross-reference and *variatio* (as it has been called, by a bit of oversimplification). Secondly, it allows the 'a' verse, *Lixte se leoma*, to play its role in the intensely concentrated and well-balanced four-verse summary of the primordial event and the 'b' verse, *leoht inne stod*, to be read with the separate statement on the light (lines 1571–72a). These lines present the simile of 'God's candle' which is not only a more leisurely kind of description, but which amounts to a lightly Christian gloss on the victorious morning light.[11]

Fontenrose has aptly said of this light, 'To the poet it was like the sun; for us it is a memory of the sun that lay hidden in the chaotic waters, as in the Indian and Egyptian cosmogonies, a memory that has clung to the tale as it moved from myth to heroic legend' (*Python*, p. 527). But from the skill with which the *Beowulf* passage is composed it appears that the move from myth to heroic legend did not leave myth behind. The memory of myth was as alive to the oral poet as the memory with which he vividly realized the heroic legend itself, for both were not so much memories in our sense of the word as the perception of types in the eternal struggle between order and chaos. The poet must have seen this struggle not only in various levels of his cultural tradition, but all around him in the stresses of his social world.

In the sense that the subsequent simile on the light is contained in the single verse 1570a, the still longer description of the 'melting' of the blade which follows at lines 1608b–11 is contained in the parallel phrase, *sweord*

wæs swatig (1569a), for the traditional audience knew about dragons'
blood (see, e.g., 897b). God's power, figured as the sun, projects both
light and heat to overcome the dark frigidity of chaos, sin, or alienation,
whatever we choose to call it. Thus the phrase *sweord wæs swatig* points to
the heat (see 1616) but implies the light, while the parallel image, *lixte se
leoma*, denotes the light and implies the heat. Compression can go no
further, as is understandable in a climactic passage which is seeking to
describe one controlling image of the myth, decapitation, in terms of the
other two, the treasure and the light.

Yet compression has gone even farther than we have so far described.
When Beowulf describes the dissolution of the sword during his 'de-
briefing' session with Hrothgar, he uses the words:

> þa þæt hildebil
> forbarn brogdenmæl,   swa þæt blod gesprang,
> hatost heaþoswata (1666b–68a).

(Then that battle-sword with its patterned blade burnt away as the
blood sprang forth, hottest of battle gore.)

These words pick up not only *æfter heaþoswate* from the simile of the
melting blade (1606a), but another example of the same formula system
that had been used to describe Hrunting at the 'briefing' for this battle
some lines earlier:

> þæt wæs an foran   ealdgestreona;
> ecg wæs iren,   atertanum fah,
> ahyrded heaþoswate (1458–60a).

(That was one of the foremost of ancient treasures; its blade was of
iron, gleaming with deadly patternings, hardened in the blood of
battle.)

It will be seen that Beowulf's social humiliation of Unferth (brought out
both in the flyting and in this passage, 581b–601a and 1465–71) and his
subsequent 'humiliation' of the treasure-sword which Unferth had in his
possession (1527b–28) are discernibly parallel to his treatment of
Grendel's dam and her weapon. Indeed the connection seems close to the
surface when Beowulf moves without transition from squelching Unferth
to predicting his success against Grendel. He ends that prediction, fit-
tingly, with a victorious reference to morning *light*, which also figured

into his description of the past success of the Breca episode, the content of the present squelch. Finally Hrunting, too, is described in traditional language as a *beadoleoma* (1523a) just at the moment when it is striking the head of Grendel's dam. Thus both the images of tempering in battle-gore (so curiously reminiscent of the second simile on the blinding of Polyphemus, *Od.* 9.391–94) and the release of light at the moment of destruction are associated with swords which in one way or another end their long career at this fateful battle. Modern scholars have seen that Unferth, the fratricide, had it in for Beowulf all along. He is of the same kidney as the Grendels, who descend from the prototype of this proto-typical evil, Cain, the first fratricide and introducer of violence into human life. Some have also thought that the failure of Hrunting when Beowulf seems to need it most is part of Unferth's plot. This may be correct, but the mythic dimension reveals that the failure of Hrunting, however the poet has worked it into his story, is an expected and a positive development. To imagine Beowulf in dismay at the failure of the sword would be, again, to be a good listener to the surface narrative, but not to the underlying myth.

Human culture does not survive on amusement value. For a myth to have survived for so long and to have projected itself so well through so many successive layers of cultural idiom, indeed to speak to us who are in a way so differently circumstanced today, it must have some practical relevancy, and we are therefore obliged to do some educated speculation about its meaning. Here a certain amount of subjectivity is unavoidable.

When Beowulf kills Grendel's dam he serves the ongoing struggle for order at a deep level, winning a demonic subterranean battle. At the same time he fulfils what he had predicted or begun at the social level with his courageous act of truth in Hrothgar's mead-hall, and what he will return to do again, as we have seen, with his magnificent gift to the aging king. But he does not win permanent security for Danes or Geats.

I have no quarrel with the cosmogonic level of interpretation which Fontenrose and others have set forth with such skill. I must confess to a bit of nervousness, however, when I read that in *Beowulf* the pessimistic aspect of the 'fabulous' element, i.e. the eventual triumph of the chaotic forces in the legend, arises from a particular historical situation, the fragility of life among the Nordic tribes. It does, of course, but it is also much more. Is our life really more secure today? Has violence been quelled at its source?

Beowulf is still read today because the problems of violence and authority are still with us. And its potential contribution to those problems is not to be most readily deciphered in terms of Indo-European cosmogony or medieval history, though all of that plays a role; rather it is to be rendered intelligible in terms of the insight of the myth, and this poet's rendition of the myth, into human nature. This is the only frame of reference deep enough, universal enough, and crucial enough to explain the impact of the story, and also to provide us with an intellectual grasp of it as scholars.

In these terms, the story looks something like this: there is a treasure, something of great creative power capable of releasing light where there is darkness and restoring harmony and peace where there is suicidal strife. It is earmarked for us, though it is also much greater than our individual selves. In the normal state of affairs, it is, however, quite hidden, buried in the depths—and here I interpret, the depths of consciousness. There it has fallen to the Enemy. This usurper, hoarding as he does our precious faculties, carries out depredations on our lives with impunity.[12] This goes on for years. Living in such a case, men lose their bearings; quite understandably, but very ominously, the social order is periodically threatened with dissolution.

To reach this Enemy, not to mention quell him, requires nothing less than superhuman effort. At first the aspirant does not even realize that his or her encounters, ferocious as they are, are only preparations and that the victory they can bring is only temporary. We slowly realize that we must grapple with this problem at its source. A titanic struggle awaits the one who has tracked this monster to the very ground of its—and our—existence; but only there can the battle be fought definitively, the warmth and light untrapped, and the treasure definitively freed. He or she who has liberated this capacity in himself has won a much greater victory than personal happiness, often the goal of modern psychology. He can also confer untold benefits on the community, for example by reorienting and re-legitimizing its institutions of authority, and through them he can provide guidance to the community towards a more harmonious and meaningful existence. This is not a 'myth' in the popular sense of the term. It has happened in history—one thinks of what St. Joan did through Charles the Dauphin, or in modern times of Gandhi and Nehru—and it is something that society needs very badly.

Here we have almost an interpretation of the myth. The way that I have just recast the story is still partly an imagistic paraphrase, while what we are after is a complete translation into concrete and pragmatic terms. Who is this Enemy, who are his legions, and what in particular is this treasure? Here we are very fortunate in that the most penetrating psychologist in the Western tradition, a man whose work was far from irrelevant to that of our poet, has written what is virtually a commentary on the central myth of *Beowulf*:

Velle meum tenebat inimicus; et inde mihi catenam fecerat et
constrinxerat me. quippe voluntate perversa facta est libido, et dum
servitur libidini, facta est consuetudo, et dum consuetudini non
resistitur, facta est necessitas. quibus quasi ansulis sibimet
innexis—unde catenam appelavi—tenebat me obstrictum dura
servitus. voluntas autem nova, quae mihi esse coeperat, ut te gratis
colere fruique te vellem, deus, sola certa iucunditas, nondum erat
idonea ad superandam priorem vetustate roboratam. ita duae
voluntates meae, una vetus, alia nova, illa carnalis, illa spiritalis,
confligebant inter se, atque discordando dissipabant animam meam.

(St. Augustine, Confessions 8.5)

(The Enemy held possession of my will; and from that had he made a
chain to choke me with. For disoriented will became desire, and
because I indulged desire it turned into habit, and when I failed to
resist habit it became compulsion. By these rings as it were linked
one to the other—which is why I called it a chain—a very hard
servitude held me fast bound. That new will which had begun in me,
to do what you find favorable and to desire to please you, God, our
only sure joy, was not yet strong enough to overcome its prede-
cessor, seasoned with long use. Thus my two wills, one old, the
other new, the former carnal, the latter spiritual, fought amongst
themselves, and in their conflict squandered my spirit.)

This passage could hardly be improved on for its psychological insight.
It identifies the crucial element which the Jungians, for example, in their
preoccupation with dreams, fantasies, and archetypes, have overlooked:
the 'treasure' of psychic energy that lies waiting to be rescued in the
depths of our consciousness is guarded by nothing more nor less than
human will. The 'enemy' is that portion of our will which has become
disoriented from the source and ground of all existence, or in the
language of the *Beowulf* poet is *fah wiþ God.* In our language it is the
subconscious desire for separate existence, the arch-desire to capture our
vital energy, as it were, and use it for separate ends. From this primordial
split in consciousness has arisen the host of self-oriented desires, habits,
and conditioned responses—the lesser demons of the myth—which
prevent us from acting spontaneously for our own welfare and which
strenuously resist whatever attempts we assay to get closer to our heritage
of psychic unity.[13]

The 'hero' within all of us is the remaining will, however paralyzed,
that can be commanded by the down-but-not-out desire to reverse the
conditioning which the demons have accomplished in their years of
roaming the countryside unchecked, or only listlessly and sporadically

checked. As long as there is both a hero and an enemy, there is going to be conflict. The former will bring into existence an unending host of positive desires for freedom, just as the latter will go on supporting an equally innumerable host of restricting desires for separate gratification. But that is our glory, the myth seems to say: as long as we are bound, the desire for freedom cannot but arise. The only alternative to unending inner conflict is to win it.

The arrival of the hero symbolizes precisely this decision to stake everything, *aldres orwena*, if need be—to win this battle once and for all. No more temporary victories on the surface, but a life-or-death fight in the yet unvisited depths of the haunted mere with the mother evil, then if God wills to hold boundless energy in our hands and at last make use of it for the purpose for which it was destined.[14]

Two things differentiate the hero Beowulf from his retainers. The first is that he and the monsters know they are made for one another. The nicors don't even sniff at Breca but go straight for Beowulf, who is right alongside him; on the other hand, when the news goes out that the Grendels are active in Denmark, Beowulf, and he alone, makes inexorably for their lair. The second, of course, is that unlike poor Æschere and the others, Beowulf wins. Interestingly, this is not because of his innate capacity alone: when he attacks Grendel's mother he bends her to the floor for a while (1539–40), but when she counterattacks she throws him and all but undoes him (1541–56). Beowulf wins because as long as he stakes his all without regard for his own life (1536b, 1565a) he has God, the ultimate will, on his side—again, a theology of which Augustine would have thoroughly approved.

Of course, the *Beowulf* poet need never have read or even heard of Augustine. He either was incapable of thinking in these terms or knew that if he did so he would lose his audience.[15] He says, not that man must gain a certain mastery over his desires before he can fight out this battle in the depths of his consciousness, but that Beowulf had to prove himself in the swimming match with Breca, and then against Grendel in the mead-hall, before he could pass so easily through the region of nicors down through the haunted mere to reach the demon, and the treasure, at their source. He says that there was a race of giants in primordial times who turned against God and whom God destroyed with flood, that in the time of *geardagum*, the present of our poem which is poised between the primordial *fyrngewin* and the present of the audience, it was the Grendel line that had to be destroyed by the sword that they were hoarding. But on some level, surely, he must have known what it all meant. He must have sensed that, as Salustius says, 'a myth is something that never took place but which is always true.' He must have known that he was implying that the unchallenged existence of a Grendel in the mere means the unchecked disruptiveness of a treacherous thyle in the mead-hall, or in our language, that an unchecked veering of the will self-ward in the depths of an individual consciousness (spawning as it does a race of anger, fear, and greed) must lead to political and social chaos in the world.

Yet I think the pessimism of *Beowulf* has been exaggerated. Historically, the poem looks back upon (and pretends to predict) disaster for both Danes and Geats; but as we now know, this epic (*pace* Thorkelin) was sung not by Danes but by Mercians and Saxons, who were muddling through. Of course, Beowulf dies, leaving an uncertain future for his people; but as we have seen, Beowulf is only the main actor on a certain portion of the stage. If evil is not quelled with the destruction of Grendel, or his mother, or the dragon, neither is good destroyed with Beowulf. Heroism is temporal, God's power is eternal.

What the poet saw reflected in his complex tradition is relevant, optimistic, and disturbing; for where there is capability, there is also responsibility. It is tempting to lose oneself in a reverie of unrelieved gloom; but if there be fiends within us—and he is surely right about that (cf. Plato's *Phaedrus* 230)—there is also a great source of energy by which to control them. This I have interpreted to mean the untapped sources of will by which we are, or could be, capable almost at every moment of choosing whether to hoard our vitality for ourselves or use it to make our fullest contribution to the forces of living order within us and around us.

University of California, Berkeley

Notes

Old English Literature in Its Most Immediate Context

FRED C. ROBINSON

[1] Elliott Van Kirk Dobbie, ed., *The Anglo-Saxon Minor Poems* (New York: Columbia Univ. Press, 1942), p. 113. I am deeply grateful to Dr. R. I. Page, Librarian of Corpus Christi College, for his help and courtesy in giving me access to Manuscript 41 when I was in Cambridge and for subsequently providing me with photostats of relevant pages of the manuscript. Professor Howell D. Chickering of Amherst College read the typescript of this article and made valuable suggestions for improving it, as did Professor Carl Berkhout of the University of Dallas.

[2] For Dobbie's *brego, rices weard* (2a), I read *bregorices weard*, a reading suggested to me by Professor John C. Pope and confirmed by *bregorices fruma* in *Genesis* 1633b; for *wynsum* (4b) I read *wynsumum*, as the grammar requires.

[3] Literally 'the tablets.' I have discussed this and other textual problems in this poem in a forthcoming article in which I offer a new edition of the 'Metrical Epilogue.'

[4] See Thomas Miller, ed., *The Old English Version of Bede's Ecclesiastical History of the English People*, EETS o.s. 95 (London: Oxford Univ. Press, 1890), pp. xvi–xvii, and 111 (1898), p. 596; Jacob Schipper, ed., *König Alfreds Übersetzung von Bedas Kirchenge-schichte*, Bibliothek der angelsächsischen Prosa, 4 (Leipzig: Georg Wigand, 1899), pp. xxv–xxvii; Ferdinand Holthausen, 'Altenglische Schreiberverse,' *Beiblatt zur Anglia*, 38 (1927), 191–92; Eduard Sievers, 'Altenglische Schreiberverse,' *Beiträge zur Geschichte der deutschen Sprache und Literatur*, 52 (1928), 310–11.

[5] The first four volumes constitute volumes II through V of the *Spicilegii friburgensis subsidia* (Freiburg: Editions universitaires, 1965–76) and include signed colophons listed alphabetically by the scribes' names, letters A through O. The colophons are numbered consecutively throughout the series and are cited by these numbers in the present paper. For a description of the types of colophons see volume II, p. vii.

[6] *Colophons*, no. 7088. For acrostic colophons elsewhere, see nos. 2805, 6893, 9997, and 12,921.

[7] *Poetae latini aevi carolini*, vol. IV, ed. Karl Strecker (Berlin: Weidmann, 1923), pp. 1056–72. The acrostic poems in *MGH* are also cited in *Colophons*, which records others besides (e.g. no. 9997, an acrostic poem in French). The 48-line eighth-century verse colophon printed as no. 5497 in *Colophons* is to be found in *MGH*, *Poetae latini aevi carolini*, vol. I, ed. Ernest Dümmler (Berlin: Weidmann, 1881), pp. 94–95, and others in *Colophons* are printed elsewhere in volumes of the *MGH*.

[8] This is the famous colophon in the Lindisfarne Gospels: see British Library MS. Cotton Nero D.iv, fol. 259^r, col. 2. For a discussion see the facsimile edition prepared by T. D. Kendrick *et al.*, *Evangeliorum quattuor codex lindisfarnensis* . . . , vol. II (Lausanne: Urs Graf, 1960), part 2, pp. 5–11.

[9] All of these can be found both independently and as parts of larger verse colophons. The request for a drink, for example, occurs as an isolated tag in *Colophons*, nos. 7431 and 7414, but as part of a poem (of two verses or more) in nos. 162, 351, 7432, 7530, 7633, 7995, 12,125,

12,900, and 14,458. Elsewhere a similar idea is expressed in different terms, such as the couplet 'Melius scripsissem, si aliquid bibere habuissem' ('I should have written better if I had had something to drink'), which occurs in a fifteenth-century scribal poem (no. 448). For examples of the repetition, adaptation, and even parodying of colophon verses, see W. Wattenbach, *Das Schriftwesen im Mittelalter*, 3rd ed. (Leipzig: S. Hirzel, 1896), pp. 491–534.

¹⁰ *Colophons*, no. 262. Wattenbach, pp. 278–82, records examples of colophons expressing this topos from the seventh century on. Ernst Robert Curtius, *European Literature and the Latin Middle Ages*, trans. Willard Trask (New York: Harper and Row, 1953), pp. 128–30, traces the use of the same metaphor by Classical, Medieval and Renaissance writers to refer to prose and poetic composition.

¹¹ It now seems clear that the manuscript was written in two scribal hands, one early and one late in style. Dobbie, p. cxvii, misguidedly revives an old, discredited view that the Bede text was written 'by three, or possibly four, scribes.'

¹² Schipper, pp. xxv–xxvii.

¹³ See for example *Colophons*, nos. 1 ('opus manuum mearum' ['work of my hands']), 83, and 279. The phrase *per manus* occurs no less than fifty times in the first thousand texts in *Colophons*, while *per manum* occurs but rarely. A fourteenth-century scribe plays with the formula in a Prague manuscript ('per manus et non per pedes' ['by hands and not by feet']); see *Colophons*, no. 11,653). A scribe in a fifteenth-century Venetian manuscript deemed this variation worthy of imitation: see Lynn Thorndike, 'More Copyists' Final Jingles,' *Speculum*, 31 (1956), 323.

¹⁴ See Ælfric's *De temporibus anni*, ed. Heinrich Henel, EETS o.s. 213 (London: Oxford Univ. Press, 1942), p. 82.

¹⁵ Wattenbach, p. 284. These verses (or mangled versions of them) are among the most popular of the tags occurring at the end of medieval manuscripts. Scribes began formulating the basic idea as early as the eighth century: '. . . qui nescit scribere putat hoc esse nullum laborem. O quam gravis est scriptura: oculos gravat, renes frangit, simul et omnia membra contristat. Tria digita scribunt, totus corpus laborat . . .' ('. . . he who does not know how to write thinks this to be no labor. Oh how burdensome is writing: it weighs down the eyes, it weakens the kidneys, and at the same time it saddens all the limbs. Three fingers write, the whole body labors . . .'). See *Colophons*, no. 13,323.

¹⁶ *Colophons*, nos. 83, 13,105, 12,403, and 12,483. For the last, see Max Förster, 'Ae. *bam handum twam awritan*,' *Archiv*, 162 (1932–33), 230, and Dobbie, p. cxviii.

¹⁷ See the forthcoming article cited in note 3 above.

¹⁸ Not all manuscripts of the Old English version are complete at the end, while the many Latin versions end in more than one way, as is discussed below.

¹⁹ M. R. James, *Descriptive Catalogue of the Manuscripts in the Library of Corpus Christi College, Cambridge*, vol. I (Cambridge: Cambridge Univ. Press, 1909), p. 82. See also Elżbieta Temple, *Anglo-Saxon Manuscripts, 900–1066* (London: Harvey Miller, 1976), p. 99. Raymond J. S. Grant, *Cambridge, Corpus Christi College 41: The Loricas and the Missal*, Costerus, n.s. vol. 17 (Amsterdam: Rodopi, 1978), pp. 1–2, sees less skill in the illustrations than do James, Wormald, Temple, and others. Also he mistakenly identifies the "Metrical Epilogue" as part of "the marginalia in Old English" (p. 2). But other comments in his monograph are valuable, such as his suggestion that "Corpus 41 could have been a product of the New Minster at Winchester, a suggestion which is borne out by its similarity to the *Missal of Robert of Jumièges* and Corpus 422, both products of the New Minster" (p. 50).

²⁰ Charles Plummer in his edition *Venerabilis Baedae opera historica* (Oxford: Clarendon, 1896), vol. I, pp. xcvi–xcvii, concludes that the M-type version was the earlier and the C-type the later. Bertram Colgrave and R. A. B. Mynors, eds., *Bede's Ecclesiastical History of the English People* (Oxford: Clarendon, 1969), p. xli, question Plummer's judgment in the matter. T. J. M. van Els, *The Kassel Manuscript of Bede's 'Historia Ecclesiastica Gentis Anglorum' and Its Old English Material* (Assen: Van Gorcum, 1972), pp. 48–49, decides that 'the question cannot be taken to be settled definitely one way or the other.'

²¹ Miller, p. xvi. Schipper similarly assumes that the poem is a statement by the scribe (p. xxvi), and Holthausen (p. 191), Sievers (p. 310), and Förster (p. 230) all refer to it as 'Schreiberverse'. M. R. James, p. 81, calls it 'the scribe's prayer.'

²² *A Study of Old English Literature* (London: George G. Harrap, 1967), p. 192. The poem

does not invite prayers for the copyist; it requests that readers *support* the scribe so that he can serve the Lord with further pious works.

[23] Since the foregoing text of Bede's *History* was written by two scribes, not one, the references in lines 4 and 5 of the poem to 'þone writre . . . þe ðas boc awrat' would be illogical if the poet were one of the two scribes. Furthermore, the metrical solecisms and the ungrammatical *wynsum* in line 4 would not likely have occurred in the author's own copy of his verses.

[24] Women were scribes from relatively early times. See Wattenbach, pp. 444–47, and G. H. Putnam, *Books and Their Makers During the Middle Ages* (New York: Hillary House Publishers, 1896), vol. I, pp. 40–41, 51–55. The grammatical endings signifying gender in Latin colophons sometimes reveal that the scribe is a woman: see for example Leodigundie's affecting appeal for prayers in *Colophons*, no. 12,402.

[25] Genuine colophons in Old English (such as those by Aldred, Owun, and Wulfwi—see N. R. Ker's *Catalogue of Manuscripts Containing Anglo-Saxon* [Oxford: Clarendon, 1957], pp. 216, 352, and 235) tend to be homely and brief. Poems like 'Thureth' and 'Aldhelm' may be the work of scribes, but if so the scribes have transformed the colophon form into something more elaborate, as did the author of the Bede envoi.

[26] 'Ic þe sende þæt spell . . . þe sylfum to rædenne . . . ond eac on mâ stowe to writenne ond to læranne' (Schipper's ed., p. 1, col. 2). ('I send you the story . . . for you to read yourself . . . and also for copying [Latin *ad transscribendum* "for transcribing"] and teaching in more places [besides].') 'In this lending of copies for purposes of transcription,' says Plummer (vol. II, p. 1), 'consisted the mediaeval process of publication.'

[27] The assumed eleventh-century date of the poem is based on the presupposition that 'the date of the writing of the manuscript . . . . may be taken as indicating also the date of the composition of the metrical epilogue' (Dobbie, p. cxviii), but in view of the possibility that the poem is a copy of a poem which was in the scribe's exemplar (a possibility which Dobbie concedes and which I have supported above in n. 23), the date of the metrical epilogue must be acknowledged to be indeterminate. One factor arguing for a late rather than an early date is the absence of the metrical epilogue from any of the other manuscripts of the *History*—if indeed it is absent from them all. It is certainly unique among the manuscripts of the Old English version, and I have seen no reference to a corresponding Latin petition at the end of any manuscripts of the Latin version. But there are 161 Latin manuscripts, all of which I have not examined, and one or another might contain a Latin version of the petition.

[28] Leningrad State Public Library MS. Lat. Q. v. I, 18, fol. 161r.

[29] See his 'Colophons dans des manuscrits de Bède,' *Revue Bénédictine*, 69 (1959), 100–01, and 'The Bede "Signature" in the Leningrad Colophon,' *ibid.*, 71 (1961), 274–86. See also D. H. Wright, 'The Date of the Leningrad Bede,' *ibid.*, 71 (1961), 265–73.

[30] E. A. Lowe, 'An Autograph of the Venerable Bede?' *Revue Bénédictine*, 68 (1958), 200–02, thought that a signature in the nominative case (rather than the genitive) in which the writer refers to himself as *indignus* 'could be used properly only by the author himself' (p. 201), but as Meyvaert has pointed out, this phrasing is precisely what we should expect of a forger trying to persuade others that Bede had written the words himself.

[31] Meyvaert, 'The Bede "Signature",' p. 285.

[32] Meyvaert, *loc. cit.*

[33] Paul Meyvaert and Thomas Mackay have both privately communicated to me their view that this colophon is ultimately of Bedan origin. The manuscripts of Bede's works (and their colophons) that survive are, of course, but a fraction of those that once circulated in the Middle Ages, and the number of colophons claiming Bede's authorship no doubt exceeded considerably those cited above.

[34] Compare the Old English poem *Durham*, line 15a: 'and breoma bocera Beda' ('and the renowned scholar Bede').

[35] This grafting process may be compared with that of the scribe Aldred when he added his personal comment to the two preceding paragraphs of the colophon to the Lindisfarne Gospels: he appears to have deleted an original *ic* and put his comment into the third person 'merely to preserve a kind of grammatical harmony with the two preceding paragraphs.' See T. D. Kendrick *et al.*, vol. II, part 2, p. 11. In the poetic corpus *Genesis B* provides an example of the grafting of one text onto another.

³⁶ MGH: *Poetae latini aevi carolini*, vol. I, p. 320, lines 11–14.

³⁷ R. A. B. Mynors, ed., *Cassiodori senatoris institutiones* (Oxford: Clarendon, 1937), p. 75.

³⁸ Perhaps we find a distant echo of this Cassiodoran interpretation in the legend of the Scottish monk in Regensburg who miraculously used the three fingers of his left hand to light the page when no lamp was at hand.

³⁹ *Poetae latini aevi carolini*, vol. I, p. 285, line 4, and p. 288, line 15.

⁴⁰ Alistair Campbell, ed., *Æthelwulf de abbatibus* (Oxford: Clarendon, 1967), p. 19, lines 214–15.

⁴¹ *Cassiodori senatoris institutiones*, p. 76.

⁴² *Poetae latini aevi carolini*, vol. II, ed. Ernest Dümmler (Berlin: Weidmann, 1884), p. 186, line 11.

⁴³ *Bedae venerabilis opera exegetica in Lucam et in Marcum*, Corpus Christianorum, vol. 120, ed. D. Hurst (Turnhout: Brepols, 1960), p. 7. For other Church Fathers who claimed to be scribes as well as authors (among them St. Ambrose), see Wattenbach, pp. 416–28. A colophon to the commentary on Mark preserved in a ninth-century manuscript in Berlin (Codex Philip. 47) shows how easily Bede's name became associated with appeals in behalf of the scribe: 'Expositionis in evangelium marci liber quartus explicit Bede famuli Christi et presbyteri. Deo laudes, Deo gracias. Amen. Orate pro scriptore ut Deum habeat protectorem.' ('Here ends the fourth book of the commentary on the Gospel of Mark by Bede the priest and servant of God. Praise to God, thanks to God. Amen. Pray for the scribe that he may have God for his protector.')

⁴⁴ *The Anglo-Saxon Minor Poems*, pp. 55–57.

⁴⁵ 'A mere formless compilation of trivia of merely antiquarian interest' is Roger Fowler's characterization of the Old English maxims in 'A Theme in *The Wanderer*,' *Medium Ævum*, 36 (1967), 2.

⁴⁶ The more recent critical interpretations of the poem include surveys of earlier approaches. See Stanley B. Greenfield and Richard Evert, '*Maxims II:* Gnome and Poem,' in *Anglo-Saxon Poetry: Essays in Appreciation*, ed. Lewis E. Nicholson and Dolores Warwick Frese (Notre Dame: University of Notre Dame Press, 1975), pp. 337–54 (the poet 'unified the poem thematically through his development of the idea that man's knowledge is indeed limited' [p. 354]); Nigel F. Barley, 'Structure in the Cotton Gnomes,' *Neuphilologische Mitteilungen*, 78 (1977), 244–49 ('It is inherently *structural*. . . . Its basic technique is the use of the rich paradigmatic associations of words and ideas' [p. 245]); J. K. Bollard, 'The Cotton Maxims,' *Neophilologus*, 57 (1973), 179–87 (see n. 47 below); and, for a bibliographical survey, Patrizia Lendinara, 'I cosidetti "Versi Gnomici" del Codice Exoniense e del Ms. Cotton Tiberius B I: una ricerca bibliografica,' *Annali dell' Istituto Universitario Orientale, Napoli, Sezione Germanica*, 20 (1977), 281–314.

⁴⁷ Bollard, 'The Cotton Maxims,' has in fact argued well for a certain unity of theme and content among the three texts, and to some extent my argument for their structural and thematic cohesion is but a further demonstration of the analysis briefly stated by him. I should also state here that Greenfield and Evert acknowledge that *Maxims II*, like its adjacent texts, 'is, to some degree, a list' (p. 354), and their shrewd observations on similarities among the texts have encouraged me in my own reading of them. But their main concern is to establish the 'aesthetic unity' of *Maxims II* as an independent poem.

⁴⁸ Nicholas P. Howe is at present preparing a Yale dissertation analyzing Old English list poems in the light of the Latin encyclopedia tradition.

⁴⁹ Greenfield and Evert cite 'three alternative meanings' for this maxim: ' "A king ought ·to rule (or preserve) a kingdom" . . . or "A king shall rule a kingdom" . . . or "A king must rule a kingdom" ' (p. 340). I would propose yet another meaning which might seem even more consonant with the generalizing character of the *Maxims*: 'The king shall have dominion' or 'A king shall hold the power' (with untranslatable gnomic force in 'shall'). Thus stated, the maxim identifies the essential characteristic of all kings, both earthly and eternal. Cf, *Christ and Satan* 258–61a: 'God seolfa him/rice haldeð. He is ana cyning . . . mihtum swið' ('God himself holds the power. He is the one king . . . strong in powers').

⁵⁰ See lines 14–15 'on Brytene, in foldan her' ('here on the land in England'), 39–40 'Gregorius . . . breme in Brytene' ('Gregory . . . renowned in England'), 98 'on Brytene

her' ('here in England'), 104–05 'Nu on Brytene rest on Cantwarum' ('Now he rests in Canterbury, in England'), 155 'in Brytene her' ('here in England'), 228–30 'Nu . . . geond Brytenricu' ('Now . . . throughout England').

[51] See Bollard, pp. 179–81.

[52] See P. R. Robinson, 'Self-contained Units in Composite Manuscripts of the Anglo-Saxon Period,' *Anglo-Saxon England*, 7 (1978), 231–38, and M. B. Parkes, 'The Paleography of the Parker Manuscript of the *Chronicle*, Laws and Sedulius, and Historiography at Winchester in the Late Ninth and Tenth Centuries,' *ibid.*, 5 (1976), 149–71. Parkes points out that the combination of genealogy, annals, and laws in the Parker manuscript 'suggests a conscious attempt on the part of this compiler . . . to preserve the tradition of the West Saxon royal house' (p. 167). Thus these contiguous texts would seem to be unified by a common theme as well as by the common catenulate structure discussed above.

From Horseback to Monastic Cell: The Impact on English Literature of the Introduction of Writing

Jeff Opland

[1] On the Conversion, see Henry Mayr-Harting, *The Coming of Christianity to Anglo-Saxon England* (London: Batsford, 1972). In its original form, this paper was first presented as the Chairman's Address at the Fourth Biennial Meeting of the Medieval Society of Southern Africa held in Grahamstown in July 1978.

[2] Recent studies germane to the theme of this paper include Eric A. Havelock, *Preface to Plato* (Oxford: Blackwell, 1963); Walter J. Ong, S. J., *The Presence of the Word: Some Prolegomena for Cultural and Religious History* (1967; rpt. New York: Simon and Schuster, 1970); Jack Goody, ed., *Literacy in Traditional Societies* (Cambridge: Cambridge Univ. Press, 1968); Ruth Finnegan, *Oral Literature in Africa* (Oxford: Clarendon, 1970), esp. Ch. i; Dan Ben-Amos and Kenneth S. Goldstein, ed., *Folklore: Performance and Communication* (The Hague: Mouton, 1975).

[3] *Beowulf and Judith*, ed. Elliott Van Kirk Dobbie, The Anglo-Saxon Poetic Records (ASPR), IV (New York: Columbia Univ. Press, 1953).

[4] *'Beowulf' and Its Analogues*, trans. G. N. Garmonsway and Jacqueline Simpson (London: Dent, 1968), pp. 24–25.

[5] See, for example, Norman E. Eliason, 'The "Improvised Lay" in *Beowulf*,' *Philological Quarterly*, 31 (1952), 171–79, and Robert P. Creed, ' ". . . Wél-Hwelć Gecwæþ . . .": The Singer as Architect,' *Tennessee Studies in Literature*, 11 (1966), 131–43. I find it difficult to accept the conclusions in either of these two articles, but find myself more in sympathy with the ideas expressed in R. E. Kaske, 'The Sigemund-Heremod and Hama-Hygelac Passages in *Beowulf*,' *PMLA*, 74 (1959), 489–94.

[6] By eulogy I mean that poetic genre that is also referred to as panegyric or praise poetry. The subjects of eulogies tend to be individuals, not necessarily heroic; the contents tend to include genealogical statements, assessments of the subject's physical and moral qualities, and reference to the major events of the subject's career. A strong argument can be advanced for the existence of eulogy in earliest Indo-European times: see for example J. E. Caerwyn Williams, 'The Court Poet in Medieval Ireland,' *Proceedings of the British Academy*, 57 (1971), 85–135; Donald Ward, 'On the Poets and Poetry of the Indo-Europeans,' *Journal of Indo-European Studies*, 1 (1973), 127–44; and Gregory Nagy, 'Iambos: Typologies of Invective and Praise,' *Arethusa*, 9 (1976), 191–205. Eulogies tend to be elliptical and allusive and are distinct from explicit narratives. This distinction has not often been observed in Anglo-Saxon studies, and has led to confusion: Alistair Campbell wrote of *The Battle of Brunanburh*,

The poet's subjects are the praise of heroes and the glory of victory. When this is realised, the oft-repeated criticism, that he does not greatly add to our knowledge of the battle, falls to the ground. It was not his object to do so. He was not writing an epic or a 'ballad'. He was writing a panegyric, and a sufficient number of similar poems of the period are preserved to show that this was then a regular form of composition . . . (Campbell, ed., *The Battle of Brunanburh* [London: Heinemann, 1938], pp. 41–42).

Traditions of eulogy are still common in Africa: see Finnegan (note 2 above), ch. 5.

[7] Strictly speaking, the thane is not an Anglo-Saxon and his performance does not take place in England, but this does not undermine my argument. I am merely using the thane as an example; the points I make are general and not specific. It is sufficient for my purpose to accept the thane as the kind of poet who could have existed in Anglo-Saxon England.

[8] A convenient start to Cynewulf studies is 'Cynewulf and his Poetry,' in Kenneth Sisam, *Studies in the History of Old English Literature* (Oxford: Clarendon, 1953), pp. 1–28.

[9] *Fates of the Apostles*, in *The Vercelli Book*, ed. George Philip Krapp, ASPR, II, 53–54.

[10] This and other translations of Cynewulf's poetry are taken from *Anglo-Saxon Poetry*, trans. R. K. Gordon, rev. ed. (1926; rpt. London: Dent, 1954). With this passage compare the conclusion of Cynewulf's *Juliana*: 'I pray every man of human race, who may recite this poem, zealously and fervently to remember my name, and pray the Lord that the Protector of the heavens, the mighty Ruler, the Father, the Comforter, the Judge of deeds, and the beloved Son will afford me help on the great day, when the Trinity, gloriously throned in unity, will decree through the fair world reward to the race of men. . . .'

[11] *Elene*, in ASPR, II, 100–01.

[12] Bruce Jackson, *Wake Up Dead Man: Afro-American Worksongs from Texas Prisons* (Cambridge, Mass.: Harvard Univ. Press, 1972), p. xvii.

[13] Bruce Jackson, *'Get Your Ass in the Water and Swim Like Me': Narrative Poetry from Black Oral Tradition* (Cambridge, Mass.: Harvard Univ. Press, 1974), pp. x–xi.

[14] Walter J. Ong, S.J., 'The Writer's Audience is Always a Fiction,' *PMLA*, 90 (1975), 9–21.

[15] A. C. Jordan, *Tales From Southern Africa* (Berkeley: Univ. of California Press, 1973).

[16] John Pepper Clark, 'The Communication Line Between Poet and Public,' in *The Example of Shakespeare* (London: Longman, 1970), pp. 70 and 73.

[17] The ritual significance of eulogy is referred to briefly towards the end of my article '*Beowulf* on the Poet,' *Mediaeval Studies*, 38 (1976), 442–67. A ritual function is clearly suggested by a semantic study of the Old English noun *leoþ*, the word most frequently employed for a poetic performance. I propose to present the evidence for my contentions about the ritual context of *leoþ* in my forthcoming book *Anglo-Saxon Oral Poetry: A Study of the Traditions*, in which I shall show grounds for the belief that traditional Anglo-Saxon poetry was associated with the cult of ancestor veneration, and that the establishment of Christianity in England initiated an alteration in the function of poetry in society.

[18] See René Derolez, 'Anglo-Saxon Literature: "Attic" or "Asiatic"? Old English Poetry and its Latin Background,' *English Studies Today*, 2nd ser. (1961), 93–105, rpt. in *Essential Articles for the Study of Old English Poetry*, ed. Jess B. Bessinger, Jr. and Stanley J. Kahrl (Hamden, Conn.: Archon, 1968), pp. 46–62; Jackson J. Campbell, 'Learned Rhetoric in Old English Poetry,' *Modern Philology*, 63 (1966), 189–201; and W. F. Bolton, 'Alcuin and Old English Poetry,' *The Yearbook of English Studies*, 7 (1977), 10–22.

[19] *Historia ecclesiastica gentis anglorum*, IV, 24.

[20] Recent efforts to characterise the nature of the tradition within which Cædmon operated include F. P. Magoun, Jr., 'Bede's Story of Cædman: The Case History of an Anglo-Saxon Oral Singer,' *Speculum*, 30 (1955), 49–63; Kemp Malone, 'Cædmon and English Poetry,' *Modern Language Notes*, 76 (1961), 193–95; N. F. Blake, 'Cædmon's Hymn,' *Notes and Queries*, 207 (1962), 243–46; Donald W. Fritz, 'Cædmon: A Traditional Christian Poet,' *Mediaeval Studies*, 31 (1969), 334–37; J. B. Bessinger, Jr., 'Homage to Cædmon and Others: A Beowulfian Praise Song,' in *Old English Studies in Honour of John C. Pope*, ed. Robert B. Burlin and Edward B. Irving, Jr. (Toronto: Univ. of Toronto Press, 1974), pp. 91–106; Donald W. Fritz, 'Cædmon: A Monastic Exegete,' *American Benedictine Review*, 25 (1974), 351–63; and Donald K. Fry, 'Cædmon as a Formulaic Poet,' in *Oral Literature: Seven Essays*, ed. Joseph J. Duggan (Edinburgh and London: Scottish Academic Press, 1975), pp. 41–61. A suggestion that Cædmon's Hymn is indebted 'to royal panegyrics

and even, perhaps, to the praise of pagan gods' can be found in *Seven Old English Poems*, ed. John C. Pope (Indianapolis: Bobbs-Merrill, 1966), p. 53.

²¹ On the matter of *Beowulf*, see the classic accounts in W. P. Ker, *Epic and Romance: Essays on Medieval Literature* (1896; rpt. New York: Dover, 1957) and J. R. R. Tolkien, 'Beowulf: The Monsters and the Critics,' *Proceedings of the British Academy*, 22 (1936), 245–95; on the sources and structure of the poem, see recently F. P. Magoun's two articles 'Béowulf A´: A Folk-Variant,' *Arv*, 14 (1958), 95–101 and 'Béowulf B: A Folk-Poem on Béowulf's Death,' in *Early English and Norse Studies Presented to Hugh Smith*, ed. Arthur Brown and Peter Foote (London: Methuen, 1963), pp. 127–40, and Arthur G. Brodeur's response 'Beowulf: One Poem or Three?,' in *Medieval Literature and Folklore Studies: Essays in Honor of Francis Lee Utley*, ed. Jerome Mandel and Bruce A. Rosenberg (New Brunswick, N.J.: Rutgers Univ. Press, 1970), pp. 3–26.

²² *The Mwindo Epic*, ed. and trans. Daniel Biebuyck and Kahombo C. Mateene (Berkeley: Univ. of California Press, 1969). It is a matter of passing interest that *The Mwindo Epic* seems to provide a non-Indo-European analogue for *Beowulf*. From Biebuyck's summary of the contents of the performance on pp. 20–32, we can extract the following: after a precocious youth, Mwindo rescues his aunt from the clutches of a subaquatic monster. He returns home with her, putting his hostile father to flight, and then undertakes a subterranean search for his father, maintaining contact with his aunt 'by means of the rope with which he was born.' Later 'Mwindo comforts his aunt, who, feeling the rope become still, thinks he is dead.' He returns with his father after defeating miscellaneous antagonists. Mwindo then becomes a mature ruler and rehearses his exploits in an extended plot recapitulation, and subsequently he confronts and defeats a dragon.

The Æcerbot Ritual in Context

JOHN D. NILES

¹ David C. Douglas and George W. Greenaway, ed., *English Historical Documents*, vol. II [1042–1189] (New York: Oxford Univ. Press, 1953), p. 162.

² References in this paragraph are to Felix Grendon, 'The Anglo-Saxon Charms,' *Journal of American Folklore*, 22 (1909), 55; Godfrid Storms, *Anglo-Saxon Magic* (The Hague: Nijhoff, 1948), pp. 178–83ff; Bruce A. Rosenberg, 'The Meaning of Æcerbot,' *Journal of American Folklore*, 79 (1966), 428; and Gert Sandman, *Studien zu altenglischen Zaubersprüchen*, Diss. Munster 1975 (Munster: privately printed, 1975), pp. 142–91. In the present essay, all quotations from *Æcerbot* are from the edition by Storms, pp. 172–76. Translations are from Storms with occasional minor modifications.

³ The two following examples are quoted from Dorothy Whitelock, ed., *English Historical Documents*, vol. I [c. 500–1042] (New York: Oxford Univ. Press, 1955), pp. 420 and 437, respectively. For another example of early eleventh-century anti-heathen legislation see *Wulfstan's Canons of Edgar*, ed. Roger Fowler (London: Oxford Univ. Press, 1972), canon 16 (p. 5), and see further Fowler, pp. 26–27, and Grendon, pp. 140–43.

⁴ For information bearing on Anglo-Saxon agricultural practices, I am particularly indebted to the classic study by C. S. and C. S. Orwin, *The Open Fields*, 2nd ed. (Oxford: Clarendon, 1954), to H. R. Loyn, *Anglo-Saxon England and the Norman Conquest* (New York: St. Martin's, 1962) and to H. P. R. Finberg, ed., *The Agrarian History of England and Wales*, vol. I, part 2 (Cambridge: Cambridge Univ. Press, 1972), pp. 385–525.

⁵ Christina Hole, *British Folk Customs* (London: Hutchinson, 1976), pp. 157–58. The currency of the custom of blessing the plough in church is confirmed by George Ewart Evans, *The Pattern Under the Plough: Aspects of the Folk-Life of East Anglia* (London: Faber and Faber, 1966), pp. 135–36. On the customs of Plough Sunday and Plough Monday, I have also consulted (among others) Sir Edmund Chambers, *The English Folk-Play* (Oxford: Clarendon, 1933), pp. 89–104; Laurence Whistler, *The English Festivals* (London: Heinemann, 1947), pp. 81–85; Enid Porter, *Cambridgeshire Customs and Folklore* (London:

Routledge, 1969), pp. 96–103; Jerry V. Pickering, "The English Plough Plays," *Western Folklore*, 32 (1973), 237–48; Russell Wortley, 'A Penny for the Plough Boys,' *English Dance and Song*, 36 (1974), 23; William Palmer, 'Plough Monday 1933 at Little Downham,' *ibid*, 24–25; and Geoffrey M. Ridden, 'The Goathland Plough Monday Customs,' *Folk Music Journal*, 10 (1974), 352–64. Wortley includes a photograph of the ancient Plough Monday plough used at Balsham, Cambridgeshire, in 1952. Porter gives a photograph of Plough Monday boys with miniature plough in Swaffham Prior, 1929 (photograph 10, between pages 270 and 271).

⁶ George Young, *A History of Whitby and Streoneshalh Abbey* (Whitby, 1817) II, 880–81, quoted in Eliza Gutch, *Examples of Printed Folk-Lore Concerning the North Riding of Yorkshire, York and the Ainsty*, Publications of the Folk-Lore Society, 45 (= County Folk-Lore, vol. II) (London: D. Nutt, 1901), p. 232.

⁷ The present idea is based on a suggestion made by an undergraduate student, Mr. Deke Houlgate, in my introductory Old English course, winter 1978. For yet another explanation of why hardwood trees are excluded from the rite, see Francis P. Magoun, Jr., 'OE Charm A 13: *Būtan Heardan Bēaman,*' *Modern Language Notes*, 58 (1943), 33–34. Magoun's suggestion—that the *proscription* of hardwood trees is intended as a *prescription* of softwood trees, i.e. evergreens—rests on the uncertain assumption that the modern distinction between 'hard wood' and 'soft wood' goes back to eleventh century precedent. In addition, evergreens are not likely to have been common in many agricultural regions of England.

⁸ St. John Chrysostom, *Homily on the Epistle to the Philippians* 13.1, quoted by Jean Daniélou, S.J., *Primitive Christian Symbols*, trans. Donald Attwater (Baltimore: Helicon, 1964), p. 137 (my punctuation). The following discussion of the symbolism of the cross is indebted to Daniélou, pp. 136–45 ('The *Taw* Sign'), and to René Guénon, *Symbolism of the Cross*, trans. Angus MacNab (London: Luzac, 1958). Of particular value to the present study was William O. Stevens, *The Cross in the Life and Literature of the Anglo-Saxons*, Yale Studies in English, XXIII (New York: Holt, 1904).

⁹ See particularly Thomas D. Hill, 'The *Æcerbot* Charm and Its Christian User,' *Anglo-Saxon England*, 6 (1977), 215–18. Hill further discusses the significance of the association of the cross and the four directions in 'The Theme of the Cosmological Cross in Two Old English Cattle Theft Charms,' *Notes and Queries*, 25 (1978), 488–90.

¹⁰ Pseudo-Alcuin, *Liber de divinis officiis, 18, in J.-P. Migne, Patrologia Latina*, vol. 101 (Paris, 1851), col. 1208; translation from Stevens, p. 65.

¹¹ In the following summary, all Biblical quotations are from the Revised Standard Version issued as *The New Oxford Annotated Bible With the Apocrypha*, ed. Herbert G. May and Bruce M. Metzger, expanded edition (New York: Oxford Univ. Press, 1977).

¹² A reading of the entire *Benedicite* prayer is perhaps the single most valuable aid to understanding the spirit of *Æcerbot*; for the text see Daniel 3.57–86 (the Canticle of the Three Children) in the Vulgate Bible. The frequent appearance of the Canticle of the Three Children and the related Song of Azarias in the liturgy of the Anglo-Saxon church is noted by R. T. Farrell, ed., *Daniel and Azarias* (London: Methuen, 1974), p. 24.

¹³ George Hadley, *A New and Complete History of the Town and County of Kingston-upon-Hull* (Kingston-upon-Hull: T. Briggs, 1778), pp. 823–25, quoted by Eliza Gutch, *Examples of Printed Folk-Lore Concerning the East Riding of Yorkshire*, Publications of the Folk-Lore Society, 69 (= County Folk-Lore, vol. VI) (London: D. Nutt, 1912), p. 88.

¹⁴ See Elliott Van Kirk Dobbie, ed., *The Anglo-Saxon Minor Poems*, The Anglo-Saxon Poetic Records, VI (New York: Columbia Univ. Press, 1942), note on *Erce* (p. 208); Sandman pp. 152–54; and Audrey R. Duckert, ' "Erce" ' and Other Possibly Keltic Elements in the Old English Charm for Unfruitful Land,' *Names*, 20 (1972), 83–90.

¹⁵ I should like to thank Joseph Harris of Stanford University and Thomas D. Hill of Cornell University for having read this essay and made several suggestions for its improvement. I am reassured to discover that the possibility of a connection between *Æcerbot* and Plough Monday had occurred to Harris independently. For several references to Plough Monday celebrations I am indebted to Mr. Tony Connell of the Vaughan Williams Memorial Library, Cecil Sharp House, London.

The virga *of Moses and the Old English* Exodus

THOMAS D. HILL

[1] All quotations of *Exodus* are from the edition of Francis A. Blackburn, *Exodus and Daniel* (Boston and London: D. C. Heath, 1907) by line numbers. I have silently expanded conventional abbreviations. Blackburn's edition has the advantage of being the most conservative modern edition of a very difficult text. In accordance with practice throughout this book, translations are provided for all quotations from Old English and Latin. In translating from *Exodus* it has been necessary to pass over a number of problems not directly related to my concerns in this article. And since, in several instances, the proper translation of the lines in question is precisely the matter to be discussed, certain lines are left untranslated. Such omissions are signified by a row of three stars (* * *).

[2] Edward B. Irving, Jr., 'New Notes on the Old English *Exodus*,' *Anglia*, 90 (1972), 309.

[3] John P. Hermann, 'The Green Rod of Moses in the Old English *Exodus*,' *ELN*, 12 (1975), 241–43.

[4] I quote from Isidore, *Etymologiae siue origines*, ed. W. M. Lindsay (Oxford: Clarendon, 1911) by book, chapter, and section references; I include references to the *Patrologia Latina* since the Arevalo edition which is reprinted there is usefully annotated: 'Virgae sunt summitates frondium arborumque, dictae quod virides sint, vel quod vim habeant arguendi' (V.xxvii.18; *PL* 82, 212). '*Virgae* are the ends of branches and trees, so called because they are green [*vi*rides] or because they have the power [*vi*m] to censure.' 'Virgo a viridiori aetate dicta est, sicut et virga, sicut et vitula' (XI.ii.21; *PL* 82, 417). 'A virgin [*vi*rgo] is so called from the greener [*vi*ridiori] age, as also a rod [*vi*rga], as is also a calf [*vi*tula].' 'Virga autem a vi vel a virtute dicitur, quod vim in se multam habeat, vel a viriditate, vel quia pacis indicium est, quod vim regat' (XVII.vi.18; *PL* 82, 608). 'A rod [*vi*rga] is so called from power [*vi*] or from courage [*vi*rtute] because it contains much force in itself, or from greenness [*vi*riditate], or because it is a sign of peace, because it governs force [*vi*m].'

[5] Isidore, XVII.vi.18; *PL* 82, 608.

[6] Marine Dulaey, 'Le symbole de la baguette dans l'art paléochrétien,' *Revue des études Augustiniennes*, 19 (1973), 13 (my translation).

[7] E. B. Irving in his edition, *The Old English Exodus*, Yale Studies in English, 122 (1953; rpt. New York: Archon Books, 1970), emends *andsaca* in line fifteen to *andsacan*, which would be the regular acc. plural form of a weak noun. But *andsaca* might be a dialectal acc. plural form as Blackburn suggests, since loss of final -n in the weak declension is quite common in late Northumbrian texts (A. Campbell, *Old English Grammar* [Oxford: Clarendon, 1959], §617, p. 249). If the emendation seems preferable, it is a very simple one. Professor Joseph S. Harris of Stanford University has suggested to me that the somewhat anomalous use of the verb *bindan* in this passage may reflect the usage of traditional Germanic magical texts in which the magician *binds* or *unbinds* his victim with the power of his spell. See for example *Hávamál*, stanzas 148–49, or *Die erste Merseberger Zaubersprüche*.

[8] Irving, *The Old English Exodus*, p. 32.

[9] Cassiodorus, *Institutiones*, ed. R. A. B. Mynors (Oxford: Clarendon, 1937), I.i.8–9, pp. 14–15 (*PL* 70, 1111–12).

[10] On Rabanus Maurus' use of Origen in his commentary on *Exodus* see Henri de Lubac, S.J., *Exégèse médiévale* (Aubier, 1959), I.i.228. De Lubac documents fully the popularity of Origen in the early middle ages; see his chapter 'L'Origène Latin,' pp. 221–38.

[11] John F. Vickrey, ' "Exodus" and the Battle in the Sea,' *Traditio*, 28 (1972), 136, convincingly explains *Exodus* 58a, 'enge anpaðas,' a strikingly unrealistic reference to the 'narrow paths' the Israelites traversed, in terms of Origen's exegesis of Exodus 14:2.

[12] Origen, 'In Exodum Homilia IV.6,' ed. W. A. Baehrens in *Origenes Werke*, vol. VI, part I, *Homilien zum Hexateuch in Rufins Übersetzung*, Die griechischen Christlichen Schriftsteller, 29 (Leipzig: Hinrichs, 1920), 177 (*Patrologia Graeca* 12, 321). This passage was incorporated by Caesarius of Arles into his 'Sermo 99; De decem plagis,' *Corpus Christianorum Series Latina*, vol. 183, p. 403.

[13] *Ibid.* This sentence, too, occurs in Caesarius, 'Sermo 99.'

[14] Origen, 'In Exodum Homilia III.3,' p. 167 (*PG* 12, 314).

[15] For references see Irving, 'New Notes,' p. 319.

[16] Irving, 'New Notes,' p. 319. This suggestion was first made by C. W. M. Grein, in 'Zur Textkritik der angelsächsischen Dichter,' *Germania*, 10 (1865), 418; it is tentatively supported in Bosworth and Toller, in *An Anglo-Saxon Dictionary*, s.v. *wig-trod*.

[17] Irving, *The Old English Exodus*, pp. 94–95; 'New Notes,' p. 319.

[18] K. W. Bouterwek, ed., *Cædmon's des Angelsachsen biblische Dichtungen* (Elberfeld: Julius Bädeker, 1849; Gutersloh: C. Bertelsmann, 1851), I, 129; II, 306. Blackburn (p. 230) suggests *witrod* should be taken as* *wit-rad*, 'path of punishment, fatal road.'

[19] One possible objection to this interpretation of the compound is that *wite* is ordinarily spelled *wite* in compounds and scribal practice is fairly regular in this respect, presumably to enable readers to distinguish readily between *wite* compounds and *wit* compounds. However a compound *witstenges* is recorded as a gloss for *eculei*, 'goads,' in a twelfth-century MS of Aldhelm's *De virginitate* (A. S. Napier, *Old English Glosses*, Anecdota Oxoniensia, 4th series, vol. XI [Oxford: Clarendon, 1900], p. 142); and the form *witern* for *wite-ærn** is attested (although one would expect assimilation in this case). Old English scribal practice is sufficiently irregular that *wit* is a permissible form of *wite* in this compound, and if one prefers, the emendation to *witerod** is a simple one. The basic reason for interpreting *witrod* as 'rod of punishment' here is that this understanding of the compound makes for smoother syntax and good sense in context.

[20] Irving, 'New Notes,' p. 320.

[21] Fred C. Robinson, 'The Significance of Names in Old English Literature,' *Anglia*, 86 (1968), 14–58, and 'Some Uses of Name-Meanings in Old English Poetry,' *Neuphilologische Mitteilungen*, 69 (1968), 161–71.

[22] J. E. Cross and S. I. Tucker, 'Allegorical Tradition and the Old English Exodus,' *Neophilologus*, 44 (1960), 122–27; James W. Earl, 'Christian Traditions in the Old English Exodus,' *Neuphilologische Mitteilungen*, 71 (1970), 541–70.

[23] Michael W. Herren, *The Hisperica Famina*, vol. I: *The A Text* (Toronto: Pontifical Institute of Mediaeval Studies, 1974), and 'Hisperic Latin: "Luxuriant Culture-Fungus of Decay," ' *Traditio*, 30 (1974), 411–19; Michael Lapidge, 'The Hermeneutic Style in Tenth-Century Anglo-Latin Literature,' *Anglo-Saxon England*, 4 (1975), 67–111.

[24] This aspect of the art of the *Exodus* poet is generally recognized, but one further possible instance of a specifically Germanic usage in the poem occurs in verse 408b, when Abraham draws his sword to slay Isaac, and the poet says that the 'ecg grymetode.' *Grymetan* is a verb ordinarily used to denote the sound of an animal snarling or roaring, and I would suggest that the poet might well be alluding to the Germanic (and Celtic) folkloristic theme of the blade which snarls or cries out as a presage of violence. The most famous example is probably Gunnar of Hliðarendi's *atgeirr* 'halberd' (see Einar Ól. Sveinsson, ed., *Brennu-Njáls saga*, Íslensk Fornrit, XII [Reykjavík: Hið Íslenzka Fornritafélag, 1954], p. 80 *et passim*), but this motif is fairly common in Old Norse-Icelandic literature. Cf. D. Slay, ed., *Hrólfs saga Kraka*, Editiones Arnamagnæanæ, Series B, vol. I (Copenhagen: Munksgaard, 1960), p. 63 and pp. 116–17; Einar Ól. Sveinsson, ed., *Kormáks saga*, Íslensk Fornrit, VIII (Reykjavík: Hið Íslenzka Fornritafélag, 1939), p. 235. Cf. also Myles Dillon, ed., *Serglige con Culainn*, Mediaeval and Modern Irish Series, XIV (The Dublin Institute for Advanced Studies, 1953), p. 1. The passage in question is conveniently translated by Tom Peete Cross and Clark Harris Slover in *Ancient Irish Tales* (1936; rpt. New York: Barnes and Noble, 1969), pp. 176–77.

[25] Since the final draft of this paper was completed, I have been able to see the recent edition of *Exodus* by Peter J. Lucas (London: Methuen, 1977), pp. xvi and 198. Lucas keeps the MS phrase *grene tacne* in line 281, which he takes (citing Hermann) as an allusion to the Cross. He accepts, however, the interpretation of *witrod* as *wigtrod* arguing that 'Bouterwek's *witerod* obstructs scansion' (p. 138). But there are other instances of irregular scansion in the poem, and in any case one could scan *witrod gefeoll* as a regular type E line, if one assumes that the second element in the compound *witrod* received less emphasis than the first. And Lucas presents a radical reconstruction of line 499 which obscures the suggestion of flogging. Since this new commentary touches on the concerns of this present

paper only tangentially, it does not seem to me to be necessary to provide more specific references. This paper was originally prepared in a seminar at Cornell which I taught together with R. T. Farrell in the spring term of 1977, and before the MLA 'Studies in Old English Language and Literature' group on December 28, 1977. I would particularly like to thank Michael Twomey, Daniel R. Ransom, Paul Szarmach, and R. E. Kaske for their comments on various drafts of the paper.

The Typological Structure of Andreas

JAMES W. EARL

[1] Part of this paper was presented before the Old English section of the Modern Language Association in December, 1975. I would like to acknowledge the contributions and advice of my 1974 seminar on the Vercelli Book at the University of Virginia, especially David Burchmore, Allen Frantzen, Lisa Kiser, and David Riede. The heroic school of *Andreas* criticism is still alive and well: R. J. Reddick, in a paper delivered in October, 1976 at the Ohio Conference on Medieval Studies, attacked the typological approach to the poem, pointing to Hill's article (note 2 below) as 'distorting' the poem; and the most recent handbook to appear, M. W. Grose and D. McKenna, *Old English Literature* (Totowa, N.J.: Rowman and Littlefield, 1973), p. 88, reflects the old opinion: 'Numerous phrases recall *Beowulf* and the resemblance extends to whole episodes such as Andrew's journey by ship with a band of companions to Mermedonia to combat man-eating beasts, just as Beowulf sailed to Denmark to destroy the monsters'—a tribute to the Anglo-centric world view, since the plot, of course, is from the Greek original.

[2] Thomas D. Hill, 'Figural Narrative in *Andreas*,' *Neuphilologische Mitteilungen*, 70 (1969), 261–73. Hill raises the question of the relationship of the poem's conclusion to the poem as a whole, but leaves it unanswered. His remark that 'the typological patterning of the earlier part of the poem strikes me as being less complex than that of the conclusion, and in the first sections of *Andreas* the poet seems to be concerned with explicit moralization rather than figural narrative' (p. 271), drove me to begin this study under his direction in 1969. I hope to show that he has erred just this once. See also his 'Two Notes on Patristic Allusion in *Andreas*,' *Anglia*, 84 (1966), 156–62, and 'The Tropological Context of Heat and Cold Imagery in Anglo-Saxon Poetry,' *Neuphilologische Mitteilungen*, 69 (1968), 522–32.

[3] Penn Szittya, 'The Living Stone and the Patriarchs: Typological Imagery in *Andreas*, ll. 706–810,' *Journal of English and Germanic Philology*, 72 (1973), 167–74. Other recent studies of *Andreas* which point toward a sophisticated and allegorical reading are by: David Hamilton, 'The Diet and Digestion of Allegory in *Andreas*,' *Anglo-Saxon England*, 1 (1972), 147–58; Joseph Trahern, 'Joshua and Tobias in the Old English *Andreas*,' *Studia Neophilologica*, 42 (1970), 330–32; Oliver Grosz, 'The Island of Exiles: A Note on *Andreas* 15,' *English Language Notes*, 7 (1970), 241–42; and John Casteen, '*Andreas*: Mermedonian Cannibalism and Figural Narration,' *Neuphilologische Mitteilungen*, 75 (1974), 74–78.

[4] Thomas D. Hill, 'Sapiential Structure and Figural Narrative in the Old English *Elene*,' *Traditio*, 27 (1971), 159–77.

[5] Joseph Wittig, 'Figural Narrative in Cynewulf's *Juliana*,' *Anglo-Saxon England*, 4 (1975), 37–55. Other such studies include: Daniel G. Calder, 'Theme and Strategy in *Guthlac B*,' *Papers on Language and Literature*, 8 (1972), 227–42; L. K. Shook, 'The Prologue of the Old English *Guthlac A*,' *Medieval Studies*, 23 (1961), 294–304; and Shook, 'The Burial Mound in *Guthlac A*,' *Modern Philology*, 58 (1960), 1–10.

[6] James W. Earl, 'Typology and Iconographic Style in Early Medieval Hagiography,' *Studies in the Literary Imagination*, 8 (1975), 15–46.

[7] All quotations and line numbers are from Kenneth R. Brooks, ed., *Andreas and the Fates of the Apostles* (Oxford: Clarendon, 1961), except where noted. All translations are my own.

[8] For a more complete discussion of the historiography of the saints' lives, see my

'Typology and Iconographic Style'; the principles of hagiographic composition are also dealt with by Charles Jones, *Saints' Lives and Chronicles in Early England* (Ithaca, New York: Cornell Univ. Press, 1947); Jean Leclercq, *The Love of Learning and the Desire for God*, trans. Catharine Misrahi (New York: Fordham Univ. Press, 1961); Hippolyte Delehaye, *Legends of the Saints*, trans. V. M. Crawford (Notre Dame: Notre Dame Univ. Press, 1961); and Baudouin de Gaiffier, 'Mentalité de l'hagiographie mediévale,' *Annalecta Bollandiana*, 86 (1968), 391–99 (a review of recent German scholarship on the subject).

⁹ Bertram Colgrave, ed. and trans., *The Earliest Life of Gregory the Great* (Lawrence: Univ. of Kansas Press, 1968), pp. 128–31.

¹⁰ Reginald of Canterbury, *Vita S. Malchi*, ed. L. R. Lind, Illinois Studies in Language and Literature, 27, nos. 3–4 (Urbana, Illinois, 1942), pp. 40–41. The translation is mine; I have tried to capture the terrible style of the original.

¹¹ Agnellus, *Liber pontificalis ecclesiae ravennae*, in *MGH: Scriptores rerum langobardicarum*, ed. G. Waitz (Hanover, 1878), p. 297; cited and trans. Jones (note 8 above), p. 63.

¹² I have treated the history of these notions in some detail in 'Typology and Iconographic Style' (note 6 above).

¹³
                 Hwæt, ðu golde eart
sincgife, sylla;   on ðe sylf cyning
wrat, wuldres God,   wordum cyðde
recene geryno,   on rihte æ
getacnode   on tyn wordum . . . (1508b–12).

(Lo, thou art better than gold and treasure; on you the King Himself, the God of Glory, wrote and revealed in words marvelous mysteries, and rightfully made known the Law in ten words. . . .)

¹⁴ It should be noted that the lines of the 'disclaimer,' 1478–91, are original in the Old English poem and have no sources or analogues in the other versions of the Andrew legend. It is interesting to compare a similar invitation to allegorical interpretation set near the end of the Old English poem *Exodus*:

        Gif onlucan wile   lifes wealhstod,
        beorht in breostum,   banhuses weard,
        ginfæsten god   gastes cægon,
        run bið gerecenod,   ræd forð gæð;
        hafað wislicu   word on fæðme,
        wile meagollice   modum tæcan
        þæt we gesne ne syn   godes þeodscipes,
        metodes miltsa (523–30a).

(If the interpreter of life, the guardian of the body, bright in the breast, will unlock great goodness with the key of the spirit, wisdom will be made known, and counsel will go forth; he will have wise words in the bosom, and will earnestly teach to minds that we are not deprived of God's instruction, the Lord's mercy.)

The Junius Manuscript, ed. George Philip Krapp, The Anglo-Saxon Poetic Records, I (New York: Columbia Univ. Press, 1931), my punctuation. For an analysis of these lines and of the relationship of the Exodus to the Harrowing of Hell and baptism, see my 'Christian Traditions in the Old English *Exodus*,' *Neuphilologische Mitteilungen*, 71 (1970), 541–70.

¹⁵ The best introductions to the subject of typology and these particular relations are: Jean Daniélou, *From Shadows to Reality: Studies in the Biblical Typology of the Fathers*, trans. W. Hibberd (London: Burns and Oates, 1960); Erich Auerbach, 'Figura,' in *Scenes from the Drama of European Literature*, trans. R. Manheim (New York: Meridian, 1959); and A. C. Charity, *Events and Their Afterlife: The Dialectics of Christian Typology in the Bible and Dante* (Cambridge: Cambridge Univ. Press, 1966).

¹⁶ Augustine, *City of God* 20.30, trans. Henry Bettenson (Baltimore: Penguin, 1972), p. 963.

[17] Bede, *De templo*, ed. D. Hurst, *Corpus Christianorum Series Latina*, vol. 119A (Turnholt, 1969), p. 116.

[18] Even Grose and McKenna acknowledge that the one episode 'mirrors' the other, p. 88.

[19] David Riede, 'A Figural Interpretation of the Pillars in the Old English *Andreas*' (unpublished).

[20] Augustine, *City of God* 20.29, trans. Bettenson, p. 957. The whole notion is described in more detail in 20.28, Bettenson pp. 955–56.

[21] A. Roberts and J. Donaldson, trans., *Ante-Nicene Fathers*, vol. 8 (Buffalo: The Christian Literature Company, 1886), p. 522.

[22] Ambrose, *Expositio in Lucam*, in J.-P. Migne, ed., *Patrologia Latina*, vol. 15, p. 1743, trans. Thomas Mossman, in Cornelius à Lapide, *Great Commentary* (Edinburgh: J. Grant, 1908), vol. 4, p. 335.

[23] Augustine, Sermon 89, *Patrologia Latina* 38.554, trans. Philip Schaff, *Nicene and Post-Nicene Fathers* (New York, 1888), vol. 6, p. 389; in this same sermon (p. 390) is a *locus classicus* of Augustine's analysis of the 'stone rejected by the workmen,' which he interprets as Christ, the cornerstone uniting in His Church the Jews and the Gentiles.

[24] Anon., 'Corpus Christi,' ed. L. McKenna, *Miscellany of Irish Bardic Poetry*, Irish Texts Society, vol. 37 (Dublin, 1939), pp. 339–43, trans. vol. 40, pp. 210–13; also Fearghal Óg Mac an Bhaird, 'Exile in Alba,' vol. 37, pp. 204–07, trans. vol. 40, pp. 120–22.

[25] See Jean Daniélou, *The Bible and the Liturgy*, trans. anon. (Notre Dame: Notre Dame Univ. Press, 1966), esp. ch. 5, for a convenient and compact discussion of the patristic traditions linking baptism, the Red Sea, the Harrowing of Hell, and the Last Judgment.

[26] Augustine, *City of God* 20.8, trans. Bettenson, p. 912.

[27] See J. A. MacCulloch, *The Harrowing of Hell* (Edinburgh: T. & T. Clark, 1930), pp. 288–99, where it is shown that the Fathers and apocryphal writings associated this resurrection with the Descent, and the controversies regarding the eschatological significance of the event are recounted.

[28] Augustine, *City of God* 20.6, trans. Bettenson, p. 904.

[29] *Ibid.*, p. 906.

[30] Hill, in 'Old English Poetry and Sapiential Tradition,' Diss. Cornell University 1967, pp. 84–85, note 41, has documented the tradition which asserts that Christ died and harrowed Hell in the same hour; see also the Leabhar Breac 'Treatise on the Canonical Hours,' ed. R. I. Best, *Miscellany Presented to Kuno Meyer* (Halle, 1912), pp. 142–66. The identification of the raising of the dead at the moment of Christ's death and the Harrowing of Hell depends upon the typological relation between the Harrowing and the raising of the dead at Judgment.

[31] Casteen (note 3 above).

[32] Hamilton (note 3 above), p. 151.

[33] Casteen, p. 78, note 1.

[34] *City of God* 20.3, trans. Bettenson, p. 899.

[35] Boethius, *De consolatione philosophiae*, Book IV, poem 4, 'Quid tantos innat excitare motus fatum sollicitare manu?,' ed. Ludwig Bieler, *Corpus Christianorum*, vol. 94 (Turnholt, 1957), p. 77, trans. Richard Green (Indianapolis: Library of Liberal Arts, 1962), p. 88.

[36] Brooks, p. 63. Brooks' suggestion that *heorogrædige* may be read 'ravenously hungry' is stretching the meaning a bit far, even if we accept the common opinion that our poet often uses herioc battle diction in strange ways.

[37] Hugo Rahner has devoted a book to this subject, *Greek Myths and Christian Mystery*, trans. Brian Battershaw (New York: Harper & Row, 1963), ch. 5: 'Moly and Mandragora in Pagan and Christian Symbolism,' esp. pp. 179–216.

[38] 'Fuit autem maga et venifica et sacerdos daemonum, in cuius habitu et opera magicae artis et cultus idolatriae recognoscitur.' Isidore, *Etymologiae* 18.28.2, ed. W. M. Lindsay (Oxford: Oxford Univ. Press, 1911).

[39] There is another tradition which grows out of the Circe legend which is related to the themes of our poem. Circe's potion is universally identified very early as the mandrake, a root which resembles a human body, but lacks a head, and which became an image of unredeemed man in Christian lore. In exegesis, the headless body of the mandrake is allegorized further in a bizarre and astonishingly widespread development: to cite Bede, 'Mandrakes are plants which resemble the human body though they have no head, and they

are a sign of the Jews who still lack the head which is Christ' (*Enarrationes in cantica canticorum 7, Patrologia Latina* 162, 1222; Rahner, pp. 270–71). At the last times, of course, the dark mandrake root will be converted and produce a white flower, and the Jews will be converted and crowned with the head of Christ. Thus the potion of Circe is a prophecy and a figure for the gathering of the nations and the conversion of the Jews.

[40] Boethius, Book IV, prose 3, 'Ita fit ut qui probitate deserta homo esse desierit, cum in diuinam condicionem transire non possit, uertatur in beluam.' Bieler, p. 72, trans. Green, p. 83. Cf. Origen, *Contra Celsum* 4.93, paraphrased by Rahner, p. 212.

[41] Boethius, Book IV, poem 3 and prose 4, trans. Green, pp. 83–84.

[42] S. Cavallin, ed., *Vitae SS. Honorati et Hilarii* (Lund, 1952), trans. F. R. Hoare, *The Western Fathers* (New York: Harper, 1954), pp. 260–62.

[43] The Biblical type for the beast-man who eats grass is Nebuchadnezzar, Daniel 4.24–33. See Penelope B. R. Doob, *Nebuchadnezzar's Children: Conventions of Madness in Middle English Literature* (New Haven: Yale Univ. Press, 1974), esp. ch. 2.

[44] It is interesting that the Old English prose version of the legend, which is commonly assumed to be translated from the same prototype as our poem, is much less sensitive to the spiritual implications of this portion of the story. The transformation into beasts is not mentioned at all; Matthew's prayer asks specifically only for the restoration of his sight; and God simply restores it, with no promise to reveal the radiance of Heaven as well.

[45] F. G. Cassidy and Richard N. Ringler, ed., *Bright's Old English Grammar and Reader*, 3rd ed. (New York: Holt, 1971), p. 218.

[46] See Hill, 'Sapiential Structure and Figural Narrative in the Old English *Elene*,' p. 167: 'The bestowal of the Holy Ghost, which is granted to Judas during his renunciation of the devil, is not given to Elene until the whole body of unbelieving Jews acknowledge the faith—a detail which might suggest the patristic theme that the final fulfillment of the church is to be achieved only in the last times through the conversion of the remnant of the Jews.' See further Gregory, *Moralia in Iob* 35.15, *Patrologia Latina* 76, 764–65, and Isidore, *De fide catholica contra Iudaeos* 2.5, *Patrologia Latina* 83, 508–10.

[47] Jean Leclercq, *Etudes sur le vocabulaire monastique du Moyen Age*, Studia Anselmiana, fasc. 48 (Rome, 1961), p. 125.

[48] Cf. God's promise to Matthew to lead him 'of henðum on gehyld Godes' ('out of suffering into God's keeping,' 117).

[49] 'Christian Traditions in the Old English *Exodus*' (note 14 above).

[50] Actually, the Old English prose version is also corrupt here. Andrew sends the host to wait under the fig-tree and eat its fruit, they ask him to come wait with them, he refuses and reassures them, and the text reports: 'And se haliga Andreas [. . .] and asetton on þa dune þær se eadiga Petrus se apostol wæs, and he þær wunode mid him' ('And St. Andrew [. . .] and they sat on the hill where blessed Peter the apostle was, and he there dwelt with them'), Cassidy and Ringler, p. 213. From the lacuna in this passage we can assume that the poet's direct source was faulty; but clearly he suppressed even those parts of the episode which are included in the prose version.

[51] It may be inferred from my references to *Elene* that I find these poems companion pieces not only in their genre, style, and their inclusion in the same MS; I detect in them parallel themes and developments as well. In fact, I have come to believe that *Andreas* is probably Cynewulf's. I find nothing in *Andreas*, *The Fates of the Apostles*, and *Elene* to dissuade me of this; the unfortunate fact that *The Fates* is not the most elegant possible conclusion to *Andreas* cannot outweigh the affinities these two poems have with each other in subject, style, diction, and of course, their situation in the MS, and the powerful similarities of the two large poems. And as an epilogue, *Fates* is not greatly more awkward than the other signatures. These conclusions I will have to elaborate in a separate study.

Tradition and Design in Beowulf

THEODORE M. ANDERSSON

[1] Dorothy Whitelock, *The Audience of Beowulf* (Oxford: Clarendon, 1951), pp. 39–55.

[2] Larry D. Benson, 'The Originality of *Beowulf*,' in *The Interpretation of Narrative*: *Theory and Practice*, Harvard English Studies, 1, ed. Morton W. Bloomfield (Cambridge, Mass.: Harvard Univ. Press, 1970), pp. 1–43 (esp. 20–22).

[3] P. G. Buchloh, 'Unity and Intention in *Beowulf*,' *English Studies Today*, 4th series, ed. Ilva Cellini and Giorgio Melchiori: Lectures and papers read at the sixth conference of the International Association of University Professors of English held at Venice, August 1965 (Rome: Edizioni di storia e letteratura, 1966), pp. 99–120. In footnote 18 (p. 107) Buchloh announces the appearance of a Kiel *Habilitationsschrift* by Dietrich Jäger entitled *Erzählformen des Beowulf: Vergleichende Untersuchungen über die Gattungsmerkmale des ursprünglichen heroischen Epos* and scheduled for publication in 1967. According to Buchloh this study entails a comparison of *Beowulf* to 'other Old High German and Old Icelandic lays,' but to my knowledge it did not appear. I owe the reference to Buchloh's paper and much else to my colleague Joseph Harris.

[4] The following Eddic references are to *Edda: Die Lieder des Codex Regius nebst verwandten Denkmälern*, ed. Gustav Neckel, revised by Hans Kuhn (Heidelberg: Carl Winter, 1962). This edition will be abbreviated NK (Neckel-Kuhn). *Hamðismál* 18–20 (NK, pp. 271–72); *Atlakviða* 1–2, 10 (NK, pp. 240–42) and 34–35 (NK, p. 246); *Atlamál* 8–9 (NK, p. 249); *Hlǫðskviða* 15 (NK, p. 306); the lost Rosimund lay in Paul the Deacon, *Pauli Historia Langobardorum*, ed. Georg Waitz (Hanover: Impensis bibliopolii Hahniani, 1878), p. 104; the *Waltharius*, ed. Karl Strecker, *Monumenta Germaniae historica: Poetae latini medii aevi*, VI, 1 (Weimar: Hermann Böhlaus Nachfolger, 1951), lines 310–12 (pp. 36–37).

[5] *The Fight at Finnsburg*; *Hamðismál* 23 (NK, p. 272); *Atlakviða* 19 (NK, p. 243).

[6] Both Atli poems and *Hamðismál*; *Hlǫðskviða* (NK, p. 306); the *Hildebrandslied* by implication.

[7] *Hamðismál* 18–19 (NK, pp. 271–72); *Atlakviða* 14 (NK, p. 242), *Hlǫðskviða* (NK, pp. 306–07).

[8] *Atlakviða* 10 (NK, p. 242) and 33 (NK, p. 245); *Atlamál* 8–9 (NK, p. 249); *Hlǫðskviða* 6 (NK, p. 303); *Waltharius* (edition cited in footnote 4), lines 215–26 (p. 33).

[9] *Atlakviða* 1 (NK, p. 240); *Atlamál* 4 (NK, p. 248); *Hlǫðskviða* 3 (NK, pp. 302–03).

[10] *Hamðismál* 3–10 (NK, pp. 269–70); *Atlakviða* 6–9 (NK, p. 241); *Atlamál* 11–29 (NK, pp. 249–51); *Hlǫðskviða* (NK, p. 302).

[11] *Helgakviða Hundingsbana I*, 32–46 (NK, pp. 135–37); *Helgakviða Hjǫrvarðssonar* 12–30 (NK, pp. 143–6); *Helgakviða Hundingsbana II*, 19–24 (NK, pp. 155–56); *Hamðismál*, 3–10 (NK, pp. 269–70); the *Hildebrandslied*; the lost Ingeld poem (e.g., *Beowulf*, 2047–56 and Saxo Grammaticus, *Gesta Danorum*, ed. Alfred Holder [Strassburg: Trübner, 1886], Book 6, pp. 204–13). For a listing of Germanic flytings see Carol J. Clover, 'The Germanic Context of the Unferth Episode,' forthcoming in *Speculum*.

[12] *Atlakviða* 12 (NK, p. 242); *Atlamál* 34–36 (NK, p. 252).

[13] *Helgakviða Hundingsbana I*, 1, 1 (NK, p. 130); *Sigurðarkviða in skamma* 1, 1 (NK, p. 207); *Atlakviða* 1, 1 (NK, p. 240). *Atlamál* follows suit with 'Frétt hefir ǫld ófo, . . .' (1, 1; NK, p. 248) and *Hamðismál* expands the invocation considerably (2, 1–6; NK, p. 269):

> Vara þat nú   né í gær,
> þat hefir langt   liðit síðan,
> er fát fornara,   fremr var þat hálfo. . . .

[14] That Bragi assigns the attack to the night hours is argued by Walther Heinrich Vogt, 'Bragis Schild: Maler und Skalde,' *Acta Philologica Scandinavica*, 5 (1930–31), 3–7.

[15] See John Nist, 'The Structure of *Beowulf*,' *Papers of the Michigan Academy of Science, Arts, and Letters*, 43 (1958), 307–14 and *The Structure and Texture of Beowulf* (São Paulo,

Brazil, 1959). Favorable notice is given Nist's analysis by Tilman Westphalen, *Beowulf 3150–55: Textkritik und Editionsgeschichte*, Bochumer Arbeiten zur Sprach- und Literatur- wissenschaft, 2 (Munich: Fink, 1967), p. 344. Another structural analysis is offered by Eamon Carrigan, 'Structure and Thematic Development in *Beowulf*,' *Proceedings of the Royal Irish Academy*, 66, Sec. C (1967), 1–51. Less inclined to structural subtleties is Kenneth Sisam, *The Structure of Beowulf* (Oxford: Clarendon, 1965), pp. 21–22.

[16] Gwyn Jones, *Kings, Beasts and Heroes* (London: Oxford Univ. Press, 1972), p. 4: 'And finally, it [*Beowulf*] is by any standards a good, even a fine poem; and there have been many to think it a great one—less for its movement and action, or fable, than because they find it a statement about human life and values by an artist who—by virtue of his technical ability, his command of words and metre, his power to present narrative, argument, reflection mood, and feeling in verse—has given lasting significance to the thing he wrote, which is now the thing we read.'

[17] See Alain Renoir, 'A Reading of *The Wife's Lament*,' *English Studies*, 58 (1977), 4–19 and 'Germanic Quintessence: The Theme of Isolation in the *Hildebrandslied*,' in *Saints, Scholars and Heroes: Studies in Medieval Culture in Honour of Charles W. Jones*, ed. Margot H. King and Wesley M. Stevens (Collegeville, Minnesota: Hill Monastic Library of St. John's Abbey and University, 1979), II, 143–78.

[18] Klaus von See touches on this idea in *Germanische Heldensage: Stoffe, Probleme, Methoden* (Frankfurt am Main: Athenäum Verlag, 1971), pp. 170–72.

[19] Arthur G. Brodeur, *The Art of Beowulf* (Berkeley: Univ. of California Press, 1959; rpt. 1971), e.g. pp. 51, 60. The ebb and flow of mood in the poem is also suggested by Joan Blomfield, 'The Style and Structure of *Beowulf*,' *Review of English Studies*, 14 (1938), 396–403, rpt. in *The Beowulf Poet: A Collection of Critical Essays*, ed. Donald K. Fry (Englewood Cliffs, N.J.: Prentice-Hall, 1968), pp. 57–65, and Herbert G. Wright, 'Good and Evil; Light and Darkness; Joy and Sorrow in *Beowulf*,' *Review of English Studies*, N.S. 8 (1957), 1–11, rpt. in *An Anthology of Beowulf Criticism*, ed. Lewis E. Nicholson (Notre Dame, Indiana: Univ. of Notre Dame Press, 1963), pp. 257–67. See also Robert B. Burlin, 'Gnomic Indirection in *Beowulf*,' in *Anglo-Saxon Poetry: Essays in Appreciation for John C. McGalliard*, ed. Lewis E. Nicholson and Dolores Warwick Frese (Notre Dame, Indiana: Univ. of Notre Dame Press, 1975), pp. 41–49. Burlin comments on 'the alternation of human security and fear, comfort and agony, the inexorable rhythm on which the poet has chosen to organize his narrative' (p. 47).

[20] Line references are to *Beowulf and the Fight at Finnsburg*, ed. Fr. Klaeber, 3rd ed. (Boston: D. C. Heath, 1950).

[21] Cf. Adrien Bonjour, *The Digressions in Beowulf* (Oxford: Blackwell, 1950), p. 7.

[22] The poem is printed in *Monumenta Germaniae historica: Poetae latini aevi carolini*, I, ed. Ernestus Duemmler (Berlin: Apud Weidmannos, 1881; rpt. 1964), 229–35. The letters written by Alcuin on the same occasion are excerpted and translated by Stephen Allott, *Alcuin of York c. A.D. 732 to 804: His Life and Letters* (York: William Session Ltd., 1974), pp. 36–41. The originals are to be found in *Monumenta Germaniae historica: Epistolae karolini aevi*, II, ed. Ernestus Duemmler (Berlin: Apud Weidmannos, 1895), 42–60 (epistolae 16–22).

The Middle of Things: Narrative Patterns in the Iliad, Roland, and Beowulf

PHILLIP DAMON

[1] Claude Lévi-Strauss, 'The Structural Study of Myth,' in *Myth: A Symposium*, ed. Thomas A. Sebeok (Bloomington: Indiana Univ. Press, 1955), pp. 81–106.

[2] Claude Lévi-Strauss, 'The Tale of Asdiwal,' in *The Structural Study of Myth and Totemism*, ed. Edmund Leach, A.S.A. Monographs, 5 (London: Tavistock Publications, 1967), pp. 3–47 (orig. pub. 1958–59).

[3] J. L. Myres, 'The Last Book of the *Iliad*,' *Journal of Hellenic Studies*, 52 (1932), 264–96; J. T. Sheppard, *The Pattern of the Iliad* (London: Methuen, 1922); Cedric Whitman, *Homer and the Heroic Tradition* (Cambridge, Mass.: Harvard Univ. Press, 1958); Fern Farnham, 'Romanesque Design in the *Chanson de Roland*,' *Romance Philology*, 18 (1964), 143–64; John Niles, 'Ring-Composition in *La Chanson de Roland* and *La Chançun de Willame*,' *Olifant*, 1 (December 1973), 4–12.

[4] Iohannes Kakrides, *Homeric Researches*, Acta Reg. Societatis Humaniorum Litterarum Lundensis, XLV (Lund, 1949), pp. 152ff.

[5] *Iliad* 9.588–92 and 595–96, trans. Richmond Lattimore (Chicago: Univ. of Chicago Press, 1951), p. 214.

[6] Ernst Curtius, *European Literature and the Latin Middle Ages*, trans. Willard R. Trask, Bollingen Series XXXVI (Princeton: Princeton Univ. Press, 1953), pp. 173–78.

[7] Pierre Le Gentil, *The Chanson de Roland*, trans. Frances F. Beer (Cambridge, Mass.: Harvard Univ. Press, 1969), p. 76; Jean Rychner, *La Chanson de geste: Essai sur l'art épique des jongleurs*, Société de Publications Romanes et Françaises, 53 (Geneva: Droz, 1955), pp. 37–40.

[8] *La Chanson de Roland* 1691–97, trans. W. S. Merwin (1963; rpt. New York: Random House, 1970), p. 48.

[9] Robert Kaske, '*Sapientia et Fortitudo* as the Controlling Theme of *Beowulf*,' *Studies in Philology*, 55 (1958), 423–57.

[10] Margaret Goldsmith, *The Mode and Meaning of Beowulf* (London: London Univ. Press, 1970), p. 225.

[11] Robert Kaske, 'The Governing Theme of *Beowulf*,' in *Critical Approaches to Six Major English Works*, ed. R. M. Lumiansky and Herschel Baker (Philadelphia: Univ. of Pennsylvania Press, 1971), p. 24.

[12] Text and translation from Howell D. Chickering, Jr., ed., *Beowulf: A Dual-Language Edition* (Garden City, N.Y.: Doubleday, 1977), pp. 188–91.

Beowulf *and Traditional Narrative Song: The Potential and Limits of Comparison*

JOHN MILES FOLEY

[1] Francis P. Magoun, Jr., 'The Oral-Formulaic Character of Anglo-Saxon Narrative Poetry,' *Speculum*, 28 (1953), 446–67; Lord, *The Singer of Tales* (1960; rpt. New York: Atheneum, 1968). Relevant scholarship in Old English is reviewed in my Introduction to *Oral Traditional Literature: A Festschrift for Albert Bates Lord*, ed. John Miles Foley (Columbus: Slavica Press, forthcoming 1980).

[2] See especially *The Making of Homeric Verse: The Collected Papers of Milman Parry*, ed. Adam Parry (Oxford: Clarendon, 1971), and Lord, *The Singer of Tales*. See further Edward R. Haymes, *A Bibliography of Studies Relating to Parry's and Lord's Oral Theory* (Cambridge, Mass.: Harvard University Printing Office, 1973), with supplement in a review by Samuel G. Armistead in *Modern Language Notes*, 90 (1975), 296–99; and James P. Holoka, 'Homeric Originality: A Survey,' *Classical World*, 66 (1973), 257–93.

[3] Lord's 'themes' are 'groups of ideas regularly used in telling a tale in the formulaic style of traditional song' (*Singer*, p. 68). Donald K. Fry defines the similar 'type-scene' as 'a recurring stereotyped presentation of conventional details used to describe a certain narrative event, requiring neither verbatim repetition nor a specific formula content' and the differently configured 'theme' as 'a recurring concatenation of details and ideas, not restricted to a specific event, verbatim repetition, or certain formulas, which forms an underlying structure for an action or description' ('Old English Formulaic Themes and Type-Scenes,' *Neophilologus*, 52 [1968], 53). In what follows, I will employ the term 'theme' in Lord's sense, thus approximating Fry's notion of 'type-scene.'

⁴ The validity of the formulaic test for orality is questioned by Larry D. Benson, 'The Literary Character of Anglo-Saxon Formulaic Poetry,' *PMLA*, 81 (1966), 334–41. On the nature of the Old English verse hagiographies, Lord remarks: 'If the religious poems were truly oral traditional songs, I would expect to find a higher degree of verbal correspondence among the various instances of a theme within a given poem, after making due allowance for adjustment to the specific position in the poem which it occupies' ('Perspectives on Recent Work on Oral Literature,' in *Oral Literature: Seven Essays,* ed. Joseph J. Duggan [Edinburgh: Scottish Academic Press, 1975], p. 23). See also Lee C. Ramsey, 'The Sea Voyages in *Beowulf,*' *Neuphilologische Mitteilungen,* 72 (1971), 51–59; and my 'Formula and Theme in Old English Poetry,' in *Oral Literature and the Formula,* ed. Benjamin A. Stolz and Richard S. Shannon (Ann Arbor: Center for Coördination of Ancient and Modern Studies, 1976), pp. 207–32.

⁵ Fry's differentiation between narrative units (see note 3) represents a real advance in theory, as does his definition of the Old English formula as 'a group of words, one half-line in length, which shows evidence of being the direct product of a formulaic system,' where a system is 'a group of half-lines, usually loosely related metrically and semantically, which are related in form by the identical relative placement of two elements, one a variable word or element of a compound usually supplying the alliteration, and the other a constant word or element of a compound, with approximately the same distribution of non-stressed elements' ('Old English Formulas and Systems,' *English Studies,* 48 [1967], 204, 203).

⁶ In 'The Theme of the Withdrawn Hero in Serbo-Croatian Oral Epic,' *Prilozi za književnost, jezik, istoriju i folklor,* 35 (1969), 18, Lord states: 'My basic assumption is that in oral tradition there exist narrative patterns that, no matter how much the stories built around them may seem to vary, have great vitality and function as organizing elements in the composition and transmission of oral story texts.' On the story pattern, see also Lord, 'Composition by Theme in Homer and Southslavic Epos,' *Transactions of the American Philological Association,* 82 (1951), 71–80; *Singer,* esp. pp. 186–97; 'Homer as Oral Poet,' *Harvard Studies in Classical Philology,* 72 (1967), 1–46; 'The Traditional Song,' in *Oral Literature and the Formula,* pp. 1–15; Mary Louise Lord, 'Withdrawal and Return: an Epic Story Pattern in the Homeric Hymn to Demeter and in the Homeric Poems,' *Classical Journal,* 62 (1967), 241–48; Michael Nagler, 'The "Eternal Return" in the Plot Structure of *The Iliad,*' in *Spontaneity and Tradition: A Study in the Oral Art of Homer* (Berkeley: Univ. of California Press, 1974), pp. 131–66; Berkley Peabody, 'The Flight of Song,' in *The Winged Word: A Study in the Technique of Ancient Greek Oral Composition as Seen Principally through Hesiod's* Works and Days (Albany: State Univ. of New York Press, 1975), pp. 216–72; Nagler, ' "Dread Goddess Endowed with Speech",' *Archaeological News,* 6 (1977), 77–85; and my 'The Traditional Structure of Ibro Bašić's "Alagić Alija and Velagić Selim",' *Slavic and East European Journal,* 21 (1978), 1–14, and 'Tradicionalna zgrada izrećinja na pesmom "Alagić Alija i Velagić Selim",' *Filološki pregled,* forthcoming.

⁷ 'Studies in the Epic Technique of Oral Verse-Making. I. Homer and Homeric Style,' *Harvard Studies in Classical Philology,* 41 (1930), rpt. in *The Making of Homeric Verse,* p. 272.

⁸ *Comparative Studies in Greek and Indic Meter* (Cambridge, Mass.: Harvard Univ. Press, 1974), esp. pp. 140–49.

⁹ *Spontaneity and Tradition,* p. 8.

¹⁰ See, for example, Frederick M. Combellack, 'Contemporary Homeric Scholarship: Sound or Fury?' *Classical Weekly,* 49 (1955), 17–26, 29–55.

¹¹ *The Winged Word,* pp. 30–117. A more thorough treatment of the comparative metrical foundations is undertaken in my 'Tradition-dependent and -independent Features in Oral Literature: The Formula,' in *Oral Traditional Literature: A Festschrift for Albert Bates Lord,* forthcoming; and in a work in progress, *Studies in Oral Tradition.* The brief descriptions of the Homeric hexameter and Serbo-Croatian epic decasyllable presented here are based, respectively, on Paul Maas, *Greek Metre,* trans. Hugh Lloyd-Jones (Oxford: Clarendon, 1962; rpt. 1966), and Roman Jakobson, 'Studies in Comparative Slavic Metrics,' *Oxford Slavonic Papers,* 3 (1952), 21–66.

¹² By taking into account the smallest and most basic unit of ancient Greek prosody, the 'mora,' we may see more clearly how consistent and conservative the Homeric hexameter is.

Counting by morae, two to a long syllable and one to a short (so that the interchangeable dactyl and spondee are understood as formally equivalent) with a single value for the final syllable of the line (the *brevis in longo*), we arrive at a constant value of 23 for each line. Whatever the syllabic deployment, then, which itself varies only within narrow limits, the fundamental measure of mora-count remains the same.

[13] See *The Winged Word*, pp. 66–117.

[14] An accented long is avoided in positions 7 and 8 and an accented short avoided in position 9. This and other rules lead to Jakobson's statement that 'it is consequently reasonable to suppose that the Slavic epic decasyllable is traceable directly to an Indo-European prototype' ('Studies,' 63). That the quantitative close might better be considered a tendency than a rule is suggested in John Miles Foley and Barbara Kerewsky Halpern, ' "Udovica Jana": A Case Study of an Oral Performance,' *Slavonic and East European Review*, 54 (1976), 19, note 36.

[15] 'Studies,' 26. In any given line, this tendency may or may not find full expression in the five 'feet,' for, as Lord puts it, 'there is a tension between the normal accent and the meter. The accent of the meter does not always fall on the normal prose accent, nor are all five stresses of the same intensity. The ninth syllable is the most prominent, has the strongest beat, and is held longest; the seventh and eighth are the weakest. The tenth may be lost entirely, completely swallowed, or hopelessly deformed' (*Singer*, pp. 37–38).

[16] Partially because of irregularities in these two areas, the exact dynamics of the alliterative line have puzzled scholars for many years, and a large number of theories has been advanced. The major works include: Eduard Sievers, *Altgermanische Metrik* (Halle, 1893); M. Kaluza, *Der altenglische Vers: Eine metrische Untersuchung* (Berlin, 1894); Andreas Heusler, *Deutsche Versgeschichte mit Einschluss des altenglischen und altnordischen Stabreimverses*, 2 vols. (Berlin, 1925–27); John C. Pope, *The Rhythm of Beowulf*, rev. ed. (New Haven: Yale Univ. Press, 1966); Robert P. Creed, 'A New Approach to the Rhythm of *Beowulf*,' *PMLA*, 81 (1966), 23–33; A. J. Bliss, *The Metre of Beowulf*, rev. ed. (Oxford: Basil Blackwell, 1967); Morris Halle and Samuel J. Keyser, *English Stress: Its Form, Its Growth, and Its Role in Verse* (New York: Harper and Row, 1971); and Thomas Cable, *The Meter and Melody of Beowulf* (Urbana: Univ. of Illinois Press, 1974). While some of these are obviously more credible than others, there remains a good deal of controversy over the finer points of scansion. For the present purpose, then, I will acknowledge only those metrical features upon which there is at least general agreement. There is a consensus on enough basic features to permit some suggestions about the Old English formula, and that is our primary goal.

[17] Robert P. Creed has derived a set of ordered generative rules for lineation, rules which operate unambiguously to determine half-line and other metrical boundaries; see our *A Systematic Scansion of Beowulf*, in preparation.

[18] The essential criterion here is that the morpheme bear one of the four heaviest stresses (SM's) per line (any of which may be more than one syllable in extent, as the laws of resolution permit), or that it bear a secondary but still heavy stress (SSM), as in the case of compounds whose first element is a stress maximum and second element a secondary stress. Note also that inflection may fall under a stress if the root syllable is short, though the inflection is clearly not part of the formulaic core.

[19] Compare Fry's description (note 5 above).

[20] 'Formula and Theme in Old English Poetry,' esp. pp. 207–20.

[21] A full account is available in my 'A Computer Analysis of Metrical Patterns in *Beowulf*,' *Computers and the Humanities*, 12 (1978), 71–80.

[22] See Paul Kiparsky, 'Oral Poetry: Some Linguistic and Typological Considerations,' in *Oral Literature and the Formula*, pp. 73–106.

[23] In 'Formula and Theme in Old English Poetry,' I showed that 'we may set formula length by the standard of the template: a whole line with verse (half-line) substitution' (p. 213). Thus the real answer to the question of the formula's length is that it forms a half-line unit but also has a whole-line dimension. Compare Peabody's discussion of the 'hybrid' nature of the Homeric line (*The Winged Word*, pp. 143–67).

[24] While the poet may recall certain verses verbatim from one instance to the next, this apparent memorization does not compromise formula generation. Metrical and verbal

relatives of the memorized verse will still appear, and even the verbatim phrase itself owes its diachronic identity to the multiform process. In studying oral traditional form, in short, we must cease being tyrannized by the written word (that which we see), that is, by the individual instances of the verbal formula.

[25] See *Singer*, pp. 245–47 and 260–61.

[26] See Lord's 'General Introduction' to *Novi Pazar: English Translations*, Serbo-Croatian Heroic Songs, vol. I, ed. and trans. Milman Parry and Albert Lord (Cambridge, Mass. and Belgrade: Harvard Univ. Press and the Serbian Academy of Sciences, 1954), pp. 3–20, for background information on the early collecting trips.

[27] According to the standard Parry Collection notation, italicized numerals indicate recorded texts (sung or recited), while regular typeface identifies texts taken from dictation. See further Lord, 'Homer's Originality: Oral Dictated Texts,' *Transactions of the American Philological Association*, 84 (1953), 124–34.

[28] On the proem or *pripjev*, see Eugene E. Pantzer, 'Yugoslav Epic Preambles,' *Slavic and East European Journal*, 17 (1959), 372–81; and my 'The Traditional Oral Audience,' *Balkan Studies*, 18 (1977), 145–54.

[29] Compare the methodology employed in Patricia Arant, 'Excursus on the Theme in Russian Oral Epic Song,' in *Studies Presented to Professor Roman Jakobson by His Students*, ed. Charles E. Gribble (Cambridge, Mass.: Slavica Press, 1968), pp. 9–16. See also my 'The Oral Singer in Context: Halil Bajgorić, *Guslar*,' *Canadian-American Slavic Studies*, 12 (1978), 230–46.

[30] This definition is taken from Lord's 'The Marks of an Oral Style and their Significance,' read at meetings of the International Comparative Literature Association in Belgrade in 1967 and printed in his essay, 'Perspectives on Recent Work on Oral Literature,' p. 20.

[31] *Ob-Ugric Metrics: The Metrical Structure of Ostyak and Vogul Folk-Poetry*, FF Communications No. 174 (Helsinki: Suomalainen Tiedeakatemia, 1958), esp. pp. 65–69. On p. 65, Austerlitz defines the terrace as 'a complex of two lines in which the latter portion of the first line is identical with the former portion of the following line.' In the Serbo-Croatian line absolute identity is impossible, since the hemistichs or cola are of different lengths (four and six syllables, respectively); but the principle behind terracing obtains in a four-syllable version of the six-syllable utterance in the former line. Inasmuch as the terrace is a pure form of what Parry and Lord have called 'unnecessary enjambment,' it would seem to be an indication of oral traditional style (see Peabody, pp. 125–43, for a summary of discussion on enjambment and the ancient Greek epos).

[32] A seven-syllable second colon yields an eleven-syllable line. The trouble seems to be a recurrent one: see *6617.34*.

[33] In using the shorter form of the future tense (*Ložiću* instead of the longer and more common *Ja ću ložit'*, a colonic form), Kukuruzović makes a short first colon and short line.

[34] This line resists translation, and I have settled for an idiomatic re-casting. Literally, it means 'while his spirit beats (or strikes) in his bones.'

[35] The unelided *je Alija* produces a long first colon and an eleven-syllable line.

[36] The *bila* pair shows an interesting priority of sound over syntax and morphology; in the opening line of the couplet it means 'white' (here left untranslated because of its proverbial character), while in the following line it is the feminine past participle of *biti*, 'to be.'

[37] Text *1868* manifests a variant ending to the ζ unit, an ending which does not lead into η. For whatever reason, this oral dictated text very often includes variant elements (see note 27).

[38] Compare Mary P. Coote, 'The Singer's Use of Theme in Composing Oral Narrative Song in the Serbocroatian Tradition,' Diss. Harvard University, 1969, esp. pp. 107–14, who distinguishes a highly repetitive 'cluster' and four types of themes, defined according to degree of verbal correspondence, internal order, idea structure, and frequency of occurrence. Compare also Joseph A. Russo, 'Is "Oral" or "Aural" Composition the Cause of Homer's Formulaic Style?' in *Oral Literature and the Formula*, pp. 31–54, who shows that the *Iliad* and the *Odyssey* exhibit a variable formulaic density.

[39] The original form of this essay included an example of the ornamental gloss which was eliminated from the present version for the sake of economy in presentation. On other sorts of patterns, such as phonemic series, end-colon rhyme, and semantic association, which also

characterize other oral genres in the Serbo-Croatian tradition, see John Miles Foley and Barbara Kerewsky Halpern, 'The Power of the Word: Healing Charms as an Oral Genre,' *Journal of American Folklore*, 91 (1978), 903–24.

40 For the text of the passages under consideration, see Fr. Klaeber, ed., *Beowulf and the Fight at Finnsburg*, 3rd ed. with 1st and 2nd suppls. (Boston: Heath, 1950; rpt. 1968). I differ only with respect to Klaeber's emendation to *naca* in line 1903b (nom. sing. and subject), for which I see no clear justification, choosing to return to the manuscript reading *nacan*, ostensibly a dat. sing. taking its inflection from the preceding *on*.

41 The *bātweard* ('boat-guard') I take to be the same person as the *landweard* ('land-guard,' 1890b), since it is the *landweard* who promises to guard Beowulf's ship until he returns (see lines 293–98).

42 Though the Geatish *hȳðweard* ('harbor-guard') is certainly not the same person as the Scylding figure of X_1 and X_2, he performs the same generic function and can thus be seen as the agent of the thematic variant.

43 See notes 41 and 42.

44 This kind of splitting of themes is not uncommon in the Serbo-Croatian tradition and may be related to Homeric 'ring composition.' On the latter phenomenon, see especially Cedric Whitman, *Homer and the Heroic Tradition* (Cambridge, Mass.: Harvard Univ. Press, 1958).

45 See Edward B. Irving, Jr., *A Reading of Beowulf* (New Haven: Yale Univ. Press, 1968; rpt. 1969), pp. 31–42; George Clark, 'The Traveler Recognizes His Goal: A Theme in Anglo-Saxon Poetry,' *Journal of English and Germanic Philology*, 64 (1965), 647–48; and Loren C. Gruber, 'Motion, Perception, and *oþþæt* in *Beowulf*,' in *In Geardagum: Essays on Old English Language and Literature*, ed. Loren C. Gruber and Dean Loganbill (Denver: Society for New Language Study, 1974), pp. 31–37.

46 Note that we have only two Old English instances here, both taken from the unique text of *Beowulf* (about whose history we know next to nothing), while the Serbo-Croatian examples are four in number and are taken from different texts of two generic songs, with all four known to be oral traditional.

47 'Formula and Theme in Old English Poetry,' pp. 220–32.

48 If a motif is split, as in E_1-E_2 in Occ. #1, a greater distance between responsions can of course result.

49 An elegant example is the morphophonemic relationship between *æhte* and *Nāh* (2248a/2252b) in the Beowulfian 'Elegy of the Last Survivor.' The poet has turned the responsional mode to his advantage in this case, lexically emphasizing the poetic truth that the speech essentially concerns 'having' and then 'not having.'

50 See Jackson J. Campbell, 'Learned Rhetoric in Old English Poetry,' *Modern Philology*, 63 (1966), 189–201; and 'Knowledge of Rhetorical Figures in Anglo-Saxon England,' *Journal of English and Germanic Philology*, 66 (1967), 1–20. Even some of the figures which Campbell cites frequently as examples of borrowed techniques (*anaphora, polysyndeton, hypozeuxis*, etc.) can be so explained. The subject deserves much fuller treatment than is possible here, and I must for the moment leave the argument at the level of suggestion.

51 'The Theme of the Withdrawn Hero in Serbo-Croatian Oral Epic,' 19; see also note 6 above.

52 A *rapprochement* between man and wife is structurally identical to a marriage of maiden and suitor in terms of story pattern; see further my 'The Traditional Structure of Ibro Bašić's "Alagić Alija and Velagić Selim" ' (note 6 above).

53 There are also smaller, story-dependent differences between the two songs. In the AA, the hero hears about the impending marriage of his wife, while in the OA the same news concerns the hero's son. This divergence causes some later discrepancies when OA and AA return to their homeland and families. None of these differences, however, conditions the overall shape of the songs, as does the W- element.

54 In 1287a the poet seems to 'abort' the full version of the song by releasing the hero's wrath in an unlikely marriage. The union serves two narrative purposes: the retribution is accomplished by deceiving Mustajbeg, the Turk who led the wedding party, and the song as a whole culminates in a W element.

55 In symbolic terms, At is really a continuation of Rt, a reflex we might call Rt_2.

[56] The traditional singer has ways of finding his way back to the story line; see my 'The Traditional Structure of Ibro Bašić's "Alagić Alija and Velagić Selim," ' and Peabody, *The Winged Word*, esp. pp. 233–36.

[57] The conversation is Parry text *6619*; the same information is also contained in the repertory listing, text 1287.

[58] Compare Francis P. Magoun, Jr., '*Béowulf* A´: *A Folk-Variant*,' *Arv: Journal of Scandinavian Folklore*, 14 (1958), 95–101: and '*Béowulf* B: A Folk-Poem on Béowulf's Death,' in *Early English and Norse Studies Presented to Hugh Smith in Honour of His Sixtieth Birthday*, ed. Arthur Brown and Peter Foote (London: Methuen, 1963), pp. 127–40. See also the reply by Robert P. Creed, ' ". . . *Wél-Hwelć Gecwæþ*. . .": The Singer as Architect,' *Tennessee Studies in Literature*, 11 (1966), 131–43.

[59] The basic research for this paper was carried out at the Milman Parry Collection of Oral Literature at Harvard University under a fellowship from the American Council of Learned Societies. I wish to express my gratitude to the Council and also to Professor Albert B. Lord and Dr. David E. Bynum, both of whom were so generous with their learning and their time. In addition I would like to thank Professors Robert P. Creed of the University of Massachusetts at Amherst, Donald K. Fry of the State University of New York at Stony Brook, and Alain Renoir of the University of California at Berkeley for their comments on earlier versions of parts of this study. The editions and translations of the Parry Collection texts are my own.

Interlocking Mythic Patterns in Beowulf

ALBERT B. LORD

[1] See my *The Singer of Tales* (Cambridge, Mass.: Harvard Univ. Press, 1960), ch. 9: 'The Iliad,' pp. 186–97, and Michael N. Nagler, *Spontaneity and Tradition: A Study in the Oral Art of Homer* (Berkeley: Univ. of California Press, 1974), ch. 5: 'The "Eternal Return" in the Plot Structure of the *Iliad*,' pp. 131–66. For further references see John Miles Foley's essay in the present volume, footnote 6.

[2] For selected examples see *The Singer of Tales*, Appendix III: 'Return Songs,' pp. 242–59.

[3] For further discussion of these elements in the Hymn, see Mary Louise Lord, 'Withdrawal and Return: An Epic Story Pattern in the Homeric Hymn to Demeter and in the Homeric Poems,' *Classical Journal*, 62 (1967), 241–48.

[4] See my article 'Beowulf and Odysseus,' in *Franciplegius: Medieval and Linguistic Studies in Honor of Francis Peabody Magoun, Jr.*, ed. Jess B. Bessinger, Jr., and Robert P. Creed (New York University, 1965), pp. 86–91.

[5] Carol J. Clover, 'The Germanic Context of the Unferth Episode,' forthcoming in *Speculum*.

[6] *Beowulf and the Fight at Finnsburg*, ed. Frederick Klaeber, 3rd ed. (Boston: D. C. Heath, 1950); translation by Kevin Crossley-Holland, *Beowulf* (New York: Farrar, Straus and Giroux, 1968), p. 109.

Beowulf *in the Context of Myth*

MICHAEL N. NAGLER

[1] Joseph Fontenrose, *Python: A Study of Delphic Myth and Its Origins* (Berkeley and Los Angeles: Univ. of California Press, 1959), p. 526. Fontenrose's comments concerning

Beowulf (on pages 524–34 of *Python*) have provoked some discussion now by Terry A. Babb, '*Beowulf*: Myth and Meaning,' *Arlington Quarterly*, 2 (1970), 15–28. Gwyn Jones, in *Kings, Beasts and Heroes* (London: Oxford Univ. Press, 1972) pp. 16–17 (note 1) and pp. 21–22 (note 1 part 4) is not hospitable to Fontenrose's viewpoint. Two other studies of a mythological orientation make no mention of it: Carl Meigs, '*Beowulf*, Mythology and Ritual: A Common-Reader Exploration,' *Xavier University Studies*, 3 (1964), 89–102, and Janet Dow, '*Beowulf* and the "Walkers in Darkness," ' *Connecticut Review*, 4 (1970), 42–48. In the following discussion, references to *Beowulf* are to the 3rd edition by Klaeber (Boston: D. C. Heath, 1950). Unless otherwise noted, all translations are my own.

I take this opportunity to thank John Niles for his very generous help with this article, and Alain Renoir, neither of whom is to be held accountable for its remaining shortcomings.

[2] Myth, as Axel Olrik said of *Volksdichtung* in general, 'hat ihre logik . . . nicht immer mit der der natürlichen welt commensurabel.' 'Epische Gesetze der Volksdichtung,' *Zeitschrift für deutsches Altertum*, 51 (1909), 9. The truth of Olrik's observation has been abundantly confirmed by modern myth studies from Claude Lévi-Strauss onwards. The question to be asked here is, to what extent does oral epic poetry follow the logic of its underlying myth?

[3] The *Odyssey* once treats this theme in a more Beowulfian style. Circe warns Odysseus—in vain, as it turns out—not to arm himself against Scylla as she is an *athanaton kakon*, which I am tempted to translate a 'spiritual problem.' The encounter with Scylla and Charybdis, who periodically swallows up the world and spews it back again, is Odysseus's closest brush with an unrationalized, primordial creation-and-dissolution myth, so Circe's warning about the inutility of worldly weapons here is quite appropriate. Beowulf, by contrast, has rotten luck with weapons all the time, as Old English scholars were quick to notice. For the Indo-European provenience of the bare-handed fighter, see Georges Dumézil, *Mythe et épopée*, I (Paris: Gallimard, 1968), 63–64, with discussion in Gregory Nagy, *The Best of the Achaeans* (Baltimore: Johns Hopkins Univ. Press, 1979), ch. 20 § 7.

[4] References to the deleterious effects of Grendel's raids on both religion and the order of civilization are prominent in *Beowulf*, but nowhere more evocative than in the difficult passage on the Danes' relapse into paganism, 175–83a. Heorot is not an ashram or a church, but its well-being is accompanied by a creation hymn which arouses the jealous wrath of the chaos demons (cf. Pindar's First Pythian, 13ff, a parallel brought to my attention by E. L. Bundy), and its depopulation by the demons leads to the decay equally of religious and social order. For a note on the similarity of house and temple in the pagan North, see H. R. Ellis Davidson, *Gods and Myths of Northern Europe* (Baltimore: Penguin, 1964), p. 88.

[5] Lines 1687b–98a. Apparently there are two separate inscriptions written on the hilt, one which refers to the *Genesis* combat story and another which tells the name of the one for whom the sword was (originally) made (with *swa* at 1694a meaning 'also,' 'in like manner'). In any case this allusive reference to the sword's first (and real?) owner is typical of the intriguing, suggestive Beowulfian style. From the Indo-European point of view the sword was made by the smith god (Tvaṣṭr, Hephaestus, Weland—see *wundorsmiþa geweorc*, 1681a) for the ruler of the sky (Indra, Zeus, perhaps Thor, but in this context the *rodera wealdend*).

[6] I.e. by banishing them—Cain or Grendel or both, the text is instructively confusing—to the watery realm (104). But the text is not confused about this being the beginning of evil (*Þanon untydras ealle onwocon*, 111) or about God giving them their final requital (*He him ðæs lean forgeald*, 114b; compare 1692b–93, *him þæs endelean | þurh wæteres wylm Waldend sealde*). The recapitulation at 1260ff. is similarly unambiguous.

That the Grendels should be identified with the watery chaos (see Babb, note 1 above) and destroyed by it is not a confusion either; it is a typical paradoxical ambivalence of myth. Adrien Bonjour, who first drew attention to these important parallel passages and the Biblical imagery in them, is a bit shy of the mark (though not mistaken) in his reference to a 'certain dramatic irony' in the ogress' death by her own weapon; see *The Digressions in Beowulf*, Medium Ævum Monographs, 5 (Oxford: Basil Blackwell, 1950), p. 66. Dramatic irony there is, but there is also profound mythic significance—and on the latter level of meaning the weapon is not hers.

[7] Indications that the hero's adventure is unique are a regular strategy of heroic epic.

Urshanabi is cursed by Utnapishtim and is forever debarred from ferrying heroes to the 'land of the far away' after conveying Gilgamesh there and back; the Phaeacians are cursed and debarred in exactly the same way for their conveyance of Odysseus (*Od.* 13.146ff). The melting of the blade also symbolizes something else, however: the sky-god's weapon is not so closely bound to the identity of the individual hero as we, and he, often think. Beowulf cannot keep this sword, as a sword, and by a sort of inversion Roland cannot destroy Durendal to coincide with his personal death (*laisses* 171–73 of the Oxford *Song of Roland*, ed. Bédier). There is only one power; there will be an endless succession of heroes and enemies to use or to usurp it: *Wæs þæra geosceaftgasta Grendel sum* (1266, with change of word-order).

⁸ Indo-Europeanists in their way, and Jungians in theirs, have helped to clarify the significance of this elixir rescued from the land of death, and I often feel that what is valid in their interpretations could be better articulated with the specific historical knowledge which is the privilege of the Anglicist. I cite as examples G. Dumézil, *Mythe et épopée*, III (1973), 21–92, and Joseph Campbell, *The Hero With a Thousand Faces* (New York: Pantheon, 1949) pp. 245–46 (cited by Meigs, p. 100).

It is interesting that both *Beowulf* and the *Odyssey* exhibit a two-stage adventure to the death realm, first a relatively rationalized place (Phaeacia, Denmark), then embedded within that a more primordial one (the nekyia, the haunted mere). At both levels the hero experiences conflict and from both he returns with treasures. From the rationalized realm, interestingly enough, he returns with things that are useful in the worldly sense (the gifts of kings Alcinous and Hrothgar and their wives) but from the primordial realm with 'treasures' which are more symbolic or which at least are not meant for his own use (the prophecies of Teiresias—see my article 'Entretiens avec Tirésias,' forthcoming in *Classical World*—and the hilt and Grendel's head).

⁹ On the solar symbolism of Polyphemus, see A. Kuhn, *Die Herabkunft des Feuers und des Göttertranks* (Gutersloh, 1886), p. 63; A. B. Cook, *Zeus: A Study in Ancient Religion* (Cambridge: Cambridge Univ. Press, 1914), I, 323; and my 'Entretiens' (preceding note). Needless to say, this solar symbolism, which we associate with the oldest and most pagan stratum of the mythology, was effortlessly christianized in the Middle Ages. Among many other examples, consider Baudri of Bourgueil's 'Tituli' *De sole detenebrato* (XIth c.):

Sol veluti plorat, quia sol in morte laborat (17)
Sol radios velat quoniam sol in cruce clamat (19).

(The sun is weeping as it were, for the Sun [Christ] is in his death agonies. The sun hides its rays for the Sun cries out on the cross.)

Phyllis Abrahams, ed., *Les oeuvres poétiques de Baudri de Bourgueil* (Paris, 1926), p. 6.

¹⁰ Even the similar syntactic pattern of the respectively subjective and objective verse from each pair— 'she + object + verb': 'man + object + verb,' etc.—reinforces the starkness and the parallelism of the effect. As Tolkien says, *Beowulf* is the 'narration' of an underlying static contrast between good and evil. These four verses, fast moving but repetitive, static and starkly final, capture that contrast in an arresting manner.

¹¹ Dawn accompanies the victories of the swimming contest (569b–72a), of the flyting with Unferth (cf. 603b–06), and of the fight with Grendel (837, repeated in 'ring composition' in 917b–18a). See also 311 on the glory of Heorot, 1965b–66a, and 2769b–71a. For a later and more completely christianized example, see *Andreas* 122–25a and 835ff. I regard this theme as complementary to the gleam in liminal situations discussed by David Crowne, 'The Hero on the Beach: An Example of Composition by Theme in Anglo-Saxon Poetry,' *Neuphilologische Mitteilungen*, 61 (1960), 362–72.

¹² In the *Mahabharata* the grief and conflict at the center of the epic is caused by king *Dhṛtarāṣṭra* 'usurper,' which he is. He is also quite blind, showing his connections with the blinded Polyphemus and Grendel, who walks in darkness. Though he is much more rationalized than these figures, Indian tradition knows him as a potent allegory of the usurping ego.

[13] Augustine's old ways and wants would say to him, 'Where do you think *you're* going?' (*quo is, indigne et sordide*, 7.7). One wonders how far back this theme can be traced when one reads the famous refrain with which the mythological creatures seek to discourage Gilgamesh from his quest for immortality: *Gilgameš, Gilgameš, eš tadal,* 'Gilgamesh, Gilgamesh, where are you going?'

[14] On the escalation from the fight with the chaos demon to the fight with his mother, see *Python*, pp. 525–26. The *Beowulf* poet for a change is rationalizing, or at least adding literary coloring, when he says that Grendel's dam 'wants to avenge her son' (1276b–78). The root meaning of the mythologem is that the hero must fight his way to the source. Part of Circe's disregarded advice to Odysseus about Scylla is to go over Scylla's head and 'call out to Krataïs ["power"], who mothered this bane to mortals' (12.124–25).

[15] For comparative purposes, the following is a Bengali devotional song which *is* a conscious allegory. Note the almost unnerving similarities of theme despite the differences in style:

> Taking the name of Kāli, dive deep down, O mind,
> Into the heart's fathomless depths,
> Where many a precious gem lies hid.
> But never believe the bed of the ocean bare of gems
> If in the first few dives you fail;
> With firm resolve and self-control
> Dive deep and make your way to Mother Kāli's realm.
> Down in the ocean depths of heavenly Wisdom lie
> The wondrous pearls of Peace, O mind;
> And you yourself can gather them,
> If you but have pure love and follow the scriptures' rule.
> Within those ocean depths, as well,
> Six alligators lurk—lust, anger, and the rest—
> Swimming about in search of prey.
> Smear yourself with the turmeric of discrimination;
> The very smell of it will shield you from their jaws.

Swami Nikhilananda, trans., *The Gospel of Sri Ramakrishna*, by 'M.' [Mahendranath Gupta] (New York: Ramakrishna-Vivekananda Center, 1942), p. 124. 'Mother Kāli' is the divine mother, a feminine personification of godhead popularly worshipped in Bengal.

Index